LAUGHING AND SPLASHING

LAUGHING
AND
SPLASHING

A Memoir

Sue Bathurst

Matador
Unit E2 Airfield Business Park,
Harrison Road, Market Harborough,
Leicestershire. LE16 7UL
Tel: 0116 2792299
Email: books@troubador.co.uk
Web: www.troubador.co.uk/matador
Twitter: @matadorbooks

ISBN 978 1803135 458

British Library Cataloguing in Publication Data.
A catalogue record for this book is available from the British Library.

Printed and bound in the UK by TJ Books Limited, Padstow, Cornwall
Typeset in 11pt Adobe Caslon Pro by Troubador Publishing Ltd, Leicester, UK

Matador is an imprint of Troubador Publishing Ltd

For Sophie

When a waiter brought the first bottle to the table and filled the glasses, my father would raise his and say,

"Here we go, laughing and splashing!"

There is a farming adage –

'Live as though you will die tomorrow, farm as though you will live forever.'

ONE

MARY

For longer than anyone could remember, the George Grigses had been inextricably linked to South Shields, the River Tyne, and the sea. In the mid-1830s the brig *George and Jane*,[1] named after her captain-owner George Grigs and his wife Jane, rescued the crew of the brig *Heldeys*, registered in North Shields, as it went down off the Dutch coast. They were the heroes of the Tyne, and in 1839 an oil painting was commissioned to commemorate the 'miraculous' event. George and Jane's numerous descendants were master mariners. Many died of disease in foreign ports, some became harbourmasters, one became a docks superintendent in Bengal. In old age those who had returned safely to home shores occupied themselves with easier jobs such as checking the buoys in the mouth of the Tyne. Salt water was their lifeblood.

So, in 1874 when another George Grigs was born, there was no question, he would become a mariner. He spent his early childhood with his multiple siblings, the youngest boy was named Septimus, mucking about on the water's edges. When the tide was out, they searched for treasure on the shore. People were still talking about the nine-pounder breech-loading cannon dredged from the Tyne in 1864; cannon balls were working to the surface of the sands of South Shields; they might even find something from King Osric

---

1   *A brig was a small two-masted, square-rigged sailing ship used for cargo and war from the mid 18th century to the end of the 19th century. A version of a brigantine, differentiated by the rigging that required fewer men to handle the sails. It also was easier to manoeuvre.*

of Deira's 7th-century palace known to have been somewhere thereabouts. As they prodded the sands optimistically, they shouted at the garrulous, scavenging gulls that swooped to forage the foreshore they'd disturbed. They inhaled the salty air and tried to imagine the far-off places their uncles and father described.

George's father (George) moved south from the great port of Newcastle to the greater port of London. The children exchanged the Tyne for the Thames, enthused by their new friends' talk of Roman coins that sometimes surfaced in the silt. George went to school in Hackney. He was a sharp, bright little boy, but those near him noticed that in some way he was different. He didn't always see things. After a while it became clear he was colour blind, he had deuteranopia, he couldn't differentiate reds and greens. Unable to see the navigation lights on ships,[2] he would be the first George Grigs for over a hundred and fifty years not to become a mariner. It was something he regarded irrationally with shame, as though he had let his antecedents down.

At Parmiter's Foundation School in Bethnal Green, he won so many prizes that the headmaster asked him if he was prepared to accept just one, so that his fellows stood a chance. He studied law and was called to the Bar, but he could not afford to practise as a barrister. He became a First Class Clerk for London County Council. He married Florence.

James and Eliza, Florence's parents had also left salt air to find a new life in London, and James had broken with family tradition too. After centuries of the family copper-mining in Cornwall, James had left the tiny hamlet of Illogan to become a wheelwright. The signs had been there, copper seams were more difficult to find and in 1866, with imports increasing, prices had bombed.

George and Florence had a daughter Mary, then five years later a son – George. They lived in Dollis Road, Finchley where the semi-detached houses,[3] had been well-built of red brick towards the end of the 19th century. They have generous bays, on two floors, topped by little peaked coolie hats. Their house, halfway down the road, was beside a grassed alley and had a long, thin garden that led to the 'new' railway built forty years earlier. It was somewhere for the children to play and as they grew older, they ventured to the end of the road where if they scrambled over the Dollis Brook, they could climb trees and play

---

2   *Ships carry red lights on the left (port) and green on the right (starboard) so that other ships can see which way to pass in the dark.*

3   *In 2020 the sale price of the houses in Dollis Road averaged just over half a million pounds.*

in the park at the end of Nether Court's grounds.[4] Occasionally they saw a gardener in the distance but nobody else seemed to go there and they remained undetected. Nether Court had been built thirty years earlier for Henry Tubbs. Mary and George thought it very funny when school friends told them that Mr Tubbs had become wealthy enough to need fifteen bedrooms by making knicker elastic. Where Dollis Road rounded the corner to avoid the brook, the sixty-foot arches of the viaduct crossed both road and brook and the vibrations echoed as the trains clattered over.

Finchley, still quite open and agricultural, was on the up. Farmers were selling off fields. The number of houses had quadrupled in the last quarter of the 19th century, and the population had doubled in the past twenty years. Eight per cent of the residents were like George, employed as clerks or in insurance, commuting from Finchley station at the end of the road into Central London. It was a good place for a young family, but Florence became ill. She couldn't eat. She lost weight. Her pain increased. Five-year-old George was told she was only tired and to let her sleep, but almost before anyone had got used to the idea that she was seriously ill, Florence died of cancer. She was thirty-seven. Attempting to make the death peaceful, straw had been laid on the road near the house to cushion the noise of shod hooves and the iron-rimmed wheels of carts. Perhaps her father had made some of those wheels.

George was left with the two children to bring up alone. Without hesitating, Mary pitched-in and took over mothering her five-year-old brother and helping her father to run the house. She was ten years old.

Within two years, forty-three-year-old George had married twenty-nine-year-old Annie. He joined chambers in Temple at Fig Tree Court,[5] moved the family to Hemel Hempstead, and they had a son – Derick. Mary blossomed at Berkhamstead School for Girls winning scholarship after scholarship, culminating in one to read English at Bedford College for Women.[6] They were again a happy family. They moved to a bigger house in Surrey. Mary went to university; young George, in his mid-teens, showed promise as an artist and his teachers were confident that he would be offered a place at one of the top London art schools. Derick had started to talk and be quite fun. The sun shone.

---

4   *Now Finchley Golf Course.*
5   *Fig Tree Court (1666 – 1941) in Inner Temple was destroyed in the London Blitz and was later amalgamated into Elm Court in Middle Temple.*
6   *Since 1900 part of London University.*

Then, aged thirty-three, Annie died. Within a year George, now nearly fifty, had married the twenty-seven-year-old Dorothy, only seven years older than Mary. Being determined to take on a middle-aged man with a toddler, and prove she could do it, she didn't want any help or what she saw as competition. She made it plain to Mary that she saw her role as stepmother not friend. It was now her house which Mary could visit, but not too often, and when she came it would be on Dorothy's terms. Henceforth Dorothy would be the person who gave succour to George. Mary was no longer needed. She could step back, thank you.

Not only had Mary lost her mother and her much loved stepmother, but now she was being kept away from her father. For over half of her life, he had been her one constant, her loved and loving anchor. Mary was miserable. She slumped back to university and buried herself in her degree. She had transferred from English to read Analytical Philosophy and Logical Positivism under Susan Stebbing and found it fascinating.[7] It was a fruitful distraction. When she was awarded a good degree, she wanted to share her achievement with her father, to touch base with her brother George, who was heading for The Central School of Art and Design; she was keen to see Derick, who by now must be running around, mischievous even. They would have fun together; the three siblings could play games and she would make up bedtime stories for the little one. She was sure that Dorothy had been caught on the back foot, had been uncertain about becoming part of an established family, and had felt the need to establish her position in it. Everything would have calmed down and be alright now.

It was not. Dorothy gave birth to twin girls and one promptly died. Yet again death scythed the family. Mary's happiness at her degree was as unwelcome as her wish to be with her father. Dorothy told her that she must find employment and she made sure *The Times* was left on the breakfast table, every day, folded at the Employment page. One hundred years later, it is difficult to imagine what life in 1920s Britain was like. Sixteen million lives had been lost in the First War and Spanish flu had accounted for fifty million people in 1919 – one fifth of the world population. British employment figures may have risen slightly above their twenty per cent low, but Mary could not find a job. One morning Dorothy prodded an advertisement with an index finger.

---

7   *Susan Stebbing 1885–1943 was regarded as the pioneer of analytical philosophy; was the first female professor of philosophy in Britain.*

"There you are. There's something, and it will give you somewhere to live."

Mary read the advertisement. It was for a governess in a private house and the annual wage was thirty pounds.[8] It was a double blow. Not only did Dorothy want her out of the house but thirty pounds was what she thought Mary was worth, even after her degree and a multitude of scholarships. Mary beat a retreat to London where she met up with a university friend who introduced her to some nuns. They offered her a bed, until she could afford the rent for a room.

She found a job wrapping parcels in the basement of Marshall and Snelgrove, an old-fashioned department store, full of grandmothers, on the corner of Oxford Street and Vere Street[9]. Sometimes she was allowed above ground to place the parcels into the elegantly gloved hands of waiting customers. She must have found it dull and dingy folding brown paper and tightly knotting string in a cellar lit by sparsely dangled 40-watt bulbs. No doubt the logical positivism helped.

One of the above-stairs girls offered her space in the eaves of a rickety house overlooking the railway lines that converged on Marylebone Station, and Mary left the nuns. Walking back to the garret one day she noticed an advertisement for an evening job as a waitress in a ladies dining club. The place was the domain of a Mrs Williams who, extraordinarily in the 1920s, was a single parent. Her husband, Frederick de Lobau Williams, maintained such a low profile as to be invisible. Their daughter Freda (Winifreda Iola Margeurite de Lobau Williams) was ten years younger than Mary, who soon had child-minding added to her duties. She found their arms open and soon became part of their lives. At birth she had been called Ethel Mary after a cousin, to curry favour with the cousin's father. Mary hated it and currying favour can't have worked because she was allowed to drop 'Ethel'. Now she changed her name to Jill,[10] which everyone who met her at that time called her for the rest of her life. Her relationship with Mrs Williams and Freda was to become life-lasting, providing her with the loving family that her father's family did not. It was a fresh start.

When Mrs Williams' restaurant lease expired, she decided that a move to the country would be a timely idea. She found a neglected 17th-century timber-framed cottage in Blewbury, a tiny village under the Berkshire Downs, fourteen miles south of Oxford. With a collection of round barrows nearby

8   *Slightly less than £2,000 in 2022.*
9   *It became the site of Debenham's flagship store.*
10   *A set of gold and blue enamel inlaid cufflinks with the initials J.G. still exist.*

and an Iron Age hill fort on the horizon, beyond which ran the Ridgeway, she thought it would make an attractive place to establish a boarding house. Those wishing to escape London, fifty miles east, would be able to catch the train to the Upton and Blewbury Station a couple of miles away and enjoy bucolic breaks. As if by magic, more likely Mrs Williams' recommendation to one of her dining regulars, just as the restaurant closed and Mary was wondering what to do next, she was offered a position as a jobbing journalist reviewing books and conducting the occasional interview.

She had not been in touch with home, and they knew nothing about her living with the nuns. Now, aged twenty-seven, with what she regarded as a real occupation, something of which she felt her father would be proud, she wracked her brains about how to end, what had been for her, the heart-breaking silence. The arrival of her first pay packet coincided with her father's upcoming birthday. She decided to find something special for him. She had wanted to visit the British Museum to see the new exhibition of Persian Art and decided she might find a nice engraving in one of those little shops in or around Museum Street.

With what she inscribed in the flyleaf as her 'first fruits', she bought the nine hundredth copy of a limited edition of Pope's *The Iliad*.[11] The English text, from the first edition of 1715, was on the left pages, and the Greek '*by permission of the Delegates of Oxford University Press*' was on the right. It had chapter headings ('*ornaments*') '*... designed, engraved by, and composed under the supervision of Rudolf Koch*'. It had been beautifully bound in goat skin, printed and made in Holland's Harlem. It was a book of which the publishers Random House, were so pleased, it came with instructions on how to open it, before cutting the pages, without breaking its spine. Mary signed it, to her father, with 'all her love'. It might have taken all her pay packet as well, but it was a fabulous present, and the perfect statement of where she had got to since she'd seen him last. Even Dorothy might notice.

When she told the bookseller that it was a present for her father and she was going to post it to Sussex, he wrapped it particularly carefully. While Mary watched with her professional eye, he asked her about herself, what she did, where she was living. When she told him that she was looking for somewhere she could live by herself, fond though she had become of her flat mate, he told her about the two rooms on the top floor above the bookshop. They had been used as a bit of a dumping ground since he and his wife moved after the birth of

---

11   *926 copies were for sale in England, 525 in the United States.*

their firstborn. If she'd help clear the rooms, it would be handy for him to have someone living above the shop and he was sure that they could come 'to an arrangement'. They did. Any young woman who gave her father such a lovely present would make the perfect tenant, he told himself. A few weeks later, with enough in her bank account to buy a bed, Mary moved to Bloomsbury. As she rearranged the furniture the bookseller had left for her, and had hung a few of the foxed prints that he said she could borrow, she asked herself 'Where could be more perfect for someone wanting to write, than Bloomsbury?'

With her next pay packet, she bought a mahogany writing desk. The hinged writing fall had warped slightly and a few of the brass handles on the little inside drawers were missing, but as the bric-a-brac dealer told her, if it had been perfect, it would have been in one of those Mayfair antique shops, not in a back street halfway to Hampstead, anyway she should expect a bit of movement in the wood after one hundred and fifty years.

No longer needed to wait at table or childmind, she spent the evenings writing at her lovely new Georgian desk and when lost for the right word, she reorganised the treasury tags, paper clips and brass paper fasteners in the inside drawers. Her first book *Bid Her Awake*, dedicated to her father, was published in 1930. The reviews must have attracted the attention of the editor of the *London Evening News* because he offered her a job. Books, all published by Hutchinson and Co, followed year on year each one as well reviewed as the last.[12] Mary had entered literary circles and was earning more than she had dreamed. She bought a car, a ten-year-old Austin Seven. Although ostensibly large enough to carry three passengers they would have had to have been the size of dolls. The chassis was just over six feet long and the wheels only forty inches apart.

When, the following Friday evening, Mrs Williams answered the door she was surprised to see Mary.

"Jill, Darling, how did you get here? Did you walk from the station?"

Mary had parked the little car round the corner. She enjoyed surprises.

"Come and look!" Mary proudly stroked the swooping front bumper, patted the wing mirror, and opened the driver's door to show off the upholstered leather seats. Over the next months, every weekend she would drive to Blewbury and help Mrs Williams look after the increasing number of guests, for whom they started to convert stables into more bedrooms. Mary scrubbed,

---

12 *'The Almond Tree' was dedicated to Mrs Williams, 'Visitors for Miss Howard' was dedicated to her university friend Rosina Graham; 'Journey by Candlelight' was dedicated to Freda.*

swept, and painted. She searched the junk shops in Didcot and Wantage for mirrors and bedside tables, proudly returning to Blewbury with what she had been able to fit into her gleaming black car.

As Mrs Williams' reputation spread so did Mary's. She was 'poached' from the *Evening News* by the *Evening Standard*, as a feature writer. This soon became a regular spot which she wrote anonymously under initials. Occasionally it raised eyebrows, meat to an editor and she became the highest paid woman journalist on Fleet Street.

With all Mrs Williams' outhouses furnished and occupied, Mary decided it was again time to see her father. She drove the little car to Sussex, taking with her copies of her latest book *Call for a Crooner*, hot from the publishers. She signed them, and gave one each to her father, brother George, and Dorothy.

Dorothy must have noticed the dedication 'To G.B. STERN – with gratitude for the lifeline she threw to this story.'[13] She told Mary that now that the littlest ones were at school, she had found time to write herself.

"Now we're both authors!" announced Dorothy.

Mary did not hold grudges; Dorothy had thrown a plank across the chasm. Dorothy started sending manuscripts to Mary, suggesting she might like to publish them, or possibly introduce her to her friends at the BBC. Mary did help. Some of Dorothy's stories were read on *Woman's Hour* and Mary herself printed a couple of them.

Malcolm Messer had been given the fledgling *Farmers Weekly* to edit. He believed that farmers' wives, generally, were patronised. That they were perceived as rosy cheeked, slightly buxom women who wore aprons out of doors and collected eggs from clucking hens nesting in thatched barns. They might be seen crossing a cobbled yard, addressing a magnificently plumed, constantly crowing cockerel, or sidestepping a hissing gaggle of geese as they carried heavy buckets of milk hanging from a yoke on their shoulders.[14] In the kitchen of the low-

---

13 *G B Stern 1890–1973. Long-time friend of (Dame) Rebecca West and H.G. Wells. Author of many books, some filmed, and plays.*

14 *Farmers Weekly's obituary for Malcolm included a panel of Messerisms. One was "The next man to print a picture of a goose travelling from east to west across one of my pages will be fired." Another was "The trouble with accountants is that they can't count." He complained, after Hultons sold, and big publishing companies were involved, that company accountants could never grasp the 'bigger picture'. In the sixties, E. J. Smith one of the originals and a critical member of staff, had a leg amputated because of cancer. Malcolm ordered an automatic car for him. The accountants blocked it as only company directors merited automatics. Malcolm pointed out that besides the human element, E.J. was worth more to the company than a slightly more expensive car. A furore followed. They never blocked Malcolm again.*

ceilinged farmhouse there would be a string of grubby children waiting to be fed wholesome food. He knew that farmers' wives were much more than that. They were essential, not only to the farmers' (and grubby children's) welfare, but also to the rural economy. What he had seen of the women's weeklies, with their knit one/purl one editorial, and short stories about falling in love with passing hussars, was he thought irrelevant to farmers' wives. He had decided *Farmers Weekly* should have a section pitched at these staunch and resourceful women, so he put out word that he was looking for someone to create and edit these pages. Mary was suggested. She protested that her experience of rural life was limited to a little light trespass in woodland as a child and walking on The Downs at weekends.

"Well just pop in anyway, come and see us," was his reply.

She did. She was intrigued. She returned now and again to give advice on how she thought it should go. She began working part time until it took over and *Farmers Weekly* gained the foremost woman journalist. It was an inspired appointment. Malcolm Messer's selection of someone who knew little about country life, even less about agriculture, raised eyebrows but she was an immediate success. Farmers' wives wrote in to say that through her writing they felt they had gained a friend. She started collating the recipes they sent. Most featured what now sound less than mouth-watering ideas of how to stretch the sparse ingredients then available. Lard was substituted for butter and if the hens were off-lay, powdered eggs could be used instead. It was recommended to remove the longest wool from lambs' tails with scissors before scalding and making an Oxfordshire lamb's tail pie. Waste not want not. The first edition of *Farmhouse Fare* was published in time for Christmas 1935. There was no mention of turkeys, but a Christmas pudding made with carrots and a gill of 'old ale' was the answer from Montgomeryshire. It ran to seven editions.

In 1936 she wrote her first children's book, dedicated to Derick and her sister Elisabeth. *The Yellow Cat*, translated into several languages, was published by Geoffrey Cumberlege at Oxford University Press, and illustrated by Isobel and John Morton Sale. Two years later the OUP published *Animal Joe* illustrated by Newton Whittaker. Mary dedicated it to her godson Amyas, Freda's new-born. Both books ran to several editions, still reprinted twenty years on.

She became a radio broadcaster, one BBC producer described her as 'a natural'. In January 1943, she was invited by the United States Department of Agriculture to visit the States to explain to farmers' wives exactly what it was like, trying to farm with a reduced labour force and produce the food for this blockaded island. The American wives were beginning to understand the problems.[15] For six months she travelled the length and breadth of the United States visiting twenty-one states and covering over twelve thousand miles. She addressed meetings, and broadcast on local radio stations. She told of the shortage of 'manpower' on the land because more than fifty thousand skilled British farmworkers had joined the armed forces in the first two years of war alone. She told of the challenges of those left behind, trying to find time to train 'town' girls while short-staffed, they continued to work the land and tend animals. Mary explained about land girls, how they drove heavy machinery and excavators to drain the Fens to increase the acreage for crops, especially potatoes. That six thousand women – Lumber Jills, joined the Timber Corps to make pit props and telegraph poles. Being farmers' wives, they weren't surprised land girls were being used to form vermin squads to kill foxes, rabbits, moles and, principally rats. It was estimated that there were fifty million rats in Britain competing for the precious grain, and one year two land girls managed to kill twelve thousand rats. Imagine asking the average 21st century urban girl to tackle that. On March 21st Mary was invited to tea at the White House by Eleanor Roosevelt,[16] whom she found impressively well informed about all matters agricultural. At the time The Farm Labor Bill with plans for the American Women's Land Army were being batted about Capitol Hill.[17]

Mary wrote weekly throughout the time she was in the States. Whether from the ship in mid-Atlantic surrounded by U-boats, between radio interviews or giving lectures, her pieces were telegraphed across the Atlantic to the *Farmers Weekly* offices in Shoe Lane and were on farmers' wives' kitchen tables every single Friday. On March 13th 1943, nearly eighty years before the Russian invasion of Ukraine, she wrote about 'Food, the Weapon of War'.

When she returned to the office, everyone was thrilled that she had made it back safely. She was met with a metaphorical red carpet and the actual popping of corks. Everyone had missed her terribly; she was someone who made everybody's day better.

---

15   *The United States entered WWII on December 7th 1941 after the Japanese attack on Pearl Harbour. Germany and Italy declared war on the US two days later. Twelve million American soldiers were mobilised, and the production of military and aviation hardware went into overdrive employing even more men.*

16   *Wife of Franklin D. Roosevelt 32nd President of the United States from 1933 until his death in April 1945.*

17   *By the end of April 1943 there was an acute shortage of vegetables in the US as there was not enough manpower to harvest them.*

TWO

MALCOLM

Andrew Messer was born in 1867. Both his parents came from the very north of Northumberland, the previous generations had been herders in lowland Scotland, latterly West Lothian. Each generation had moved another thirty miles south. His mother, Elizabeth, was from North Berwick, his father, Walter, worked as a policeman in the tiny village of Akeld on the edge of the Cheviot Hills. They married in Alnwick. By the time Andrew was born, Walter was keeping the law in Hexham about twenty miles west of Newcastle-upon-Tyne. Andrew was born in the police station.

His parents had married relatively late, his mother was heading for forty, and they had given up hope. The cherished, only child of older parents, he benefited from their attention, and in common with many Victorians, for whom education was deemed everything, they helped him learn to read earlier than most. For the next eighty years he had a book in his hand or pocket.

It was a fortuitous time for those with educational aspirations for their children. The 1870 Education Act set the parameters for all children between five and twelve to go to school. There had been objections, some on the grounds that it would remove children from the labour force. Another was that those recently enfranchised in the 1867 Reform Act might learn to think for themselves – not necessarily advantageous to those who needed their votes. A third objection was that money would go to certain religious groups – hitherto, along with the dames' schools, the providers of primary education. The non-conformists didn't want their pupils taught by Anglicans or Anglicans enriched for teaching 'their' children.[1] The Welsh were against The Act because teaching would be in English, which their children didn't speak.

Secondary education had come under scrutiny at the same time. Strange though it may seem, public schools were just that. In 1861 a commission was set up under the chairmanship of the Earl of Clarendon following complaints about the situation at Eton College. It sat for four years and investigated seven boarding schools that had been founded as charity schools.[2] The resultant Public Schools Act was passed in 1868. The Taunton Commission followed looking into the remaining endowed schools of which there were seven hundred and eighty-two grammar schools. The Endowed Schools Act was passed in 1869. New schools, often called grammar schools, were created emulating the public schools' ethos with an updated but classically based curriculum. Andrew benefitted from these changes. He won a scholarship to grammar school followed by a scholarship to Edinburgh University to read medicine, where he continued to excel. Having graduated, he was invited to remain to teach and practise in the hospital, which he did for five years. When he returned to Northumberland he was a surgeon, a sleeves-rolled-up GP, with terrifying instruments in his Gladstone bag.

Many of his patients were miners. Over half a century before the days of free health care, he persuaded them to put aside one penny at a time, whenever they could, to pay for medicines should they be needed in future. He believed that much of the ill-health in the mining community was caused by the appalling housing, so he remonstrated with the Duke of Northumberland who owned the mines and houses, and improvements were made. The 8th Duke and the policeman's son became friends. Everybody respected 'Doctor Messer of Lemington'; many loved him.

In 1893 he married Elizabeth, the twenty-one-year-old daughter of one of the Duke of Northumberland's mining engineers. He opened a practice based in Lemington, then a little village five miles west of Newcastle. Two boys

---

1   Scotland had a differently administered system but there were remonstrations about language too, as most spoke Gaelic.
2   Charterhouse, Eton, Harrow, Rugby, Shrewsbury, Westminster and Winchester.

predictably named Walter and Andrew (Andy) – quickly followed and then after five years, the baby Malcolm. There is a miniature of Malcolm as a two-year-old. He looks more like an Elizabeth.

Neither Andrew nor Elizabeth was fenced in by horizons. In the late 1890s, before Malcolm was born, Elizabeth had crossed the Atlantic with the Lemington Mixed Choir to tour Canada. Before the First War, once the two eldest boys were at school and with Malcolm left safely with aunts, Elizabeth and Andrew had sailed with friends to Cape Town and ventured across South Africa. Fifty years on Elizabeth still made herself cry with laughter describing to her granddaughter the challenges of decorously mounting an ostriche, while wearing a swirling ankle-length skirt. Then they had ostrich raced across the Veldt.[3]

Andrew had experienced what he found to be a stultifying 'chapel' upbringing and was determined that his sons would be brought up with as little religion in their lives as possible, so he sent all three sons to Ackworth, the Quaker school in Yorkshire. In 1915 Walter and Andy volunteered with the Friends War Relief Victims Service and later registered with the Religious Society of Friends (Quaker) Ambulance Unit. A month after arriving in France, Walter was driving German wounded from the front to a field hospital, when his ambulance was strafed by the *Deutsche Luftstreitkräfte*. Andy, aged 19, was near the rear of the convoy and watched as his elder brother's ambulance, with limbs and torsos, was blown towards the sky, landing either side of the road.

The family had a couple of scruffy Dandy Dinmont terriers whose passion in life was cat rousting. If felines, that strayed into the garden, failed to take these rather jokey-looking dogs seriously, they were dumped triumphantly as trophies, on the doorstep. Elizabeth's first job in the morning was to make sure that the threshold was clear before the first patients arrived for surgery. The cats were buried among the roses and were privately credited for the abundance and depth of colour of the blooms. Elizabeth was cutting some of her favourites to arrange for the hall, when she saw the policeman open the garden gate and walk towards her. She knew exactly what he had come to say, she just wondered which of her sons had been killed. She hoped not both; some families were losing all their sons. Although it fell to local policemen to

---

3   *An ostriche can reach speeds of up to 45 miles an hour – about the same as a thoroughbred horse. They can cover over 16 feet in one stride.*

tell families, and they were doing it many times a week, he and all his family were Andrew's patients, and he had known Walter and Andy all his life. It must have made it even harder, such personal news to carry.

Walter is buried in Malo-les-Bains and is believed to be the only conscientious objector to be commemorated on a UK war memorial, in Lemington Cemetery. He had been a gentle giant who had played rugby for Edinburgh, where he had already begun studying at the School of Agriculture, hoping to become a farmer. Andy continued with the Ambulance Unit in France until the end of the war and then went up to Edinburgh, to read politics, philosophy and economics, as did Malcolm. Andrew thought no one was properly educated until they had read PPE, which he insisted they did before specialising. The boys shared an elderly car that managed to negotiate the climb over Carter Bar, the nearly fourteen-hundred-foot pass on the Cheviots. As the younger, it fell to Malcolm to climb out and clear the windscreen at regular intervals. If conditions were too bad, it was necessary to keep the windscreen fixed open and the snow piled up on their well-rugged laps.[4] After graduating, Andy remained at Edinburgh to read medicine and became a leading pathologist. Malcolm went up to Oxford to read agricultural economics. Andrew, helped by a stalwart Matron,[5] added running Newcastle General Hospital to his brief.

Whenever Elizabeth said that there was no room in the house for more books, Andrew would claim that those he extracted from the copious inside pockets of his greatcoat had been around for some time. They had. All new purchases spent time in one of the coach houses so he could tell her, with a clear conscience, that they were not new. She was never fooled but it was a good game. After his death those books which Malcolm and Andy couldn't house formed the foundation of a public library. Like his parents, Andrew was a passionate believer in education, and established a school for adults.

During WWII he was appointed Inspector of Military Hospitals. One day, as the top brass ushered him along the chequered marble corridors of a requisitioned stately home, sweeping orderlies aside as they went, the highly polished shoes clattered towards the wet mop-head of a recuperating private. He looked up and exclaimed in broad Geordie

"Eeeee it's THE Doctor!"

---

4   Automatic wipers were not fitted as standard until 1919. It wasn't until 1939 that GM introduced heaters. They did not become standard in all vehicles until the '60s.

5   She bequeathed her favourite necklace and matching earrings to Andrew's granddaughter 'in memory of a truly great man.'

Andrew had delivered him, his parents, and siblings. They were delighted to see each other. The soldier hadn't seen his family since enlistment and Andrew was able to bring him up to speed, including the recent births of two cousins. Unknown to either of them the fathers of the babies were in North Africa as part of the 'recce corps'.[6] The accompanying top brass stood aside, moustaches and fingers twitching, irritated at having had their planned progress impeded.

*

Malcolm thoroughly enjoyed his time at Oxford. Older than his peers and with one degree already under his belt, he felt confident enough to spend time producing plays for the Oxford University Dramatic Society (OUDS), including an open-air production, in Headington Hill Park, of *A Midsummer Night's Dream* with Jack Hulbert and (Dame) Cicely Courtneidge, who came down from London to take leading roles. Agriculture was a course that attracted the sons of those who had more acres than it was critical to count, as well as the cars that they were allowed to enable them to drive out of the city to look at agriculture in action. Malcolm played poker with them and was soon in debt. He had punched above his bank balance. Andy bailed him out. Having learned a bruising lesson from the younger guys, he concentrated on socialising with postgraduates and the increasing number of theatrical friends.

He had needed to wear spectacles since a child and during the last year of his degree, while playing tennis, a ball smashed into them sending a shard of glass into his eye. He was not allowed to read for months but already had been offered a post as a Junior Research Fellow at the Universtity of Oxford Agricultural Economics Research Institute. Instead of studying for his finals he spent the summer wearing an apparently fetching eye-patch and being punted up and down the Cherwell with the girls of the moment and plentiful supplies of hock. He was given a degree without sitting one single exam.

He had matured, lived in comfort, and ate well. He took a room in the turret at the top of the Randolph Hotel, a short stroll across St Giles to his old college St John's, and on Sundays he would drive the fourteen miles to Thame

---

6   *The 4th Battalion of the Royal Northumberland Fusiliers was transferred to the Reconnaissance Corps in April 1941 and sent to North Africa as part of the 50th Division.*

to enjoy prolonged meals at John Fothergill's 'Spread Eagle'.[7] Fifty years later, when asked why he had not been given a gong for services to agriculture, he explained that one had been offered but he had declined as he thought he would be expected to sit on committees which he was not prepared to do.

"Anyway," he said, "a complimentary mention in John Fothergill's book is more exclusive than a 'K'."[8,9]

He found working at the Oxford Agricultural Economic Research Unit intellectually absorbing. He had over six research papers published by the Ministry of Agriculture, as well as The Agricultural Atlas of England and Wales. It is still available in twenty-five World Cat Libraries.

By 1865 a farming magazine *Scottish Farmer and Horticulturalist* had evolved into *The Farmer*. In turn, it evolved into *The Farmer and Stockbreeder*, that started weekly publication in 1889. By the mid-twenties it was the leading farming magazine. In the early thirties, with agriculture in a state of flux, the press barons, Leverhulme and Rothermere, saw the commercial opportunities of farming journalism. In 1934 they decided to launch a rival publication – *The Farmers Weekly*.

Frank Prewett, the Canadian WWI poet, friend of Siegfried Sassoon, Robert Graves and Lady Ottoline Morrel, and a member of her Garsington Circle, was also an agriculturalist undertaking research at the Oxford Agricultural Economic Research Unit. He was appointed the first editor. Malcolm was offered the job of technical editor for an annual salary of eight hundred pounds. It was the amount he had borrowed from Andy to settle his gambling debt, so he accepted it *pro tem*. He didn't realise how temporary it would be. Prewett, prone to depression and erratic moods, stormed out during one press night after a row with the barons. In the emergency the editorial reins were thrown at Malcolm. They were to remain in his hands for over thirty years.

It may be difficult to imagine, although now in 2022 with Ukraine trashed in battle,[10] we might do well to refocus, rural Britain was not always

---

7   *John Fothergill 1876-1957. Self-described as 'Pioneer Amateur Innkeeper'. Painter, writer, gardener, cook, archaeologist, aesthete, eccentric, and friend to the glitterati.*

8   *An Innkeeper's Diary by John Fothergill. A paperback of the 1931 book, with a forword by Hilary Rubinstein, was published by Faber and Faber in late '80s and '90s. ISBN 0-571-15014-4. An excellent, highly amusing read and handle on those times.*

9   *He already had been awarded a 'C' – CBE in 1949 for wartime services to the Red Cross.*

10 *In the last harvest before the 2022 Russian invasion, the Ukraine was the 7th greatest global wheat producer at thirty-three million tons.*

regarded as a recreational facility to be 'rewilded'. It was the factory floor of food production, critical to feeding the island's population. The changes in agriculture between the 20th-century wars could not have been envisaged, and they continued after the Second World War.

Since the Enclosure Act of 1773 the health and fertility of the soil had been managed by mixed farming and rotated crops. Dependant on the soil and local climate, and the suitability for specific crops, rotations ran for between two to eight years. They reduced disease; deep-rooted crops such as carrots and potatoes aeriated the soil; animals and naturally nitrogenous-fixing plants increased fertility as well as improved soil structure. As importantly, rotations created consistent employment for the agricultural labourer throughout the year. That changed in 1914. About one hundred and seventy thousand of those working the land were conscripted.[11] At the same time five hundred thousand farm-horses were requisitioned by the army. The muscles of food production had been excised. The first Ferguson tractors were built in the 1930s; in 1938 Harry Ferguson and Henry Ford got together, and although later they fell out over patent breaches, tractors began to work British fields. In 1942 English and Welsh farms had fewer than one hundred and thirty-two thousand tractors. Within ten years that number had more than doubled. The nitrogen factories that had made explosives during WWII started making synthetic fertiliser. In 1947 the all-party Agriculture Act was passed to guarantee prices and markets that would enable stability and efficiency. Between 1948 and 1962 output per man-year in agriculture increased by eighty-four percent.

It was a time of huge change and, before universal television ownership or the internet, the only way for farmers to keep up with progress and innovative ideas was through the agricultural trade press. The press barons had been right. In 1937 Sir Edward Hulton founded Hulton Press and bought *Farmers Weekly*. Malcolm persuaded him that the paper should have its own farm so that new ideas could be tried out and results passed on. Yields and harvests would be reported honestly to the readership. It would enable the feedback of failures and problems as well as successes and would create a common bond. It was an idea that worked and over the decades the portfolio stretched to twelve farms from Scotland to Normandy, Wales to Cambridgeshire, Devon to

---

11   *About twelve per cent of males.*

Northumberland. Varying enormously in land and acreage, with their specific advantages and disadvantages, some were owned, some leased and some share farmed. The first was Grove Farm at Tring.

THREE

THEN THERE
WERE THREE

1945–1951

The office was buzzing with happiness when Mary returned from America. Malcolm and Mary were euphoric too. After eight years working side by side, they had been separated and had realised that it wasn't only their working lives that were incomplete without each other. A fortnight after her return on July 3rd 1943 they were married.

They delayed risking what proved to be my conception until they were pretty sure that they wouldn't have to '*Heil Hitler*' on Horse Guards' Parade; that the *Sturmabteilung* was not going to swarm along our Roman roads. That the Allies would win the war. It was mid-March 1945. The Allies had crossed the Rhine and the Soviets had repulsed the Germans at Lake Balaton and were heading for Vienna. By the end of the first week in December I was late. My parents had become impatient, so Malcolm took Mary to the theatre every night in the hope that laughter would trigger parturition.

Although they had a flat in Tufton Street, Westminster, Mary had found an obstetrician in Carshalton, fifteen miles away, who had developed an 'easier' way for women to give birth, so it must have seemed to her worth the drive. Malcolm did not hang around. He returned to the Travellers Club in Pall Mall and undoubtedly drank a lot of whisky with his friends, under the cast of the Bassae frieze in the library, until he was called to the telephone by the head steward. He had become the father of a girl. He drove straight to see Mary, whom he adored. I had arrived on the 16th of December.

The family of three celebrated Christmas at Grove Farm. The red brick farmhouse had been built to suit the wants of a hands-on Edwardian farmer with nearly three hundred acres, comfortable but not there to impress. There was no gravel sweep, no gryphoned gateposts. Visitors arrived via the farmyard. The east elevation was bang on Marshcroft Lane that only went to the canal and on out over the 'marsh'. Two high-ceilinged 'reception' rooms with south-facing bay windows overlooked the lawn. Between them, where one would have expected a garden door, a *Magnolia grandiflora* grew against the wall, sparring with the gutters. The lawn stretched towards the road, a cut-through between Tring station and the Icknield Way, but in practice most traffic was only for the farm. Nevertheless, the garden was screened from it by a high brick wall. To the west of the house, the vegetable garden was divided from the lawn by espaliered fruit trees of which more grew against the wall backing farm buildings. The scant, narrow, brick-edged flower beds under the walls were more of an apology than a statement. Across the Marsh Lane was an orchard with more apple and pear trees. The war had barely ended; food still took precedence over *flora*.

I don't remember ever going into the dining room, with one of the bay windows, but I have clear memories of being trotted out, literally, in the drawing room with the other bay, to do the party trick, which was (learning) to walk its length with an empty Gordon's gin bottle in each hand, used as stabilisers. The nursery, my bedroom and Nanny's were up the back stairs. Mine overlooked the lane and orchard. The hub of the house was the kitchen with its ancillary larders and scullery. There was always cooking, preserving, or conserving going on and it led to the back door – the way to all that was exciting in the wide world – the farmyard, a collection of brick and black-pitched timber buildings built at the same time as the house.[1]

My parents left Tring on Monday mornings for London, returning on Friday afternoons after the editorial meeting for the next issue. I remained at the farm with Nanny. I was her last charge before she retired, and she was finding it difficult to push the big pram that I think was named after some

---

1   *Farmers Weekly sold the house, gardens, and yards for building in 1976.*

royal residence. The sprung chrome chassis was attached to four gleaming wheels with solid rubber tyres, perfect for Kensington Gardens and urban pavements but it made for heavy going on country lanes. Quite why a tiny baby needed anything so big I have no idea, but I imagine it was to allow room for a 'spare' and those were the prams of the era. My parents decided that the solution for the daily intake of fresh air would be a pony and trap. Nanny would not have to push the pram and as Joe the carter had less to do each time a shire horse was replaced by a tractor,[2] it would give him interest and something to do. Daddy bought a Welsh mare, Betty, who had spent the war pulling the milk float round Aylesbury. Joe located a dogcart[3] for her to pull and for him to drive. Every weekday afternoon Joe, Nanny and I went down the lane on a leisurely outing to the Grand Union Canal, clip clop and back. Usually there were barges to watch and at the right time of year ducklings and cygnets.

When hounds met nearby, someone would be persuaded to wrap me in enough warm clothes, and Joe would lead Betty to the meet. Once delivered, I would be put on her saddle and Joe would hold my leg to stop my falling off the other side. When Nanny retired and days in the dogcart were no longer needed, Daddy gave in to Betty's demands for a mate. She had developed the habit of banking the five-bar gate from the orchard to reach the remaining cart horses. He put her in foal. She produced two good colts. The eldest, a rig was typically unreliable and sold as a three-year-old.[4] He went on to win at the Horse of the Year Show. The other remained with us for life. He was thirty-three when he died in his sleep, on the day after my father.

On Friday afternoons I would become thoroughly over-excited and usually ended being sent back to the nursery, soon after my parents arrived home.

"Nanny, I think Susie is ready for bed!"

Having been building to a crescendo for most of the day I was indeed ready for bed and fell straight asleep, only to wake up full of bounce as soon as the cockerels started to crow. After breakfast Daddy would take me round the farm with him as he inspected the stock and crops and talked with the men.

---

2   *In 1945 there were nearly 680,000 working farm horses but by 1955 there were only 235,000.*

3   *A dogcart – so named as it had a ventilated box in the back for carrying sporting dogs. Open topped, it had seats, back-to-back, for four people and was very popular for those wishing to watch country pursuits. The forerunner of the 'car-follower'.*

4   *A rig is a male horse that either retained an undescended testicle or was incompletely castrated. With testosterone still in the body, a rig can behave like a stallion and have an unpredictable temperament.*

He would prop me on top of the gates so that I could look at the cattle, yarded for the winter. He piggy-backed me across fields in summer. He was delighted when told by Nanny that, the previous week, she had taken me to see the cows and I had told her, "Not cows, Nanny, bullocks!"

She must have been the perfect Nanny, very loving and cosy, because I have nothing other than a warm glow when I think of her. She wore sensible shoes; wool and tweed in winter and cotton in summer and she never went out without her brown felt hat, even on the hottest days. I remember being very sad, crying under the eiderdown, when long after she had retired, Daddy told me that she had died. I hadn't seen her since the day she left, and I hadn't thought about her much. What had happened? Why hadn't we seen her? Where had she been? It was an early, but not always remembered lesson, about keeping in touch with people who matter.

Mummy would let me help her cook. She had the reputation of being able to conjure up delicious meals even during wartime rationing. Having a productive garden and orchard as well as farm produce must have been a great help, but it would have been dearth or glut. Although fruit and some vegetables could be preserved by bottling, deepfreezes were still a novelty. I was transfixed when watching her sewing all the wonderful clothes she made for me with the fabric she had bartered in Aylesbury market for pork, eggs, and cream cheese.[5,6] She drew for me; bathed me and wrapped me tightly me in a huge warm towel. She told me her own stories and hugged me lots. When she had to be away, she posted me letters written in blue biro on an A4 sheet of airmail paper. Verbs, adjectives, and adverbs were punctuated with clever, economically drawn sketches instead of nouns. Trains puffed clouds of smoke; station masters with rounded cheeks blew whistles and waved flags; steamships sailed across to France's shores, marked by a blue striped *tricolore*. I always knew she'd come back.

Mr Ferry was the farm manager, but he was more than that. My father had met him when visiting Winterdyne, an innovative farm in Staffordshire that he was managing, and he must have seemed just the person with whom to try

---

5 *Clothes rationing was introduced in 1941 and lasted nearly 4 years. Adults initially were given 60 coupons a year, later reduced to 48. Children qualified for 10 more. Child-sized coats or mackintoshes were 11 coupons; girls' woollen dresses 8 coupons; boots or shoes 3 coupons.*

6 *Food rationing began in 1940 and for some items lasted until 1954. At its height, typically, an adult's weekly allowance was 1 egg; 2 oz of cheese; 4–8 oz of bacon; 2 oz of butter and 3 pints of milk.*

out ideas. He and his wife had arrived at Grove Farm in 1943. They had three daughters and then a son, Howard, who was a year older than me and became the ideal big brother

Nanny retired and was followed by a succession of girls from Finland who came to learn English. How my mother linked up with Finland remains unclear, but they obviously loved life at Grove Farm because they continued to send cards at Christmas, with all their latest news, long after they married and produced their own children. When my parents were in London, Mrs Ferry became my fall-back mother and the Ferry's house my pit stop.

Like all toddlers, as soon as I could, I spent most of the time trying to escape the house. I would scamper out of the back door and head for the yard to watch the men milking, making ricks and Joe tending the horses. Before the Hertfordshire Agricultural Society had a permanent showground the annual show travelled the county.[7] When it was held nearby a handful of competing shire horses were stabled in the yard. It was fascinating watching the men plaiting the great beasts' manes and tails, but the most memorable time was when a display team of Gurkhas camped on the farm. They stayed for about a week and Howard and I were transfixed. Besides the funny way they tilted their hats, we had never seen Asian faces. They gave my parents a large *kukri* with a buffalo horn handle in a holster, complete with *karda* and *chakma*.[8] I was given a small version. They were kept for decades until the holsters perished, and the rusty *kukri* and *karda* looked too much like offensive weapons to be left lying around.

After a few years of living at Grove Farm my parents started looking for a farm to buy for themselves. Despite both earning significant sums they lacked capital, but a friend of my father's, Gordon Saunders, the senior partner of John D Wood & Co, had made enough with lots to spare, and without any offspring to consider he volunteered to ante-up most of the purchase price and to go into farming partnership with my father. The plan was that my father would buy him out over the years. My parents would start a new chapter. Daddy would be handy for Oxford and could return to the Agricultural Economics Research Institute. Mummy would continue writing. They would retire from *Farmers Weekly*.

---

7   *Since 1962 the permanent showground has been at Redbourn.*
8   *A Kukri is Nepal's national weapon used for anything from close combat fighting to chopping undergrowth or raw materials in the kitchen. It has a lethally sharp curved blade that can slice bone. A Karda is an ordinary short, straight-bladed knife and the Chakma is used for sharpening them. Traditionally they are holstered together.*

They settled on Lower Grounds Farm at Aynho. Aynho village, and much of the surrounding land, had belonged to the Cartwright family for over 300 years, but by the early 1940s financial 'embarrassment' meant much had to be sold and Lower Grounds Farm was available. When my parents found it, the house was derelict, which gave my mother a welcomely clean slate. The land and buildings were also post-war deprived.

Mr and Mrs Ferry agreed to come with us. For over a year there was constant traffic between Tring and Aynho. Joiners made a small sweeping staircase and pine panelled doors; plasterers plastered; plumbers plumbed, and painters painted. Halliday's of London made a carved wooden fire surround for the drawing room; an avenue of chestnuts was planted, flagstones laid. Tumbledown stables and calf pens behind the house were converted into a service cottage and beyond the crumbling walls of old calf yards a house was built for Mr and Mrs Ferry. A new electricity generator replaced the old and a telephone line was connected. The Cartwrights were Aynho 1, the doctor Aynho 2 and my parents became Aynho 3.[9] Two Agas with six ovens and a boiler were assembled with strained grunts in the kitchen.

On winter weekends we became lunchtime patrons of The Cartwright Arms and steamed dry in front of its open fire, and in the summer we picnicked on the grass in front of the house. We became familiar with the contours of the southerly view down towards the Ockley stream, to Souldern village and the fields, our fields, and beyond. The farmhouse, oxygenated with new life, basked in sunshine and the tall pines whispered approval.

Fields were ploughed and corn drilled. Gradually pasture filled with stock where thistles had been topped and ragwort pulled. Hay was mown, baled and filled the barns. A milking parlour was created next to new asbestos-roofed barns. The two cellars started to fill with dairy and pork products and the grass under a great sycamore tree outside the drawing room, began to look more like a lawn. A formal rose garden was planted. We lived in a state of contagious optimism and excitement.

The Ferrys went ahead to manage things; the house looked almost liveable. Betty, her yearling and the three-year-old colt grazed the park beyond the

---

9   Telephones were not widespread, especially in rural areas. Calls were operator-connected, and the name of the exchange enabled operators to place the call. Large towns were divided into areas. The first three letters of the area generally preceded the number so MAY (fair)1234 or in our case REG (ent)5591. STD (Subscriber Trunk Dialling) was introduced in 1958 and its roll-out continued over the next 20 years.

metal railings in front of the house. We left Grove Farm and arrived at Aynho, just in time to put the kettle on for the removal men arriving with the furniture. Brew, the ginger tom that Mummy had brought into her marriage as dowry, found a plentiful supply of rodents to amuse him and justify his existence. Button, the dachshund, who somehow had managed to fill the gap left by Garron, the deceased Scottish deerhound, had located the Agas when he was too muddy to be allowed in front of the sitting room fire.

As the corn began to turn and harvest approached, the sweet smell of baking wafted from the kitchen. All eyes were on the weather prospects, and by the time the combine had trundled into the first wheat field, the outsized thermos flasks had been located and extracted from the last of the packing cases. After lunch Mummy started putting picnic things into her car. Harvest was a team effort and was the one time of the year when the extended farm family worked together. Lambing, calving, farrowing, and milking happen despite the weather, but harvest happens when the grain is fit, and the weather allows. Everyone, whatever their role on the farm, often joined by their relatives and the retired, helped to get it safely stored before the weather turned. When Mummy's car was seen weaving slowly between the bales, down the rows yet to be baled, and towards the combine, the driver finished his row and parked up. Pitch forks were speared into bales, tractor engines switched off, and everyone headed towards the rugs that the first comers were helping to spread out. It was a joyous meal. Copious mugs of tea washed down the chunks of fresh, homemade bread that were smeared with butter and honey. Rationing for butter wouldn't end for another four years, but we made our own. It was kept, covered in salt in the dairy larder under the house, in big, brown earthenware jars called fat hens. Honey (sugar was still rationed) was in combs from local hives. Dried fruit and syrup rationing ended that year (1950) and the slabs of moist fruit cake were especially appreciated and topped the feast. When the last field was cut and the final sack of corn and last bale of straw were heading for the barns, my father would go off, to reappear with a crate of beer and everyone would celebrate the fruition of their year's efforts.

Three of us, six Ferrys and assorted livestock had exchanged life in Hertfordshire for Northamptonshire. Except that the southern half of the farm was in Oxfordshire. The land was unequally divided in four.[10] The Ockley stream was the county boundary and meandered east to west through the

---

10 *The M40 motorway now dissects the farm.*

farm. There were fields on the north side of the Aynho road to Clifton and there were fields on the west side of the brick viaduct where the trains of the Great Western Railway sent plumes of steam into the sky as they whistled past high above. The barges on the canal beyond plied between Oxford and Coventry and in winter, when the fields flooded looking like vast lakes, they seemed to float across the meadows.

In term-time I went with my parents to London during the week, to go to the kindergarten of Camden House School in Gloucester Place. I enjoyed quite a lot of school, as I believed it to be, but the best bit was the school-run with Mummy. As we passed the scurrying people and the honking traffic, we chatted away in our four-wheeled bubble. Just us the two of us, so close, so cosy.

A married couple, jokingly referred to by Daddy's amused friends, who visited at weekends as 'The Butler and The Cook' was taken on to look after the house when we were away. I didn't register the weekends' axis shift from Aynho to London because I was despatched to stay, as a 'treat' with Mrs Williams in Staffordshire. I now know it was caused by Mummy's need to spend increasingly frequent and longer spells in hospital.

When I did go with Daddy to the hospital, he would take my hand and lead me down the long corridors. Normally when my hand was in Daddy's I would skip and jump, and he would swing me over puddles or the joins in paving stones with a "wheeeeee!", but our progress through the hospital was a sedate business. I tried to keep in step with him, but my footsteps were out of time. Nurses in heavily starched deaconess caps and cardboard-crisp white aprons crossed ahead of us. From doors on the right, they went left; from doors on the left they went right. Metal clanked against metal in kidney-shaped dishes. Towels were draped over arms and sometimes the nurses stopped to check the time on the watches resting on their bosoms, or to whisper to one another. They would stand aside for doctors, with their backs pressed against the walls, or follow them in obsequious trains. Everything was hushed except the clatter of footsteps and there always was this dreadful smell, a cocktail of carbolic and formaldehyde.

Mummy, when we finally reached her, was propped up on pillows and would give me a huge smile as I climbed up to be hugged. "Careful!" a nurse might say. Mummy would ask me if I was behaving at school, if I was helping Daddy, if I was being a good girl. No sooner had I had settled down under her arm, Daddy had pulled up the chair, and we were bringing her up to speed about the animals and the farm, than a nurse would sweep into the room.

"Excuse me, Sir" they'd say to Daddy, "now we must tend to your wife." It was time to leave her in her echoing white metallic world, and we would retrace our steps along the maze of corridors. Daddy would promise a treat. We returned to the silent flat. Everything was flat.

I began to hope that I wouldn't have to do the visits with the smells, the sobriety, the watery smiles, the gloom. Yes, I wanted to be with Mummy but with her at home not at the end of those long, soulless corridors with the crease-free nurses who worried about rumpled sheets and frowned at laughter. The hospital had become no laughing matter.

My heart sank when Mummy told me that she was going back into hospital but then she told me that while she was there, I was going to Bishton, to stay with Mrs Williams. My heart bounced straight back. I would not have to visit her in that hospital. When she came out of hospital Mummy and Daddy and I would be together again but now, I was off to Staffordshire, away from London to the country. The following morning, she walked down the top few steps of the stairs from the flat, turned and hugged me, long and tight. When she released me, her eyes were level with mine.

"Now be a good girl, Susie, and look after Daddy for me."

FOUR

BISHTON

1951

During the previous fifty years, dames' schools had evolved into preparatory schools, so-called to prepare children for entrance to public schools. Married couples replaced dames and in the years before regulatory interference, the quality of education and the way children were treated depended entirely on the characters and competence of the couple in question. The best schools were a good introduction to life away from home with a daily absorption of facts made fascinating by those who, although not necessarily qualified, knew their subjects and inspired interest. The worst schools sound to have been almost as grim as the religious orphanages. What most had in common was that they were housed in redundant mansions or stately homes that had been leased or bought inexpensively.

There were numerous reasons that such houses had become available. Some had been requisitioned during the two wars to be used as hospitals and had been neglected beyond the repair of family pockets. Some had belonged to families whose fortunes had dipped irreparably, and the heir had failed to save the day by seducing an American heiress. For others there was a shortage of staff to man them, or families decimated by two world wars had no heirs to inherit. All this had been exacerbated by the massive increase in estate duty (inheritance tax), that had risen from fifteen per cent on taxable estate in 1907 to eighty per cent by 1949. If fathers and sons were killed in rapid succession, any remaining family was clobbered by a double tax whammy with crippling financial results. Houses were either demolished or if buyers or tenants could be found, offloaded.[1]

Besides having lots of bedrooms for dormitories, libraries, dining rooms, drawing rooms, halls, stable blocks and a few acres of parks and gardens (ideal as playing fields), these frequently beautiful houses were congenial places for the heads to live with their families, especially in school holidays.

In the two decades since my mother had been her child-minder, Winifreda Iola Margeurite Williams had married Cecil Henry Stafford Northcote. They bought Bishton Hall, and in 1946 had started a Catholic boys' prep school, St Bede's,[2] and Mrs de Lobau Williams had retired from running her boarding house, to live with them. In my mother's eyes they were her family and I believed they were mine. It was not for some years, when I was at prep school, that I worked out they weren't relatives at all. There had been another yawningly boring sermon, when the only distraction had been to leaf through our prayer books feigning piety. We happened across The Table of Kindred and Affinity. After the service we ran down the little hill from chapel giggling hysterically. Why would any girl want to marry her 'father's mother's husband' or a 'daughter's, daughter's husband' or anyone so old – even if still alive? Having briefly felt short-changed that I had neither a brother nor sister to provide me with their grandchildren's husbands that I could not marry, I started to ponder my known relatives, counted them off on few fingers, and realised that the Stafford Northcotes weren't among them.

Winifreda was called Freda, sometimes Freddie, but I called her Aunt Wall because I often encountered her blocking the light and my way, when I was up to mischief rushing along the school passages. Cecil, for some reason, was known as Ben. They had three children, Amyas, the eldest was eight years older than me, so grown up that he seemed part of another generation. Gentle, sometimes wistful, he always smiled when our eyes met and called me Swooze but appeared to take life seriously. He must have been working for his Common Entrance exam to Ampleforth College and I imagine his parents expected him to set an example to the other boys. Hugh seemed to have escaped Amyas' responsibilities. He was fun and noisy with a

---

1 It is estimated that 1,200 country houses have now been demolished.
2 St Bede's closed in 2018, after 72 years and 3 generations of Stafford Northcotes at the helm. Bishton Hall now belongs to Hansons Auctioneers.

predisposition to burst into shrieks of laughter, at himself as well as others, and he was a terrific tease. Julia, four years older than me, was expected to play with me which she did, endlessly. She was a very tolerant, kind, older sister. The four of us called Mrs Williams 'Granny' and I felt one of them, never an only child.

While at Bishton my life was defined by Granny's gravitational pull, with deference to the school bell. Granny was reputed to have been born in Kensington Palace, had the short, pigeon-breasted silhouette reminiscent of Queen Victoria and glass engraving diction. Throughout her life she received Christmas cards from the dethroned heads of Europe and fable or not, she had the authority that came from such provenance. Although it was her daughter's and son-in-law's school, I don't doubt she had the final word, and she certainly had the final say on the family's dealings with me. Looking back, she treated me rather like the chick from an egg that had been placed under her, that once hatched, she was going to see safely fledged. Her wing would stretch out and keep me close if she felt I needed protection. Although an ostensibly male society, it felt matriarchal. Aunt Wall oversaw what now is called 'pastoral care'. As large as her mother was small, she administered with an equally precise diction although more *basso profundo*, especially when delivering rebuke. Matron was in control of thermometers, Gee's Linctus and Germolene but Aunt Wall was very much in charge of her.

Bishton Hall is a mid-18th-century Grade II* Listed Regency house in Staffordshire between the Trent and Mersey Canal and The Trent Valley Railway. The main block, facing south, has a four-column portico above which are three room-height sash windows on two floors topped by a big pediment and a flagpole – the union flag rules. Set back slightly is the main elevation with two windows on each side of the portico and above. To the east there is a generously elegant two storey bowed wing with three matching bowed windows. Attached to it is a little brick bungalow.[3] The west wing looks like an afterthought, as though money ran out before another elegant, bowed wing could be attached. It has a flat roof and is topped by a tower with one window in it and double chimney stacks. The lack of symmetry makes the house attractively quirky and friendly rather than grand. In the autumn the entire façade is festooned from footings to gutters with deep red Boston Ivy.[4]

---

3   *The bungalow became Granny's final home.*
4   *Parthenocissus tricuspidata Veitchii. A variety of Virginia Creeper, reputed to do least damage to masonry.*

The hub of the family and of the house was the hall – the family sitting room, approached via the portico. Internal doors led to all quarters and like the set for a Whitehall farce, there was rarely time without someone crossing the scene from left to right or right to left or front to back, collecting or leaving letters, keys, books umpires whistles, dog leads and a *bon mot*. Rather battered soft furniture was arranged around the fireplace and was protected from the wind that whistled under the semi-glazed outside doors by a glass screen.

To the east of the hall, was the 'Morning Room', a chilly room: I don't remember the fire being lit. With porcelain figurines and sedate Louis XVI furniture, it was rarely used except when prospective parents, under the misapprehension that they were interviewing the Stafford Northcotes, were themselves being interviewed. A convincing reproduction of Canaletto's take on the Doge's Palace in Venice must have caught the eyes of those new to Bishton.

Granny had the big airy bedroom above the portico, with a lovely view cross the front lawn, to the games fields and the canal beyond. I knew the canal was there because sometimes I could see the barges, against the dark backdrop of the trees beside the tow path. They made steady progress between Rugeley and Stoke-on-Trent, as unrushed as they had been for nearly one hundred and seventy-five years.

I slept in a little school bed at the foot of Granny's large metal-framed one with its highly polished brass knobs at each corner. Above her bed was an ivory and ebony crucifix. A well-thumbed leather-bound missal and her rosary beads sat on her 18th-century bedside pot cupboard, and the dressing table glistened with an ornate, monogrammed, silver dressing set. On one side of the room there was a dainty satinwood-inlay harpsichord.

Her bedroom led directly to the windowless first floor landing lit by a skylight –Dormitory Square – and my day was heralded by the first school bell, followed by the thundering of feet as the boys converged from all corners, funnelling into a room overlooking the stable yard, where there were rows of half-pint size, low hung washbasins. Someone would appear at Granny's door with a tea tray and if the door was left ajar, one could hear matron chivvying Somebody Mi.[5] to wash behind his ears or to stop dawdling. There was a cup and saucer for me too and tea has never tasted better. It must have been the milk from Aunt Wall's house-cow that did it.

---

5   *Boys were called by their surnames. Brothers were differentiated thus – the eldest Ma. (Major), the younger Mi. (Minor). A third would be Minimus.*

After breakfast I joined the boys, ranged around the walls of the landing, as our surnames were read alphabetically. We had to confirm that we had cleaned our teeth and gone to the lavatory 'properly'. It was not worth letting one's voice falter.

"I can't hear you! Have you or have you not?" Any suspicion of an irregular bowel resulted in an overgenerous spoonful of Milk of Magnesia.

As soon as the next bell rang the boys were off like a flock of starlings, clattering along the dipped, worn brick floor of the back passage to the stable yard and across the gravel to the chapel. The house went quiet. While the entire community, except Granny and me, were in Mass, only the distant songbirds and the snuffling of the family pugs broke the silence. When people hear that I spent time at a Roman Catholic school they sometimes say, especially if they are members of the Church of England, that I was lucky to escape attempts to grab me into their church, but there was never any suggestion that I should join Bishton's congregation. I was oblivious of this, but since have reflected on the ridiculous religious jealousies as rife between the assorted Christian congregations as those who worship differently. They all preach the Golden Rule.

I knew it was time to join the youngest for lessons when I heard the boys filter back, markedly hushed by the experience of trying to communicate with God. My attendance at the lessons before break gave Granny time to get up and dressed. I was four years old when I started staying at Bishton during term-time and had been at Camden House School for over a year. The teaching had been excellent, and I appear to have been quite bright. I had enjoyed learning to read and write and had started to master arithmetic – known at Camden as 'Numbers'. Although I must have been three years younger than most of the bottom class at Bishton, I had enough self-confidence to raise my hand occasionally and was indulged, but Latin flew over my head and was not expected to land on it. I did try to begin with, because of inherent competitiveness, and I tried to join in as the boys declined *amo, amas, amat,* that reminded me of what at Camden had been called 'Rhythmic Exercises' (I had a good sense of rhythm according to a report), but when they started on *mensa, mensa, mensam* it became repetitive and I had no clue what was going on when the teacher said that *amo mensam* meant 'I love the table'. Why?

The window looked over the stable yard and the back door so I could watch the comings and goings. They not only involved staff going into the stables, by then converted to senior classrooms, but all the kitchen deliveries. I hoped I would be allowed one of the 'toothpaste buns'[6] that the baker carried in a huge tray, and I wondered what it was that the butcher found so heavy and we would be given for lunch. There were two doors into 'our' classroom. One led to the back hall with its rows of hooks and lockers for coats and boots, the other led to Uncle Ben's study. Occasionally Uncle Ben would pop his head round with a smile and an administrative question for the teacher but usually we knew he was there by the sound of his voice muffled by his walls of books. It was not muffled when a boy had transgressed. Then his voice would rise in controlled contempt and after a short silence we would hear the yelp as his cane whacked whatever part of the boy he deemed appropriate. Sometimes a sob and "Sorry Sir" followed. I never heard a boy plead for clemency. Punishment was taken on the chin or buttock. The first time I heard it I was struck by the pained look on my classmates' faces, as though they themselves had been caned. There followed an awkward request from the teacher that we should concentrate on what was our business absorbing the subject of the hour. We learned that rules were there to be obeyed; testing the water was not recommended and if tempted to push one's luck it was advisable to think it through first, thoroughly. I remember the last time my father sent me to my room and he thwacked my bare bottom with the Mason Pearson hairbrush. I must have been about seven and it seemed to me entirely reasonable. This was what had happened at Bishton when boys misbehaved, and I had asked for it. I don't remember what I had done but I do remember deciding that I was very foolish to be caught and to be more circumspect in future. I was never caught or smacked again.

I lunched with the boys in the school dining room, built as a ballroom, with a compliment of portraits and a lot of silver sports trophies. Uncle Ben and the senior staff sat facing us at the top table, under a larger-than-life, full-length portrait of a serious Victorian *grande dame* in her coronation robes. Long tables were set at right angles to the top table, then smaller ones and I sat with my form mates at the furthest end of the dining room with a junior teacher in charge of us. The end of the meal was signalled when Uncle Ben rang the bell, silence fell, he thanked God for what we had eaten and delivered the notices for the next twenty-four hours. He then led a crocodile of teachers out of the room accompanied by muted gasps of exhilaration or despair at what he had announced, and the cacophony of eating irons on china as the designated boys cleared tables.

---

6   *A long bun like those used for hot-dogs, with a stripe of sugar icing on top.*

In the afternoons Granny or Aunt Wall, sometimes both, would take me hand-in-hand, over Bellamour Lane, that ran below the retaining wall of the lawn, to watch rugby or cricket. Matches generated the greatest interest and a three-line whip of support. Encouraging shouts from beyond the boundary –

"Well done, Wood One!" "Good ball, Ingilby!" were accompanied by clapping. It was always jollier when the home team won and if I was lucky, I was allowed to share their match tea. Sometimes I went with Aunt Wall to take swill from the kitchens to her Gloucester Old Spot pigs.[7] I particularly loved it when the piglets rioted. They looked like exploding scatter-cushions as they rushed about. Rare at the time, they were called orchard pigs as they often were seen in the orchards of the Berkeley Vale. They were Aunt Wall's pride and joy that she sometimes showed and won rosettes at the Royal Show. She did much to help publicise the breed that is now no longer truly 'rare'.

I had supper in the library by myself, watched by Granny and spent an hour in the hall with whichever members of the family did not have tasks or prep. The boys' first bed-bell indicated it was my time too and I think I must have fallen asleep as soon as my head hit the pillow. I never heard Granny coming to bed.

I knew the boys were admonished for playing chopsticks, so as it was not allowed, I thought it would be a rather cool accomplishment and I was practising on the harpsichord in Granny's room when she came in. I expected to be told off too, but as she closed the door quietly behind her, I realised by her expression that I was not in trouble. She took my hand and told me that Mummy had died. I was very sad but it was difficult to stifle the excitement when she told me that Daddy was coming to collect me. I loved being at Bishton, but I loved being with my father more than anything.

I do not how long it was before he arrived – a week? Two? Mummy must have been cremated during that time. There were postal deliveries and collections twice a day, and each day until he arrived, Aunt Wall sent him two scribbled notes to assure him of my cheerfulness, my welfare being a given. They read like a report on an animal that was prematurely weaned. 'She is eating well and had a second helping at lunch,' or 'She ran across the field to the touch line and loved watching the First XV.'

---

7   *Feeding swill to pigs was banned by the EU in 2001 following the outbreak of Foot and Mouth Disease, thought to have been caused by feeding uncooked food waste.*

I was excited, therefore happy, that Daddy would arrive soon, but it was as though the dank February mists came inside and swirled round the family. Teachers who previously had walked past me without acknowledgment now looked down at me and smiled without a word. When I saw the long nose of Daddy's Alvis glide up, I rushed to the hall door, but the brass knob was too big for my hand, and even trying to use both, I couldn't turn it quite far enough to release the catch. Aunt Wall opened it for me, and I leapt at him, throwing my arms round his neck, and locking my ankles in the small of his back. I loved the residual scent of the Imperial Leather soap and the softness of his skin where his jaw met his ear. I greeted him that way for some years until there was a danger of knocking him over and I was made aware by others, never by him, that it wasn't a very grown-up thing to do.

The whole family were in the hall to see him. It was noticeably lacking in the usual laughter. Not even Hugh laughed. Now I realise they had had to plan their sentences and speak with care; they were worried about triggering tears. Two decades later I met the chairman of a large publishing empire. His first job on leaving school had been as the office boy at Hulton Press, pushing the tea trolley round the office or rushing to catch the last post. After nearly forty years, it still brought memories of my mother's kindness and encouragement:

"She was so sweet to everyone, even me – a spotty, little gecko."

Aunt Wall sent me to collect my things and as I left the hall, I heard her tell Daddy that I had been very good. Yes, there had been a few tears, but I had been 'fine'. Mummy would be pleased that I had been good, I thought, as I rushed the stairs. We left quickly, and it was wonderful to be with Daddy swooshing along the roads in his elegant leather and mahogany speed machine. He asked me what I had been up to. I asked him nothing. Somehow, I knew that it would be like scratching fresh scabs from new wounds if I asked anything about Mummy. The last thing I wanted to do was hurt him. We didn't talk about Mummy for over thirty years, until a few years before he died. Sometimes he mentioned her in passing:

"Your mother had a very good recipe for cabbage, I wonder whether we can find it." but I didn't probe. I never wanted to risk spoiling the moment.

Of course, I didn't understand the finality of death. Before one can read a clock, time means nothing beyond satisfying a tummy rumble. Gradually horizons extend to weekends, weekends to weeks, to months, to terms and to holidays. The finality of death is difficult to grasp until one has lost one's first pet and by then its finality is history. My father's deerhound had eaten poison put down for the farm rats and I had experienced the pall hanging everywhere at his death, Daddy had been particularly melancholy. I had not seen the deerhound again, perhaps I might not see Mummy. Beyond that I didn't think. It was exciting to be going home to Aynho.

I left Camden House at the end of the Summer term in 1951, but my last report records that I had only attended forty-eight times out of sixty-five. I spent the rest of the time at Bishton and the senior boys must have been told what had happened and to look after me. Having passed Common Entrance, and with places at their public schools confirmed, they had ample time to apply themselves to the job. It worked for them too and gave them the excuse to test boundaries. Once before lunch they were sending me, in the redundant S-N pram, to each other at top speed. The good length of the long passage by the dining room enabled them to run a few paces for greater impulsion. We all shouted with delight. Alerted by the noise, a master swept round the corner from the staff room.

"Just WHAT is going on here?"

"Oh Sir, we're looking after Susie."

"Oh… oh I see." he said as he retreated. He must have heard the boys giggling that they had got one over him.

They taught me how to play a version of billiards, lifting me up so that I could operate the cue. They taught me how to score, placing a chair under the mahogany score board enabling me to move the brass markers. I felt useful. A reproduction of Bellini's Doge Leonardo Loredan was hung from the picture rail and looked on unamused.

I learned the rudiments of cricket 'Hit the ball, don't get caught and run for it,' and as importantly 'Catch the ball d-o-o-on't drop it!' One day on the way to the pavilion I tripped, landed on a bumble bee, and was stung on the nose but I had learned that boys don't cry, much.

Unfortunately, Aunt Wall and Granny Margaret were always one step ahead of me and they decided that a photographer should come out from Stafford to take a portrait of me.

"Daddy would like it," they said.

What I hated most was dressing up, but there was no escape. It was made clear to me that a portrait photographer, driving the eight miles from Stafford, merited the ribbons that matched my gingham checked dress. They would be threaded into the rubber bands on my replaited pigtails, and carefully tied in bows. I would wear clean white ankle socks and my Clarks sandals.

The backdrop, as I saw this horrible experience, was to be the temple at the far end of the garden. As I recall, I hope correctly, I never contradicted either Granny or Aunt Wall and anyway I knew that a strop would not be tolerated. Perhaps to head one off I was allowed to take along my teddy bear. The only redeeming thing I could think of was that as all the boys would be in lessons, they wouldn't see me dressed as some Judy Garland lookalike dressed to skip along the Yellow Brick Road.

The photographs have survived. In them a small, perfectly groomed little girl smiles, revealing a missing incisor. In one photograph she holds a posy – clever of Aunt Wall to persuade me to do that – in another she sits cross legged on a step with Teddy in her lap. In the one that was enlarged, Teddy swings from her hand and the smile is more convincing. Perhaps I had been promised that the ordeal was nearly over. 'Just one more.' Behind her the mid-19th-century Listed Grade II* screen stands majestic with its Greek Doric columns. It is a black and white photograph and I do not remember whether the checks were scarlet or blue. Neither do I remember being dressed up like that again. The screen (according to its listing) is of pink sandstone, and it is thought to have been built to shield the house and gardens from the 'new' railway built in 1847 running only a field away.

My father never framed any of the photographs. The one he always kept, next to that of my mother, on his dressing mirror, was taken while we were on holiday in Devon the following summer. I am standing in front of rocks. Sand sticks to my wellington boots. I had just returned from a morning spent in a small boat, fishing for mackerel. Offshore breeze had caught wisps of hair that had escaped from my pigtails and both I and my blue, belted gaberdine mackintosh look thoroughly sodden by sea-spray. I have a dozen mackerel hanging from my hands, many of the tails touch the ground as I am so short. A different tooth is missing. I, thrilled with the bounty, obviously had not had to be told to smile for the camera. My father, who took the photograph, never needed to cajole a smile from me.

It would not be too much of an exaggeration to say that during the months after Mummy's death I had a ball. Other than The Episode of The Photographs I remember nothing but sunshine and fun. I had been enveloped by love and continuous distraction.

Decades later Bill Williams, our doctor, my father's greatest friend from Oxford, and Bill's second wife Paula, gave me lunch in Le Caprice. My father had been dead for some years and as the waiters flourished table napkins and *amuse bouches* were set before us to absorb the champagne cocktails, they started to talk about my mother's death, about which I had never enquired. Paula had been Bill's mistress at the time and she told how he had arrived at her flat in tears. It was not what she expected. She had cooked a delicious dinner and planned much fun.

Bill had walked from his Wimpole Street consulting rooms where he had just seen my mother. She had a lump in her breast which she believed had been caused when she had been hit by a taxi while crossing Fleet Street. The swelling had not reduced. Could it be some form of contusion? Bill had realised immediately it could not. He was pretty sure it was a tumour and already it had grown to the size of an orange. If he was right, it would be inoperable, and his great friend was going to lose his adored wife after only eight years of blissful marriage. Survival rates for breast cancer were only twenty-five per cent.[8] He and Paula would lose the integral member of a foursome that had spent so much time together. Bill had had many terminally ill patients, but Paula had never seen him gutted over their prognosis. She knew that this was not pessimism.

In the event he did manage her pain by prescribing heroin. My father, seeing Mummy so cheerful, popped out of the hospital for a cigarette. When he returned, she had stopped giggling and the nurses either side of her bed were straightening the sheets. When they saw him, they stepped back. She was dead. She had died on a heroin high on February 16th 1951.

The three of us had eaten a delicious lunch washed down with rare wines. Bill prescribed the best on the list, "These will do you no harm!" His professional advice was always easy to follow. After I hugged them goodbye at the corner of Arlington Street and watched them, two eighty-year-olds, supporting each other arm in arm, walk back down Piccadilly towards Albany,[9] I decided it prudent to walk myself. Had the tourists looked up as they ambled towards Buckingham Palace, taking selfies feeding pigeons they might have noticed I was smiling. I was imagining how pleased Daddy would be that I had enjoyed such a generous afternoon with his old friends; that we still talked about him and Mummy lovingly; that laughing and splashing continued in great style. I hoped he was watching.

---

8   *Survival rates for breast cancer in 2020 are nearer 80%*
9   *When we moved to Water End my father gave his set in Albany to Bill.*

FIVE

BRADENHAM

1951–1954

Nearly seven months after Mummy died, I started at Bradenham House School in Buckinghamshire.[1] It had been founded by a retired Winchester College house master and his wife, Mr and Mrs Howell.

People raise eyebrows when they hear I went to boarding school when I was five – albeit as a weekly boarder. It was fine, far more entertaining for me, and easier for everyone else, than my being left alone at home. Had I gone to the village school I still would have needed a nanny or minder of some sort while my father worked in London. Private education was not as proportionately expensive, therefore not as socially divisive, as it is in the 2020s. School fees for a 'top' girls' preparatory boarding school in the mid-fifties were circa two hundred and forty pounds a year, equivalent to six thousand pound in today's money. Fees at the same school now are in the region of twenty-seven thousand pounds a year. We didn't have 'facilities' at home, few of us even lived in houses with central heating, so why would we need 'facilities' at school?

---

1 *Dating from 1670. At the time of the school, it was known as Bradenham House. It, with the village, was bequeathed to the National Trust in 1955 by Ernest Cook, grandson of Thomas Cook the early travel agent, and is now known as Bradenham Manor.*

Bradenham Manor is a Listed Grade II* three storey, red-brick house that looks southwest over Bradenham's village green. It was on the route from London to Aynho and therefore was easy for my father to drop me off and pick me up. Once leased by Benjamin Disraeli's father and where the prime minister spent much of his childhood, it has generously wide and shallow steps leading up to the double front doors with four elegant sash windows on either side. I didn't feel at all apprehensive as Daddy led me up those steps or as I was welcomed into the school by Mrs Howell. Daddy would be back in under a week to take me home. He always did what he said. I was used to being away from him for far longer than a week, albeit at Bishton, and I had the self-confidence of someone who had never been let down.

Mrs Howell took me up the sweeping staircase to the first floor. There were four big airy rooms, used as dormitories, with the same sash windows, 'my' dormitory was the one that had a door to through to the west wing that housed 'surgery', the sick bay, and matron.

Although I had yet to sleep with anyone other than Granny Margaret, I compared it favourably with those dormitories at Bishton that I had racketed through with the boys when on the run from matron. My dormitory was all very neat, there were no lurking smelly socks or dropped muddy rugby shorts. Instead, there was a lingering whiff of talcum powder or was it Mrs Howell's *eau de cologne?*

"Don't worry, Susie, Matron is just through that door, she will look after you."

That may be what Mrs Howell thought. I never liked the woman. The first thing she decided was that I should not suck my thumb. Last thing before lights out, when I was captive in bed, with the sheets stretched tightly across me and rammed under the mattress, restricting any movement, she bore down on me with the dreaded little bottle and some cotton wool, and covered my right thumb with bitter aloes. Once she realised that I switched thumbs, she took care to daub both. My habit was a challenge to her and although she explained that the sucking of thumbs made teeth grow crooked '… and no one likes girls with crooked teeth.' I continued to suck them at weekends whenever they weren't plastered with that horrible stuff otherwise I resorted to biting my nails. In my forties I fell in love with someone who told me that he loved my crooked teeth. Matron had been wrong.

Illnesses, however minor, were taken seriously. I think matron liked to justify her existence. At the first sign of anything we were removed from our dormitories to her domain. It was obsessively cleaned without anything as germ harbouring as a picture on the walls or a book to read. Mental torture. If we had a cold, we had to sit, three times a day, with a towel over our heads inhaling the decongestant steam from Friar's Balsam and boiled water, that rose from a large, porcelain jug with a narrow neck into which one had to keep one's face rammed. The porcelain was hot, it hurt.

"I can't breathe."

"Don't move. Inhale or you'll never get better!"

If we had tummy trouble, we were deemed too ill to wash ourselves and she subjected us to blanket baths. Lying on the scratchy blankets being vigorously rubbed first on our fronts then our backs, with an elderly flannel, occasionally dipped in an enamel bowl of tepid water, did nothing to warm one's naked little body in the unheated room with its linoleum floor. She must have been a sadist. Mercifully, when whooping cough hit, we were sent home. As I only whooped once a day, the doctor prescribed fresh air and a watchful eye.

My father let me have a day's hunting with the Heythrop Hunt on a borrowed pony. Hunting wasn't embroiled in the political correctness that it is today. Foxes killed the lambs and hens that were raised as human food. They needed to be controlled – remember the vermin detachments of the Women's' Land Army, organised by the Ministry of Food in the war. People wore a 'uniform' designed historically so that they wouldn't be confused with trespassers or poachers. Was such a uniform any more ridiculous than the checked jerseys and plus fours worn by golfers? Integral to rural life, hunting was by arrangement with the farmers and landowners and there were rules to be obeyed to protect the sward and crops. It was a welcome opportunity for country people of all backgrounds to get together in the winter, do something they all enjoyed, the while keeping a covert eye on what neighbouring farmers were up to. Those without horses followed on bicycles. It was a great way to take exercise, learn respect for others, and see terrain and vistas that one wouldn't otherwise see. Daddy did not hunt, he had other interests, but he was delighted for me to do so. I returned to Bradenham fully recovered, full of fresh air, and exhilarated.

Bishton could not have prepared me better for life in a boarding school and, unlike those in the beds near to me, I did not sob myself to sleep. There was a handful of boys and they slept with us, some sniffling, in the same dormitories, but they had to leave as eight-year-olds. Having overheard some wanabe-stepmother disapprovingly tell my father that I was becoming a tomboy, I was enjoying honing the role. I hoped the boys and I would become comrades, but I found them frustratingly wet. I was chucked out of the Brownies for roughhousing with the Cubs. To misquote their almost canonised leader, Lord Baden-Powell, they had not "... *smiled and whistled under all circumstances.*" or thought that "*fun, fighting, and feeding were the three indispensable elements of the boy's world.*" For me the few minutes of ragging had been much more enjoyable than working for my sewing badge and I was delighted to be released. The boys must have been the victims of crushing domestic circumstances to have been sent to Bradenham in the first place. Poor little guys what can have happened to them at their next schools?

Lessons were interesting and I found them easy. We were allowed to run around on the close-mown grass that doubled as games pitches and there were big woods within the curtilage that were ours to enjoy, but it was very tame after a boys' school. Nobody bounced balls, whistled, or ran along corridors because it was 'unladylike', and it was noticeably quieter. The timbre in boys' schools is totally different to that in girls' schools.

I spent nearly four years at Bradenham and over time my father felt able to leave me there for the odd weekend. It was good practice for full-time boarding. Just as private education for a day pupil is very different to that of a weekly boarder, that of a weekly boarder is different to that of a full-time boarder. Exeats didn't exist and half-terms were often only in the two longest terms winter and summer. There was a camaraderie that developed between full-time boarders who didn't see their parents from one end of term until the other. If your bed happened to be next to someone who irritated the sh*t out of you, you learned to put up with it (her) because that was how it was going to be for the next twelve weeks. An early lesson in tolerance.

Until I spent a weekend in school, I had had no idea how long weekends seemed for the boarders. Saturdays for me started fine as instead of having lessons, the whole school sat together and took a general knowledge test. The questions were on the lines of 'What is the name of the Queen's sister?' 'How many ounces in a pound?' 'What is the capital city of France?' My father always listened to the news so I had absorbed a lot of the answers by osmosis and was well above my age group. I enjoyed the opportunity to shine. Otherwise, unless you had been selected to play in a team, which as the smallest in the school I never was, Saturdays dragged on and on and on.

Sundays were no better. We had to dress in Sunday clothes (mine were always chilly) and put on Sunday behaviour. After breakfast we walked in pairs down the front drive to St Botolph's just outside the big wrought iron gates. It is a charming little Grade II* Listed church dating from 1100 AD faced with flint and stone. Its charm escaped me and the sermons, which seemed interminable, made no sense. It is sad that nobody had the imagination to explain to us who St Botolph was. I knew it was his house as his name was on the board at the entrance to the churchyard but why had anyone expended considerable energy carefully arranging all that flint in the walls? It must have been sharp and painful to handle. Had we known that Botolph had lived in Norfolk, France and Holland and that various bits of him had been buried in Ely and Westminster Abbeys, and that he was a hot favourite in Denmark and Sweden, it would have made geography lessons more pertinent. It would also have been a signpost to what people had to do to be given their own houses, although he seems to have escaped the usual deprivation or torture and had just been thoroughly charming, travelling about to spread The Word.[2]

On returning from church, we had to sit silently at the long dining tables to write the weekly letter home. We had an hour to achieve the challenging task of making life sound exciting in our Sunday Best handwriting, covering both sides of an A5 sheet of Basildon Bond writing paper. Even before the days of the additional line for a post code, it usually was possible to make the address occupy a third of the first side, then there was the date and then the '*Dear…*' to parents. Those with two parents managed to take up more room. Mrs Howell circulated behind us, looking over our shoulders to make sure we did not write anything derogatory or concerning to those at home. My early letters (my father kept them all) went '*dear daddy i hope you are well. i am. as it is rainin we are not aloud out. love Susie*'. They progressed through '*Dear daddy, i hope you are well. i am. it is raining. I have lost a tooth. i am third sheperd in the play about Jesus. love Susie.*' and towards the end of my time ended up '*Dear Daddy I hope you are well. It is raining so we are not allowed out in case we get wet. I hope granny, the ferryes and button are well. I was 2nd in arthmertic. love Susie xoxoxoxox.*' It always seemed to rain when I was stuck at Bradenham. Irritatingly but inevitably, as handwriting improved it took up less space on the page, but hugs and kisses couldn't be censored and grew to a good line.

My father felt that he could bust me when he wished. Until the early '60s the Royal Agricultural Show travelled the country to different locations. It was the annual jamboree when all of England's farming folk gathered to

---

2   *Otherwise known as St Botwulf of Thorney, he is the patron saint of travel among other things.*

meet each other, exchange news and views, and show and be shown prized animals and gleaming new machinery with painted black tyres. One year it was not far from Bradenham, and Daddy told Mrs Howell that he would be taking me. The French teacher remonstrated because I would miss one of her lessons. Daddy dismissed her objections on the grounds that half an hour of French missed at eight years old was unlikely to make the critical difference in gaining, or not, an Oxbridge place ten years hence. HMQ visited on the first day of the show but after that the good and the great of the farming world were invited to use the Royal Box. I sat, as my father's guest, in the front row in a chintz-covered wicker armchair with matching cushions. I loved seeing the horse and cattle parades and particularly enjoyed it when everybody wheeled towards us, halted, and saluted.

The best thing about Bradenham, as far as I was concerned, was Miss Fegan. Miss Fegan leased the stables belonging to the house and part of the deal must have been that she taught those of us whose parents were willing to shell out for us to have one riding lesson a week. The tack was always clean, and the ponies were excellently looked after and well humoured. It cost our parents one pound a lesson and would have cost her every penny of that. She was to be seen in twill jodhpurs with chamois leather knee pads, highly polished jodhpur boots and a waisted green Harris tweed coat tightly buttoned over her shirt and tie. In the summer she removed the tweed jacket but never her tie. She wouldn't let us jump, not even a pole lying on the ground, until we'd stopped bouncing in the saddle at a canter. I imagine she was frightened of the furore had we fallen off, after all we were not allowed out in the rain in case we got wet. That was quickly corrected at my next school, Hanford, where we were sent up and down the jumping lane, reins knotted with arms outstretched and coins between our knees and the saddle. We had to sing a song as we went to prove we were relaxed, and we were allowed to keep any coins that were still there at the end of the exercise.

Every summer holidays Miss Fegan organised a camp, pitched in fields of the farm behind the church in Compton village, on the edge of the Berkshire Downs a few miles south of Didcot. Ownership of horse transport was not universal and far beyond her reach, so this involved all her ponies being ridden from Bradenham to Compton, about thirty miles. Once there, they remained for six weeks. Children could be left for as long as parents wished. I loved it and went for a fortnight, four years running. Holidays abroad, even for privileged children, were yet to come.

Ponies, unless too wayward in which case they were loosed in the farmer's orchard, were tethered with chains attached to metal spikes driven into the ground. Four surplus military bell tents were pitched in a row; a trench was dug for the long-drop beyond the hedgerow, and there was an old canvas marquee for dining, tack cleaning and wet weather diversions. We slept on groundsheets in sleeping bags, about eight to a tent, with our feet to the central pole. I was particularly proud that Granny had lent me Uncle Andy's WWI three-layer, camelhair sleeping bag. It was big enough for a fully dressed soldier with his boots still on and it had three big horn buttons to make it easier to get into. I could get lost in it.

Miss Fegan allocated ponies according to ability, which she already knew, and they were our responsibility for the duration. The first couple of days involved lessons, hacks across the farmer's land and along local bridle paths. After that we hit The Ridgeway that passes nearby. It is believed to have been used as a trade route from Dorset to Norfolk for over five thousand years. Following the top of the Downs it gave travellers far reaching views, so offered protection from thieves. Other than crossing the Cheviots I had never seen such views. I loved the sky and the space and the song of the little birds that fluttered high in the sky singing their hearts out. I now know they were skylarks. On Thursdays we rode to The White Horse at Uffington, where we picnicked and walked round the perimeter of its chalk body, being very careful not to trash its grass edges. We ran down to the Blowing Stone at Kingston Lisle and tried, but failed, to blow it.[3] It must have been a round trip of about thirty miles, no mean feat for children under ten, which most of us were. Something of which we boasted to the less fortunate, as we saw them, who went to Pony Club Camp. On the last evening of each week, we sat around the campfire, ate potatoes that had been baked in the embers and sang strangely inappropriate WWI songs like 'The Soldiers of The King' and 'It's a Long Way to Tipperary' diluted with Gilbert and Sullivan. We didn't think about the lyrics.

When the Howells retired and surrendered the lease on Bradenham House, Miss Fegan found alternative stables in Surrey. Faced with her usual transport problem she asked the parents of those she thought could make it whether they would let their children ride the ponies from Compton to Surrey after the last week of camp. Having been woken and given a good fry-up,

---

3   *The Blowing Stone is a sarsen stone which if successfully blown makes a deep boom. Legend has it that it was used to summon the troops for Alfred the Great before the battle of Ashdown in 871.*

we tacked-up our ponies by torchlight, tied little canvas bags with an apple and a bar of chocolate to one of the D rings on the saddle, water bottles to another. With bridles over the ponies' halters and ropes round their necks, we felt like the Canadian Mounties as we rode out of Compton in the dark. She had recced the route. We went through woods, across fields, down green and tarmac lanes, avoided towns and major roads, (motorways were yet to slash the country) and at lunchtime someone in a car pitched up with sandwiches and more apples. We snoozed with our ponies for an hour, remounted and reached her new stables at dusk.

My father had arranged for us to stay the night with Jim Davies, the then head of the Milk Marketing Board, at Thames Ditton. We must have ridden nearly sixty miles. I was nine. As I was brushing my teeth, I overheard his wife telling my father that he should never have let me do it. I stopped brushing.

"… she's totally exhausted." I held my breath to hear his reply.

"Yes, but she'll sleep, and she'll never forget it." I did and obviously haven't. My father was always right.

SIX

AYNHO

Returning to Aynho from Bishton after Mummy's death was exciting for me but it must have been desperate for my father, to return to the house they had made together, where they had planned to spend the rest of their lives. It was the first time he had been there since her death. At every turn he must have seen her standing in doorways; sitting on her striped, high-backed Regency sofa by the fire with the sheaves of papers beside her waiting to be edited; writing at her Georgian desk; scrambling eggs at the Aga, on Sunday evenings. He must have remembered their discussions about wood, and mouldings and paints and fabrics and seen her ideas. The results were all around him. He must have wished she was in bed beside him; wished she was complaining about his cold toes on the soles of her feet. They had their joke about her ticklish soles and his cold toes. They always were so happy together.

The house was quiet when we arrived; the butler and cook were more than usually low profile. The Ferries welcomed me into their kitchen with their reliably wide arms; Button the dachshund continued to badger for a walk; Brew continued to return to the house with his half-eaten trophies of vermin entrails left for us to tread on, and then curled up satisfied, on Mummy's sofa. The horses whinnied, hoping for carrots, when they saw us walk in front of the

47

house. Instead of Mummy going off with Daddy to visit neighbouring farmers it was me who went with him. Each year before the details of agricultural guaranteed prices were finalised and put before parliament, Daddy would be summoned to The Minister for his reaction.[1] I sat in the car, parked outside The ministry while Daddy was with the minister.[2] The last thing the government of the day wanted was a critical editorial in *Farmers Weekly*. If, as in 1957, the 'Yellow Peril's' editorial reaction to the price review was favourable, it would be quoted verbatim in parliament as proof to MPs that it was good for the industry and it would be voted through.

On Saturday mornings, as soon as I heard 'the butler' take Daddy his early morning tea, and lay out his clothes for the day, I would run along the passage to join him and plague him with questions about what he had been doing in London and what he planned that we (both of us together, because he was my best companion) would do that day. I would sit on the closed loo seat in his bathroom to watch him shave, fascinated by the way he started near his ear down the edge of his jaw to his chin, first one side and then the other. How he stretched his cheeks with his left hand to make sure that he hadn't missed any; how he would pull his top lip down over his top teeth, or put his tongue between teeth and lip, to shave below his nostrils, and then stretch his bottom lip up over his bottom teeth to finish his chin. Finally, with sweeping upward strokes to jawbone he shaved his neck. Then he would turn his head to left and right in the light to be certain he had made a clean job of it. I never tired of watching this ritual.

After breakfast, if he needed to go to Brackley market to catch up with farming neighbours or had stock to buy or sell, he took me with him. He would lift me onto the top rail of the metal pens in the marketplace so that I could see everything. It was so different looking at the steers from above instead of through a maze of knees; to be able to see the gleaming backs of fatstock; the spines and slightly hollowed quarters of stores. I watched as the expressions of farmers, standing next to the auctioneer, changed as the gnarled stick – the auctioneer's gavel – hit the metal rails of the pens. Wry smiles for a good price raised; the downturned mouths of disappointment, especially when a bony old cow with an udder nearly scraping the ground had had to go.

---

1   *The 1947 the Agricultural Act was passed to encourage farmers to produce more food. Prices for crops were guaranteed for the following eighteen months; prices for stock, milk, and eggs for the following two to four years. It enabled farmers to plan.*

2   *When my father retired the 'industry' gave him a dinner at The Savoy. The current and six previous Ministers of Agriculture attended.*

"You've got years left in that one there, Bert. She always throws a good calf and does them well."

Some Sundays we drove to have 'pre-lunch' drinks with his friends. Daddy always took me with him and once there I was expected to keep quiet. It was not difficult. His friends were sympathetic to the motherless daughter of their friend, but quite besides the fact that conversation took place over two feet above my head, there is a limit to how much interest those forty years older than me had in my life and vice versa. In fine weather I was encouraged to 'explore' the gardens. In winter I sat on hearth rugs scratching the stomachs of dogs, and soon learned that if I smiled at those who shimmied between guests with plates, they would lower them to my level. Willy Freund, a Czech friend who lived in a house bigger than I had ever been in, with stone balustrading to prevent the deer jumping from the park to the terraces, congratulated Daddy on the way I could hoover up blinis – what I called 'fish jam' sandwiches. I never looked back.

Daddy and I ate together; inspected the fields and animals together. He gave me the *Observer Book of Grasses* and any grass that I took to him and managed to identify for the first time was worth six pennies.[3] It doubled my week's pocket money. Every night, having tucked me tightly into bed, he read a chapter of the latest book, usually by Arthur Ransome. It was so cosy to be with him and always such fun.

One Sunday he said that we were off to see my grandfather for tea. Mummy's father lived in Northampton about thirty miles away. I was excited. Daddy's father had died four years earlier and I missed the way, his having lifted and hugged me, as I had sat on his bony knees held by his long arms. He had let me fiddle with the tiny silver box for matches, attached to his gold watch chain, and I had been fascinated by his always smiling eyes in his crinkled face. His lap was a haven and while in his arms nobody suggested I should be anywhere else or that it was 'time for bed'.

I ran to the front door. There was no hugging and no lap. Mummy's father sat with his back to the bay window. His wife brought a tray with the tea and a cake which she placed on a low table in front of her. She sat opposite him. Daddy and I sat next to each other on an unforgivingly sprung sofa and faced the smouldering, coal fire. As usual my feet did not touch the floor and I tried to balance the plate on my unstable lap. My step-grandmother was friendly. My

---

3   *£4.00 in 2022.*

grandfather hardly spoke and watched, expressionless. Uncharacteristically, I worried in case I dropped a crumb or said something wrong. I remained silent and refused a second slice. I did not like the old man and was delighted when Daddy said we had to 'get back'.

Recently I learned that my grandfather had not been 'up to' attending my mother's cremation. What was wrong with him was not revealed, but in the years before a rainbow of incontinence pads was advertised nightly on television, and nearly a million people in the UK were said to be suffering with dementia, neither affliction was talked about. Perhaps neither were his problem. Perhaps it was simply an old man's thoughts as he looked back over his seventy-seven years, and he was bitter at the hand he had been dealt. He had been born 'afflicted' as he saw it and unable to be a mariner and, unlike his relatives, he had seen nothing of the world. Called to the Bar but without the money to follow through, he had to take dull jobs in local government. He lent money to a friend who never repaid him. In 1937 he had been appointed to help restructure Guernsey's legal system.[4] He left these shores, saw one coast sink into the sea and another grow out of it. It may only have been the Channel but at last, after sixty-three years he had felt sea swell. He had been given something interesting to get his teeth into but in under three years, on June 30th 1940, as the Germans landed on one side of the island, he rushed to catch the last boat as it pushed off from the other side, leaving family belongings behind. He had lost two wives and two of his five children which alone would have paralysed most people's laughter lines.

*

I didn't know Granny Messer as well as I knew Mrs Williams because the only time I had spent with her had been at Christmas, and once a year on holiday in Northumberland. She was totally different. Equally small but not all Victorian although they were about the same age, she commanded respect generated from universal affection. Her long grey hair was kept in a bun in the nape of her neck. It fascinated me when I watched her brush it. It almost reached her waist, even when brushed forward over her shoulder. I watched as she plaited it and then rolled it into a tight bun which was held

---

4   *Much of Guernsey law was still based on Duchy of Normandy law dating from the 13th and 14th centuries.*

in place by a handful of targeted hair pins. It never fell. Although widowed she didn't wear black but had a variety of tweeds and linens in pale, subtle colours and whenever she went off site, she wore large-brimmed, starched, sometimes shiny, linen hats held in place by vicious hat pins. She spoke gently with the faintest hint of a burr and her vocabulary had a scattering of Northumbrian. *Bairn* for child; *breeks* for breeches; *tatties* for potatoes, she laughed at herself for that one; both she and my father called turnips *neeps*. She wore a *pinny* when in the kitchen on cook's day off; the cattle lived in *byres*; those of whom she approved or were kind, were *canny* and she called me and Daddy, *Hinny*.

She began to spend school holidays with us. When Daddy was in London it was just the two of us at Aynho and I fell for her unreservedly. In the mornings I would listen out for the 'butler' coming upstairs with her tea tray and would run along the passage to the landing, round the corner to her room, and jump into bed with her.

"Careful, Hinny!" she would say, holding her cup and saucer, as I burrowed under the bedclothes and snuggled up to her.

Soon she had a cup put on the tray for me and, as we sat together looking across the valley towards Souldern, she recounted stories of my father when he was a child. Of how he had been mischievous. Of how when Andy went Off-To-War someone had come to relieve her of his rapidly multiplying doves. Daddy, protecting his brother's birds, had tried to bite the man's ankle as he climbed the loft ladder. Of how, almost as soon as he could walk, Daddy would be put on the back of his uncles' cart horses, which would meander down the village street to the farrier. Once shod, the farrier pointed them back, patted them on the quarters and my father, still on top would arrive home. The ideal toddler-care. I loved these stories about him.

"More, more, Granny, pl-e-e-e-a-se."

Summer holidays were spent at Bamburgh. Until Grandfather died, he and Granny would stay as guests of the Armstrongs in Bamburgh Castle. We stayed in the Blue Bell Hotel at Belford about five miles inland. Every morning we met on the beach below the castle and my father and Uncle Andy would construct complicated sandcastles with moats, keeps, baileys and towers. If they went off for a round of golf, Granny, already in her mid-eighties, would kneel on the sand and help shore up collapsing towers and walls and divert the rivulets draining down from the castle's one-hundred-and-fifty-foot cliff, to keep the moats watered. Andy's wife Elaine, forty years older than me, was the next youngest member of the family and when the brothers returned from golf, she would encourage everyone to play French cricket. It became noisier and noisier until someone hit a six and the incoming tide snatched the ball and we watched it carried off towards the Farne Islands. It signalled time for lunch or a huge vacuum flask of tea.

Before someone had come up with the idea of three lane roads let alone dual carriageways, the drive up the A1 from London to Northumberland took two days of slog; tiring for the driver who had enough to do concentrating on oncoming traffic without distraction from a bored child. Granny would come down to London for a few days to collect me. Despite being totally unspoilt and very modest she was a great 'laugher and splasher'. Daddy would take her out to supper and ask her what she'd like to drink.

"Well Hinny, you know what I really like is champagne." The wine waiter would open the wine list at the right page and give it to Daddy.

"Of course, what would you like?"

"Well Hinny, you know what I really like is Krug!"

They both knew that he knew what the answer would be. It was one of their jokes. They were great friends and he loved treating her, so a bottle of Krug it always was.

Granny and I would go North on the Flying Scotsman. Daddy followed by car. To start with the trip was exciting: the guard's slamming of doors as he walked the length of the carriages along the platform, then his whistle: then a whoosh of steam from the engine and the slow creaking of wheels. We picked up speed over the joins in the rails, the tempo of clackety-clack began to increase, and we passed the backs of tall, blackened brick houses with their windows partially covered by drooping, greyed net curtains. By the time the engine had got into its stride, back yards had become back gardens. It was engaging to spy on such different lives with their parallel lines of flapping laundry; the neighbours chatting over paling fences, ersatz football posts, discarded prams, and upturned cycles waiting for punctures to be mended. Once we reached countryside with the familiar sights of dairy herds, and tractors turning the rows of hay, I couldn't wait for the first-class buffet steward to pop his head round the compartment door and announce lunch.

"Oh, Granny can we go? Now Granny?" and she would place her newspaper and a folded coat where we had been sitting, next to the window, and off we went. My excitement mounted as we neared the restaurant car and could hear the silver cutlery chattering to the upturned glasses on the crisply ironed, white linen table clothes. The steward, having walked the length of the train, caught us up just as we arrived. The same went for tea.

When Granny pointed out Durham Cathedral, I knew it wouldn't be much longer. The train began to slow, then brake to walking pace, and the carriages clattered over the bridge across the Tyne and into the station where Uncle Andy would be waiting on the platform, grinning broadly, his pipe clenched between his teeth.

All the station staff knew Granny.

"Mrs Messer, oh welcome home!" the station master would say as he directed a porter to trolley the bags to the back of Andy's highly polished, pre-war sports car. I was bundled into the dicky seat in the boot and west we sped.

In the 1910s Granny's father had built a pair of semi-detached houses, on the Hexham Road in Throckley. After Grandfather's death she moved to Tyne View West. Her youngest sister Maggie, also widowed, lived next door in Tyne View East.

I slept in the tiny room above the front door and was fascinated by the twinkling lights of Ryton on the south bank of the Tyne. Once tucked into bed with a stone,[5] I fell asleep listening to Granny playing Chopin preludes on her baby grand piano. I spent the day with Granny and Great Auntie Maggie. Their lives were interlaced and the gardens that rose steeply behind their houses were undivided. Maggie had the fruit trees and Granny the vegetables and flowers. I ran between the two. Maggie splashed batter onto a flat iron on her range and made delicious griddle cakes that she let me smear with home-made jam. Granny cooked the best ham and pease puddings ever tasted. Once I burst into Maggie's kitchen to hear them discussing 'Basil' in hushed tones. They stopped talking as soon as I entered. Years later I asked my father who Basil was. Their nephew by their sister Ann Cheesman, Basil Bunting was the poet and author of *Briggflatts* therefore Daddy's first cousin. Famous and successful though he was, his aunts may well not have approved of his marrying, second time round, a Persian girl thirty-six years younger than himself, especially as he had done little to provide for the children of his first marriage.

Once my father, who stayed with Uncle Andy and Elaine, had caught up with sleep, we all headed north to Belford. We stayed there every August for about ten years and were recognised as part of the furniture. One evening, Lady Brunskill, the hotel owner, asked me whether I would like to go cubbing

---

5   *A stone was an earthenware hot water bottle.*

with her 'on foot' the following morning. I crept out of the hotel before anyone was awake. 'On foot' turned out to be on wheels, in her Rolls Royce. She drove up onto the hills where hounds, a handful of men on horses or with push-bikes had congregated at a crossroads. Collars were up against the wind. Well known to them, she was treated with a deference that made me even more in awe of her. I spent the next three hours paying attention and jumping to – whether following her index finger as she pointed out a covey of partridge breaking cover, "There he goes!" or listening as she asked whether I could hear hounds speak or spot the curlews flying up.[6] I was still trying to make out what the hounds said to each other when, without warning she would shout "Quick – OFF!" and we would jump onto the big leather seats, close the doors as, already moving, she set the Roller crunching down a farm track. As the sun rose higher in the sky and the landscape started to shimmer, we rounded a bend on the side of the hill to see stationary, steaming, blowing horses. The huntsman was on his feet. Hounds thronged round. They had caught their fox and the huntsman held its brush above his head out of their reach.

"Would you like it, My Lady?"

"Give it to Susie... and she should be blooded."

Triumphantly I rushed into the Blue Bell's breakfast room with a blood smeared face waving a dripping fox's brush. I'm not sure which caused most shock. After a visit to the taxidermist The Percy fox's brush followed us from house to house for six decades until moths achieved what hounds hadn't.

A concern after Mummy died, had been what would happen to the 'motherless mite'. Who would look after her? The problem didn't arise. When my father was around, I was never far from him. When he was in London, and I was not at school, either Granny came down from Northumberland or I went to Bishton. Mrs Ferry always was the much-loved backstop at home. The unanticipated problem was that of household staff. It sounds like a first world problem but at the time my mother's absence made it real. It was in the era when the rich households were still staffed by a team of maids and footmen, supervised by a housekeeper and butler. The more modest households had a 'girl' or two, who either lived in the attic or 'came up' from the nearby village.

Socially, my parents fell between the two. We lived too far from a village, didn't have the accommodation for live-in staff and there were heavy jobs,

---

6   When hounds first get onto the scent of a fox, before they are in 'full cry', they are said to 'speak'.

more easily done by men. The answer was the married couple but like all employees, they needed supervising and that now fell to my father. The trouble with my father was that he expected everyone to 'behave' and to have 'manners'. His interpretation of those words did not relate to how a knife was held or not to expectorate into the gutter, as these are tribal mores. 'Manners' in his head reflected how people should be treated. He had total integrity and honesty himself and expected others to be the same. The Golden Rule, do as you would be done by and others would reciprocate, he believed. Sadly, it was not always so. The job of the married couple at Aynho was a shoo-in. My father was in London all week. All they had to do in his absence was upend coke scuttles into the Agas and remove the clinker; empty the ash and refill the log basket in the drawing room; top-up decanters; move dust; keep the silver from becoming tarnished and make sure there was enough food for the weekend. My father rarely entertained and in term-time weekends it was just the two of us. Admittedly when I was home from school and Granny came to stay, it was more of a full-time job, but it was hardly onerous, and Granny was wonderful with staff – it was she who had taught her sons how to 'behave'.

Inevitably those who did not share my father's attitude became lazy and took advantage of a man who was disinclined to check up on them. He had more on his mind and was still in the fog of bereavement. Occasionally a married couple were caught out. One Christmas Granny slipped on the polished stairs and broke her wrist. The butler was asked to drive her to hospital for physiotherapy. As they wove the wrong side of traffic islands round Banbury, it confirmed her suspicion that he 'was drinking'. She may have given the impression that she was a benign octogenarian but the only things sharper than her eyes were her wits. As alarmed as she had been careering down the wrong side of a main road, what really got her was that her son was being exploited, so she told him. The couple had left without demur, unsurprisingly as it turned out. The butler's habit had been fuelled by my father. Every bottle of gin, and my father bought drink by the case, had been drained and refilled with water. A decade later, when it had been decided to retreat from the large house in Hertfordshire to a flat in London, my father gave another couple six months' notice, as he thought it 'only manners' to let them know what was planned. They left in six weeks, taking with them two of the four solid silver candlesticks made in London in 1888, that had until then lived on the dining room table. I have the two they considerately left behind and every time I clean them, I am reminded of the way they treated my father. Possessions are transitory, manners are not.

One couple arrived with their son during term time. By then I was older and in the hiatus before Granny was able to leave the North, they were asked to keep an eye on me. They were keen for me and their son to become friends. That was fine but I already had my friend Howard and just as the new couple were crisply turned out, so was the son. I was a ragamuffin, and it became obvious that the boy was not happy in mud. As he showed no inclination to join us rampaging round the farm, in order that we should become friends, his parents thought a bit of bath-time bonding would be a good idea. I had decided that I didn't need the precious boy's friendship, and I certainly didn't see why he should be in my bath, especially as I knew he had his own in their cottage behind the house. I stayed at the Ferry's until the coast was well clear even if it did mean missing supper. The Ferry's supper, frequently delicious beef dripping on the toast we made on a long fork over the coals in the open Rayburn, was always better than the fish-in-white-sauce anyway. I still don't see the point of white sauce.

The couple, much appreciated by my father and grandmother, were too posh for us. She was a brilliant cook and he had perfectly creased grey striped trousers, a dark grey coat and wore white gloves and a starched apron to clean the silver, but they discovered that rural life, that had sounded so romantic, wasn't what they'd imagined it to be. With 'great regret' they left to work for Sir Hartley Shawcross, the chief prosecutor at the Nuremberg Trials and sometime Attorney General. He lived in grand Chelsea style, which suited them better. When in London, Granny often had tea with them, sitting in the basement kitchen, and was much amused that a socialist should live in such splendour. He later became a crossbencher in the House of Lords, nicknamed Lord Floorcrossed, although he hadn't crossed it all the way.

There had been a slight frost between us and the village after the woman who took Sunday school required I wore a skirt. Daddy had pointed out that as I and the other farm children cycled the good mile from the farm, dungarees especially in winter, were more practical. She believed that I should 'set an example to the village'. She didn't budge. No skirt: no Sunday school. Daddy, a 'lapsed Quaker', as I once heard him describe himself, told me that it was up to me. Once he had walked the farm, and when not off to see friends, he spent Sundays at home catching up on papers and reading the Sunday papers. He made it clear he would not be getting the car out just to drive me to Sunday school. I'd enjoyed collecting the little illustrated bookmarks and listening to the Bible stories. I thought it was clever of Jesus to do that with the loaves and fishes and assumed that Moses must have found a causeway like the one to Lindisfarne, but I didn't think they were worth pushing a cycle up the hill for, especially in sleet; anyway skirts were for school. That was the end of Sunday school.

There was only one television set in Aynho in 1953 and it belonged to the schoolteacher who invited all the children in the village to watch The Coronation. We cycled up from the farm and crammed in, sitting cross-legged on the floor of her front room. Being the only child not at the village school, and no longer linked to them by Sunday school, I kept a low profile, sat to one side, and didn't see much, but I was riveted by the pack of Alsatian dog figurines. arranged in diminishing sizes, up the tiled steps of the fire surround. Thanks to the sepia photographs in *The Illustrated London News,* I caught up with what the new monarch looked like when fully kitted out with her orb, crown, and sceptre. She looked much younger than any of our teachers, far too young to be a queen. The King had looked so old and sad.

It would be romantic to claim we were feral, but we did run free across the farm from breakfast until supper. As none of us had watches we only dropped back when our stomachs told us it was time for food. One summer we decided to make a boat out of a discarded tin bath. Well out of sight of the farm buildings and adults we launched onto the Ockley. The current swept us surprisingly fast the not great distance to the millpond. With rusty seams and pinpricked with holes, we were sinking fast, water was up to our waists, and we bailed out. Relieved of our weights, the tub pirouetted round and round, crashed against Aynho Park wall and disappeared underneath it.

The area below the viaduct was strictly off limits. A swampy willow copse, crossed by the Ockley and bordered by the canal, it was fenced off to prevent stock straying into it, becoming stuck or drowning. As it was Out of Bounds it was a magnet to us, and one winter, after many days of hard frost we decided to venture over the fence. To start with it was fine, even if our shouts echoed eerily under the great arches of the viaduct, but after we had got some way, the ice began to crack. I can still feel the fear, remember the skin on my skull tighten and the goosebumps. Jumping back, from willow to willow, root to root, we were out of there as soon as we could reach the nearest fencepost. We never returned.

In spring we collected eggs from nests in the hedgerow along a track on the north side of the road to Clifton and we ran through the blanket of cowslips in the little five-acre beyond the barns. In summer we helped with harvest. I was put on an old grey Massey Ferguson tractor attached to a flatbed trailer. As usual my legs were frustratingly short, and I couldn't reach the pedals, but it was put into gear, and the speed set with the hand throttle, and I steered between the bales. The men, walking behind, forked the bales up to the one stacking them on the trailer. When harvest was finished Daddy would put me on his lap letting me steer as we careered across the stubbles in Mummy's already battered old Austin Seven.

As soon as my father left for London on Mondays, I scooped cigarettes from one of the silver boxes on the dining room table, and we scampered off across the field in front of the house, with some matches, down to the derelict mill.[7] There we climbed up the rotten timbers to what had been the top floor and tried to smoke the things. Their attraction to adults remained a mystery. It seemed to make no difference whether I had scooped Virginian cigarettes from one end of the box or Turkish from the other, for us it was all about coughing and spluttering and starting to feel sick, which had nothing to do with the churning water that we could see as we looked down between our feet pressed against the floor joists.

Mrs Ferry's mother had died giving birth to her and she had been brought up in rural Radnorshire by an aunt and the neighbouring vicar, who had given her private lessons. Besides being the mother of four children, her own childhood must have made her particularly sensitive to my situation. While Howard and I, accompanied by whichever children of farmworkers wanted to join our 'gang', had enormous freedom and roamed the countryside, we always knew that we would be welcomed back at the Ferry's house. I rushed the last strides through the back door to avoid the flapping wings of the live chickens hung upside down to drain the blood from their flesh before they were killed. Sometimes they looked dead, but hearing footsteps would flap pathetically and let out a strangled, rasping, squawk. One could never take their demise for granted. Daddy didn't shoot but he let the neighbours shoot across the farm and Howard and I augmented our pocket money as beaters. One day a drive was through kale, planted as winter fodder for the cows. It reached my shoulders. I picked up a shot partridge thinking it dead, but it was only wounded, and it flapped frantically. I dropped it and off it hobbled. Size for size, it could have been

---

7   The Mill at Souldern was saved and 'done up' and for a while belonged to and was the bolt hole of Sir John Mills.

a goose. What with that and the flapping chickens it took decades for me to touch birds and if beating I took care to kick them to make sure they were dead. I still do. Runners I ignored.

When Granny wasn't staying with us my days began with the dawn chorus. Having dressed I tiptoed downstairs, picked up my wellies and, having carefully shut the back door behind me, sat on the top step to pull them on. Then I ran as fast as I could, in case anyone tried to stop me, until I reached the milking parlour. Daddy wouldn't have tried to stop me, but The Couple might have.

It was exhilarating being in the hive of activity while everyone else was still asleep. I loved the metronomic pulse of the machines, the steady munching of cows as they chewed their breakfasts and perversely, I liked the familiar, rather sweet smell of semi-digested grass on their breath. I watched the cowman with his big red rubber apron and white skull cap as he moved about with quiet purpose, putting his hand on the cows' rumps gently thanking one.

"Well done, girl, now off you go back to the field," and coaxing another "Move over you big woman, you!"

I watched him wipe mud from their udders and attach the clusters. Dnk; dnk; dnk; dnk and the milk rushed through the tubes to the cooler. I watched the milk ripple down the cooler and swirl round the big funnel and down into the galvanised churns. I knew it was important work and I tried to keep out of the way. When the last cow had lurched off towards the field, he'd tip the heavy churns towards him, rolling their bases this way and that up the ramp onto the concrete platform to be collected by the dairy's lorry, later in the morning. After hosing down he'd scoop milk from the remaining half-filled churn and fill his can. I knew that I hadn't got in his way if he'd scoop some into a chipped mug kept on the windowsill and pass it to me. Sometimes he'd let me turn off the lights. He'd shut the last gate, give me a big smile, and set off down the track to his home and breakfast. I'd scamper back for mine as pleased as if I'd done something to help.

Andy had become concerned about my father, who was driving to and from London, about a hundred miles each way, every weekend. It was an exhausting drive after a full week's work and the destination was a miserable, repetitive reminder of the life he would have been enjoying with my mother. Andy suggested he should choose between *Farmers Weekly* and Lower Grounds Farm and understandably he chose *Farmers Weekly*, to be with his colleagues by day and friends in the evenings, keeping busy.

Gordon Saunders, still the majority owner of the farm, decided that Mr Ferry should be replaced. My father, his resolve weakened by Mummy's death, did not fight hard enough to keep him and Mr Ferry was replaced by a Dutchman, Jerry. It may have been a commercial decision and in time Jerry might have proved an excellent manager, but we children hated him, and of course knew nothing about the plans. We had created a den in the gutter between the roofs of the barns, only reachable by those thin enough to climb up past the new grass drier. From that vantage point we tried to throw stones at Jerry when he walked down the yard. We always missed, probably because we ducked to avoid being seen before we had completed the follow through. Shortly afterwards our den was rumbled following a violent thunderstorm. Torrential rain, dammed by our den, backed-up and overflowed onto the machinery below. The den was dismantled. We were in deep do-do and Jerry took over.[8]

Daddy knew enough about horses to know that he knew nothing. Captain Stannard who had a yard at Charlton, a small village north of Aynho, was entrusted with all matters equine from breaking-in Betty's offspring to finding ponies for me. He was a slight, quiet, brilliant horseman. Gentle though he certainly was, he had high standards and expected them to be met. If Howard and I cycled the four miles, we were rewarded by being allowed to plait the straw at the entrance to the loose boxes, to stop it being tracked out when the horses were led into the yard. Sometimes we were allowed to polish bits and stirrups. Everything had to gleam against the dark panelling of the tack room. Captain Standard had been commissioned to find a pony for a boy who lived nearby. The boy, for whatever reason, showed no inclination to ride Jonny, the perfect boy's hunter. He was a tough, benign cob who would have followed hounds until dusk and pulled out sound two days a week. I imagine it was thought that if the boy was told that someone half his size, and a girl to boot, enjoyed riding him he would be shamed into it. That didn't appear to have worked because I was never jocked off.

---

8   *Sixty years after leaving Aynho I managed to track down Brenda Ferry. Only then did I learn that her father had what must have been a nervous breakdown, and never worked again. There was absolutely nothing fair about Mummy's death, but it is particularly unfair that while my father managed to cope, and I sailed through life, it had a cataclysmic effect on the Ferry family, particularly Howard, who was barely in double figures when it happened. I'm sure my father never knew. It was desperate to learn, but resuming friendship with Brenda was wonderful, and a kind of salve.*

Daddy was against 'pot hunters' but Captain Stannard persuaded him to let me ride Jonny at a village show in Astrop Park.[9] It was a warm sunny day, the trees in Capability's park afforded shade, the breeze kept flies at bay, and I had been entered for The Best Young Riders class. Having hacked two miles down the green lane between the villages, Jonny and I were happy and relaxed. A photograph shows a pea on a drum with her feet barely reaching below the saddle flap.

"Just follow the others." I was told as Jonny took me into the ring.

We did a circuit at a walk. I remembered to keep my heels down, my back straight and my chin up. I managed the same at a trot. Once we started cantering, Jonny gained on the smaller pony in front. It humped his quarters as warning to back off. Jonny jinxed to avoid a thwack on the jaw, and I fell off. Thinking that anyone who fell off could not possibly be a Best Rider, I left Jonny where he stood grazing in the ring. I ducked under the ropes and walked towards the car, but intercepted, I was put back on and the spectators clapped. I kept the rosette for Second Best Young Rider and rested on my laurels, for life.

One March morning in 1954 Aynho 2 dialled Aynho 3 and the doctor told Daddy that Mr Cartwright had been killed in a car crash. Driving home from Eton with his son for the Easter holidays, Mr Cartwright had not seen overhanging planks on a timber lorry, no flags had been tied. Both had been decapitated. His widow had to sell up to settle death duties.

I didn't know it, but our lives at Aynho were coming to an end too.

---

9   *Astrop Park was built in 1740 for Sir John Willes, the longest serving Chief Justice of the Court of Common Pleas. Single storey wings were added by Sir John Soane in 1805 increased to two storeys late in the 19thC. The wings were demolished in 1961.*

SEVEN

HANFORD

1955–1959

I t was a cold sleety January day. It threatened full-blown snow and the windscreen wipers on Daddy's car were doing their best to keep it cleared. It was the first time I hadn't worn dungarees since the start of the school holidays and the heater blew hot air at my bare knees. Daddy drove with a lit cigarette between the well-manicured second and third fingers of his right hand. He had never done any manual work. When not taking a gasp, he always referred to cigarettes as 'gaspers', he peered over his nose through his thick lensed glasses, between his knuckles kept at ten to two on the wooden wheel, trying to see the road through the increasingly thick snowflakes that rushed towards us and suddenly veered off just before they hit the windscreen.

As it was a Spring term there would be no coming home until the Easter holidays but Daddy said cheerfully that he and Granny would be allowed to take me out on two consecutive days in February, only a month away. The Spring term was always the shortest he said. They would easily find a hotel in Bournemouth as it was full of holiday hotels and out-of-season. He sounded enthusiastic. I had no idea what the season was or the whereabouts of Bournemouth, but I knew that Dorset was some way off. Daddy had said it would take three and a half hours to get there if the snow didn't worsen.

After Christmas Granny, with the school clothes list carefully folded into her crocodile-skin handbag, had taken me to D H Evans, a department store in Oxford Street. A stern woman in the school uniforms department on the third floor, proffered Granny a chair and sighed disapprovingly that Hanford wasn't like other schools because it didn't have a proper school uniform '… only for games…' Granny placed the list and her gold ball-point pen, a Christmas present, on the glass display cabinet above the carefully arranged scarves and school caps on the tiered shelves underneath. Together they ticked off the three pairs of this and that (one clean, one on, one in the wash) and the six pairs of socks, some for games. I was delighted that the new school didn't require uncomfortable liberty bodices, so called as they were meant to liberate the body after the wasp-waisting Victorian corsets. There was nothing liberating about them. Neither were we expected to wear the excessively hot and baggy 'flesh' coloured bloomers over our knickers called 'linings'. I was allowed to choose new pyjamas, jerseys, shirts, and skirts in any patterns that I liked. I asked for a dressing gown like Christopher Robin's.

"But that is for boys!" said the increasingly sour-faced shop assistant.

Although the dark-blue serge sports-shorts itched when I tried them, they were proper shorts and not girly divided skirts. The buff games jersey was unforgivingly stiff, but Granny assured me both would soon soften. Granny always told the truth. Blue and Buff had been chosen as Hanford's games colours at the suggestion of Mary Beaufort,[1] the wife of 'Master', the 10th Duke.

Granny had spent the following week sewing nametapes woven with my name in black capitals to absolutely everything. I had been allowed to choose the font for my nametapes and a week before I was due at school a gleaming trunk had been delivered with my name painted on it in the same font. I had been given a red leather writing case with my name in gold stamped across one corner, as a Christmas present from Uncle Andy and Elaine.

"So that you can write and tell us how you're getting on at school. We've included some stamps to go with the envelopes and paper." It even had a loop inside the spine for my new fountain pen.

---

[1] *Members of the Duke of Beaufort's hunt wear a dark blue coats with buff collars, collectively referred to as 'The Blue and Buffs'. The hunt staff wear green coats. George once tackled Master about his hounds having hunted a Bathurst fox – as one of the Duchess's Godsons George was braver than some, and Master pointed out that historically 'his country' stretched to the Heythrop. The distance between the Beaufort and Heythrop hunt kennels is over fifty miles. The Bathursts, he said, only hunted the area in between by invitation – presumably the reason the Heythrop hunt staff also wear green. Most hunt staff wear red.*

An adventure was on the horizon. I liked the prospect of this school without liberty bodices and lots of new clothes to wear so I was rather excited when at last we spotted the little black and white signpost to Hanford School. The drive turned a sharp left, and there it was. Hanford is described in Pevsner as 'A major Jacobean house, externally almost unaltered.' Even in the wet snow it looked warmly honey coloured. It was built by Sir Robert Seymer in 1623 and lived in by his direct descendants for over three hundred years. Hanford sat between the arms of Hambledon and Hod Hills, with their skirting beech-woods. It sits well and maintains the feeling of confident permanence.

Faded silver oak double doors, wide and high enough to admit horse drawn carriages, were opened right back, and trunks were being piled on either side of the outer hall. Those nearest the doors already were lightly covered with snow. I could just see the stone niches with seats for the postillions behind them. Glass doors led to a dark, dingy hall with refectory tables laid up for tea with blue plastic beakers and pink Bakelite plates. Standing with her back to them was an elderly lady (she was fifty-two years old) with frizzy greying hair and a hook nose, Mrs Canning: my new headmistress. Daddy left immediately for London, another long drive, in increasing snow. Contemporaries were told to show me around.

I had moved from the high, perfectly proportioned rooms of Bradenham House, naturally lit by tall sash windows, to a rabbit warren of corridors and small rooms ranged round the stone and panelled central hall. Originally an Italianate internal courtyard (the first in England), it had been glazed over in 1873 and the glass didn't look as though it had been cleaned since. It would have been difficult. Under the settling snow it let in no light. Such light as there was came from the tiny bulbs that represented the carpels of the flowers carved in the mahogany frames that supported the glass. The surrounding passages were barely illuminated by widely spaced forty-watt bulbs hanging on worn woven thread flexes. Dingy wasn't in it. The dormitories, off corridors that circled the hall on the two upper floors, were painted an assortment of pastel colours that seemed as though they had been chosen from bankruptcy stock. Worn linoleum covered the floors. Photographs of parents, dogs and ponies balanced precariously on recycled orange boxes, the pretend bedside cupboards that separated each chipped metal-framed bed. Rugs and quilts brought from home turned out to be essential as Mrs Canning believed in open windows. A dusting of snow on an eiderdown when one woke up was not unknown; frosted windows were the norm. Some dormitories were obviously named: North and

South; White with its white painted linen cupboards from when it had been the house linen room and Oak, completely panelled skirting to ceiling. Others were named after late 16th-century poets: Shakespeare, Marvel, Stuart, Milton, Herrick, Fletcher, Spenser, Ben Jonson and George Herbert. Only now do I wonder the reason some merited their forenames names and others did not.

At Bradenham we had used the elegant central staircase with its painted ceiling complete with urns and putti. Although there were two highly polished dark hardwood staircases at Hanford, they were off-limits. Ours was the softwood 'backstairs', each tread worn to a saucer by the feet of chambermaids rushing with coals and linen over the centuries. Little tacks, sitting proud of the treads, sometimes snagged the soles of shoes. A loo on the first landing, 'Half-Way', overlooked the slate roofs of tumbledown 18th-century outhouses, towards the majestic brick stables (Listed Grade II). The snow persisted. It was unedited January gloom.

Conversely the atmosphere inside was cheery. No one seemed sad to be back at school. There were no tears and a lot of laughter. Staff, usually accompanied by at least one longdog, many named after cigarette brands (Gold Flake, Sobranie, Lucky Strike) asked about holidays, Christmas presents, hunting, and parents' welfare.

"Did you get bucked off on Boxing Day?"

"Ha! Ha!"

"I hope you were you proud of your brother singing at Kings?"

"Did you finish your Thank You letters?"

There were lots of nicknames, jesting and more laughter.

The following day when not spent unpacking and having our clothes lists cross-checked by the matron, was largely taken up with learning the layout of the place. The Victorians had converted the large 17th-century barn into hunter stables, which were used for the school equines of every size and shape and the five senior classrooms were in a row of converted carriage-horse stables. Between both stable blocks were tumbledown brick and flint sheds housing firewood, coal, rubbish bins and the anthracite for the two commercial Agas. The area was approached by the original back door and stone steps worn to shining dips. Growing out of one tumbled shed was a tree we climbed, The Monkey Puzzle Tree.

Mrs Canning's drawing room was directly above the cloakroom with its thundering hot water pipes. Whereas at Bradenham we had not been allowed outside when it rained, at Hanford we were driven out, whatever the weather.

It took us time to realise that as the floorboards, barely covered with worn Persian rugs, had gaps between them, she could hear everything going on down below. However hard it poured, however wet we became, our clothes would dry on the pipes. If a cold bug was working its way through the school, morning lessons were cancelled and we walked to the top of Hambledon Hill for the germs to be blown out of our systems, off across the Blackmore Vale. In snow we took the battered blue tin trays from the school pantry to use as sledges and spent the afternoon swooshing down the ramparts of Hambledon, and Hod Hills' Iron Age hill forts.

Dogs were everywhere and access to the stables, when we didn't have lessons or games, was encouraged. Catching ponies, grooming and tack-cleaning earned popularity but climbing on the hay bales was deeply frowned on and temporary suspension from the stables was the humiliating punishment.

"How would you like someone walking over your food?"

As always points made were moot and the farmer's daughter, used to spending hours high on hayricks avoiding grown-ups, learned that horses were not to be confused with livestock.

At Bradenham we had been treated as micro ladies and expected to behave as such. Everything had been fair, efficient and hygienic, although unlike Bishton the place hadn't smelled of Lifebuoy soap. At Hanford we were treated like hound puppies having been out at walk with our parents,[2] we now were in kennel, encouraged to run free but not allowed to riot;[3] we had to enter the pack as part of a team; we had to be kind to each other, develop any skills or aptitudes that we had and foster any shoots of those that might emerge. Excellence was not critical; endeavour was. We were not expected to hunt mute, and Hanford in full cry was joyous music,[4] but the when the whip was cracked, we knew it. Talking in dormitory after 'lights

---

2   When hound puppies are weaned from their dams, they are sent out, usually in couples, to 'walk' for about six months. A good 'walk' is a farm, or house in a rural spot, where the puppies grow up, are free to roam all day, see the sights and sounds of country life, and socialise. They become part of the extended household until doing too much damage (they love digging gardens); start roaming too far and become too much of a responsibility, or a bitch comes in season. If you can keep your puppies for nine months, you have done well. Then they go back into kennel and will join the pack and start hunting with the older hounds the following hunting season. The person who looks after the puppies is known as a 'puppy walker'.

3   Hounds that hunt the unintended quarry, for instance a foxhound on the line of a deer, are said to 'riot'.

4   The sound of a pack of hounds in full cry is known as 'music'. Hounds that make good 'music' have a wonderful 'cry'. When a hound first picks up scent and makes a noise it is said to 'open'.

out' was rewarded by a spell silently lying flat on the splintered planks of the balcony that crossed the hall. We were at Hanford to be prepared for life, the while being educated.

The Reverend Clifford Brooke Canning had retired as headmaster of Canford School in 1947, a position he had occupied since 1928. Prior to that he had been a housemaster at Marlborough where, aged forty only seven years younger than her father, he had married the (head) master's daughter Enid Norwood. There were twenty years between them, and it was assumed that on his retirement, he had told her that it was her turn to run a school as she wished, and he would support her. Hanford School had been going for just over seven years when I landed, and the first intake was already impressing headmistresses and Oxbridge wardens.

The Cannings had looked at possible premises in Dorset and narrowed them down to two houses, each with a bit of land and coincidentally only a mile apart. Stepleton, a Grade II Listed mainly late 17th-century square house, with two wings, had been built by the parents of Peter Beckford who wrote the seminal *Thoughts upon Hunting*. Service cottages, the other side of the main road between Blandford and Shaftesbury had been built as kennels for his hounds. With its 18th-century pleasure grounds including a lake, the Cannings deemed it just too perfect to become a boarding school and they plumped for Hanford, equally Grade II* listed but less perfect, larger, and not sliced by a road. Initially renting, they bought it from Vivian Seymer in 1951.

Mrs Canning's father, Sir Cyril Norwood, the son of a Lancashire vicar, was one of the most famous educationalists of the 20th century. He achieved first place in the Civil Service exams of 1899 and entered the Admiralty but soon realised he wanted to be involved in education. Before his mastership of Marlborough he had been headmaster of Bristol Grammar School. He went on to be headmaster of Harrow and ultimately president of St John's College, Oxford. He was knighted in 1938 for Services to Education and the 1943 Norwood Report on secondary education led to the establishment of secondary modern, grammar and technical schools. In 1945 he was sent to India by the India Office to investigate the state of Indian education. Throughout his life he was a committed Christian and for a decade was president of the Modern Churchmen's Union. Lady Norwood, a London doctor's daughter, was awarded the *Medaille de la Reine Elizabeth* by the Belgian government for her work for Belgian refugees during WWI and had died in 1951. In 1956 he retired to a house in Iwerne Minster just over the hill from Hanford.

The Cannings had three daughters, Rose, Ela, and Sarah. Rose and Ela had been despatched to the US at the beginning of the war where they had been separated and something cataclysmic had happened to Rose. We never knew what. Some said she had been raped (we didn't know what rape was), others said that her true love had been killed in the war, others that she had had a nervous breakdown. What was that we wondered? Rumours came and went in waves, and some added in that she had been given Electric Shock Treatment. On the farm we often had got caught by the electric fencing that retained the pigs, but it hadn't done more than make us more careful. Whatever it was we understood it to explain the way she spent a lot of time wafting around in her own cosmos. She sometimes taught French and art to the youngest, equally badly, although she was an accomplished painter. She started a Sunday evening Gramophone Club when those who wanted were allowed to sit on the floor of the drawing room and listen as she played whatever thirty-three-and-a-third inch gramophone record that she had bought in Blandford Records earlier in the week. Every time I hear Paul Dukas' Sorcerer's Apprentice I think not of Disney's Fantasia but of Hanford's drawing room, of Rose sitting on the sofa with her eyes closed, swaying slightly; of trying to readjust my legs to relieve the pins and needles without making a noise, and of looking at the painting above the 18th-century chimneypiece with its marble Bacchic frieze and caryatids. I wondered why a chapel appeared to be in the middle of the sea.[5]

Ela did not have a torrid time across The Pond and had made a cheerful life for herself as a secretary in London while socialising with her parents' interesting friends and Canford old boys. From them her friends had fanned out, some of whom she brought to stay for weekends. Sarah, the baby, at eight deemed too young to be despatched to safety, had enjoyed a blissful childhood as an only child surrounded by the boys at Canford, riding and partying. After a glittering spell at Sherborne School for Girls, where she was head girl, she was up at Somerville College, Oxford, reading Classics and continuing to party.

There we were, eighty little girls benefitting from an unrivalled combined experience in education, care, and parenthood with its spectrum of tragedies and trophies, all supported by an unshakeable faith. Fortuitously for us it was twenty years before the Health & Safety Act was passed; forty years before the

---

5   *Maurice Utrillo's Chapelle en Bretagne was sold by Sotheby's in 2020 for over £30,240. More than £10,000 above its top estimate.*

days of Ofsted and sixty years before the Food Safety and Hygiene legislation was laid before parliament. All areas were supervised by the Cannings' personal experience and common sense.

The teaching was the best I was to have in any school and much more inspirational than anything that followed. The Cannings had friends throughout the academic world, several of whom taught us in their retirement, including at least two boys' public-school headmasters. Prepubescent girls must have seemed delightful. Our annual school visit to Lulworth Cove each summer was augmented by a day for each top scholarship gained to a public school. One year we had four, an impressive percentage of the eight or ten girls at the top of the school.

Mr Canning called 'Tin Can' to his face, for a once explained but long forgotten reason, taught us Latin and some French. In 1882 the first Married Women's Property Act was passed. It permitted women to hold property and assets independently of their husbands. In 1920 women, some of whom had matriculated up to forty years earlier, were granted Oxford University degrees. In 1928 women were given the right to vote. It had begun to look as though some people thought women had brains in those pretty little heads of theirs. Just as now, maths and English GCSE are the minimal requirements, in the 1950s to apply for Oxbridge, Latin 'O' level was a perquisite. Parents wished their daughters to be taught Latin on the off chance their heads might not be full of cotton wool.

Tin Can was in his seventies and, with failing health, did not get up until mid-morning. He slept in a high single bed in a corner up against the wall. Mrs Canning's bedroom was through a connecting door. To our amusement it was rumoured, turning out to be true, that she slept on a mattress resting high on planks above a big, cast-iron enamelled bath. We were allowed to use 'their' loo, housed in a light shaft that rose the two stories to a glass panel in the sky. It was packed with books of Latin poetry and prose, Library Loo.

Tin Can took the first two lessons after morning prayers in his bedroom. If we were lucky enough to have the first lesson, we rushed to get there early because he would share his breakfast with us, toast and butter with Frank Cooper's Coarse Cut Oxford Marmalade. Sheer luxury compared to the white sliced bread and margarine that admittedly we were allowed to dot with either honey or Marmite. These were the only spreads allowed and depended on our parents providing them, so a jar frequently had to last the term. Jam, if sent, was confiscated.

The first arrival at a lesson got the spot by Tin Can's pillow in the corner on his left, the next on his right. They would spend the lesson with his long bony arms round them as he held *Juliana*, the 1937 textbook, on his chest. Later arrivals would range down by his legs with their backs against the wall and the last would sit on the floor. Imagine Social Services' apoplexy had it existed. For parents' day, that took place at the end of every Summer term, he directed every girl who learned Latin, in a play that he had written (in Latin) for the occasion. Everyone was dressed in tunics made with yards of butter muslin, tied together with their own dressing gown cords. Those at the top of the school declaimed, the rest of us marched around as legionnaires or cohorts or stood to attention carrying a *pilum* of bamboo with silver painted cardboard blades. The favoured rode ponies bareback, declaimed an impressive lot and carried a *pilum* if the pony was amenable.

At the end of the 1957 Summer term, Tin Can wrote in my Latin report 'Susan has worked well and made good progress, but next term will bring much harder work. She must come back prepared!' What none of us were prepared for when we returned in September was that Tin Can was no longer there. He had died during the holidays. We missed his grand-paternal presence; his humour; his enveloping arms and his buttered toast. We were not prepared for Latin lessons taught by his daughter Sarah in a freezing classroom. One windowpane was missing, and the wind whistled under the door across the concrete floor that had been painted dark red to masquerade as linoleum. She was tough and we were left in very little doubt that she would rather not have been with us. Until her father died, she had planned to pursue a career in the law but home she came to support her mother in a crisis. In return Mrs Canning indulged her with a flat above the stables and ample time to hunt in the winter and show jump competitively in the summer. As the rows of rosettes grew longer and the silver cups filled the glazed cupboards on either side of the chimney breast in the tack room, it became obvious to her that, like it or not, Hanford not Chancery, was to be her lot.

She began to teach riding as well as Latin. She had an acerbic tongue and pulled no punches. In one end of term report, she wrote a single sentence: 'Despite her shape, Susan has ridden very well this term.'

Over time she became a very good teacher and could make things fun. 'Picture Latin' happened on Fridays. She wrote five sentences in Latin on the blackboard to test the vocabulary we should have learned during the week. We had to translate and draw. Any mistakes were drawn by us in our exercise books and never repeated. Sometimes she would make those who failed to grasp things run round the area in front of the stables shouting basic grammatical rules:

"By, with and from take the ablative!" Humiliating it might have been, but no one forgot them either. Later she was commissioned to rewrite the GCSE Latin syllabus.

Tin Can's death was the death of the Latin play and riding displays filled the vacuum. A manège had been laid and fenced off in the stable yard. The first display was the 'Funny Ride' and was designed to give parents a chance to see their not yet brilliant equitators act out some theme in fancy dress on the motley collection of school ponies. A father recently returned from South Africa, lent a couple of Zulu drums complete with crisply dehydrated tiger skins. Smiley was an unfortunate skewbald cross of pony and horse that Sarah had rescued from a Somerset orchard where she had found him chained to an apple tree. She thought he cried out to be a drum horse. Because Sarah knew Daddy wouldn't mind if I was dumped, I had been the one who rode him every day while Sarah re-broke him. Inevitably I became the drum major. Besides the fact that the drums came below his knees, his muscled neck was that of a grown horse, he had a mouth of iron, and he was difficult to steer even in his best mood, trying to use the reins with one's feet was at best a challenge.

"Get on with it, soldiers manage!"

I was sent out through the high stable arch towards the seated parents to Kong Frederik VIII Honnormarch. Smiley might not have followed the planned figure of eight but I had fun twirling the drumsticks above my head and enjoyed the audience's laughter.

After the Funny Ride came the Serious Ride when Hanford's top riders, most from passionate hunting homes, displayed their expertise. Inspired by The Trooping we wheeled and criss-crossed the school at trot and canter with impressive precision. Half passes, rein backs, shoulders-in and serpentines ended with synchronised four-square halts and bows to the parents.[6] Smiley didn't aspire to being a dressage horse, but Sarah gave no quarter and even if her threat to jock me off reduced me to tears after alternate rehearsals, I was the one in his saddle on the day. At the time I didn't see it as such, but it was a training feat that stood me in good stead.

---

6   *These are precise movements required in dressage competitions, quite difficult enough for adults to achieve perfectly even on well-schooled horses, very challenging for children on ponies.*

Although Mrs Canning's drawing room faced North and East it always seemed bright and sunny. From it she kept an eagle eye on the front drive, the chapel, the cedar tree, and the lawn on which we cartwheeled and played for fun as well as rounders and netball. She also kept a huge white German Shepherd dog Ferne, that lived on the sofa. Mrs Canning had been persuaded to take it from Ferne Animal Sanctuary started by one of her friends Nina, Duchess of Hamilton. Ferne's unfortunate beginnings apparently justified her habit of rushing at our ankles for a quick nip. Although she never drew blood Mrs Canning denied Ferne ever nipped at all, indeed she never did when Mrs Canning was watching. Very occasionally, after another near miss with a visiting grown up, she wore a muzzle, but it spent most of its time on the floor by the sofa.

The drawing room was up a few steps from the hall and often Mrs Canning would appear, at first unnoticed, and observe us from above. She went to the hairdresser in Blandford once a week and one teatime we became aware that we were being watched. Looking round we were astonished to see that her hair was not only permed but had gone pale purple. At about this time she rescued Tinkerbelle, a black cat so called because of the bell on a ribbon tied round her neck, to warn the songbirds of her impending arrival. Tinkerbelle was often at Mrs Canning's ankle. It had been a mystery to us that wherever we were, indoors or out, Mrs Canning knew what we were up to. Now we understood: her hooked nose, her lilac hair and a black cat explained it. She had supernatural powers; she must be a witch.

She taught us art in a dark and dingy room in an old outhouse, part of the original laundry. We used powdered poster paints on grey paper that changed the colours when wet and again when dried. It is amazing that we managed to create anything at all. Once spring arrived and the shrubs had started to bloom, we went out into the gardens and did our best for the lilacs and laburnum. She also took us for an hour a week for 'art appreciation'. This usually involved in-depth analysis of Renaissance Virgins with Child. She taught us how to look. How to look properly. How to see lines and shapes and colour. Every day, nearly seven decades on, I thank her. I sent her postcards from every exhibition I visited until she died.

We were taught English by Dorothy Preston-Tuart (DPT). Grammar was parsing made easy by our learning Latin, then there was literature, essays, and vocabulary. Ten new words to be learned each week including those so frequently in our conversation such as 'onomatopoeia'.

"Try and include something onomatopoeic in your essays!"

Literature was Shakespeare and the major poems, *The Rhyme of the Ancient Mariner, Paradise Lost and Regained, Cargoes.* Each term we did a Shakespeare play thoroughly and had to learn all the soliloquies by heart and declaim them verbatim in front of her and the rest of the class to prove that we had learned them. Those who failed word perfection had to try again at the start of every lesson until they succeeded. 'Is this a dagger which I see before me, the handle towards my hand? Come, let me clutch thee. I have thee not, and yet I see thee still.' 'Friends, Romans, countrymen, lend me your ears; I come to bury Caesar, not to praise him. The evil that men do lives after them; the good is oft interred with their bones; so let it be with Caesar.' I can still do the first four lines of most, but it took me well into middle age to want to revisit Shakespeare.

After lunch we had to rest and read in total silence in dormitories in winter, on our rugs in the box gardens in summer. We were told it was to aid digestion but none of us were under any illusion, it was so that DPT had us captive and could monitor our reading matter. Any book about ponies, or even worse those written by End Blyton, were confiscated on the spot. Sometimes we could hear her approach and managed to substitute with an alternative kept under our rugs.

"You were on that page last week!"

What she thought acceptable were Walter de la Mare, Robert Louis Stephenson, Rudyard Kipling, Elspeth Huxley, Swift, or Arthur Ransome. She made it embarrassing to ask for any books to be returned at the end of term. Had we not learned anything from reading proper writing?

After a spell in the army, Michael Sharp had married the school secretary Anne, whose father, Major Goldingham, had taught riding at Canford and had moved with the Cannings to Hanford. Mr Sharp was the first man I had noticed wearing a signet ring. His pinkie finger must either have been broken or had early arthritis as the last joint was slightly bent. His default expression was of undisguised amusement with twinkling eyes. He was kind, witty and fun but one couldn't get anything past him. He taught us maths, geography, and sometimes French. In the winter terms after prep, he would read to those for whom the 'bed bell' had not tolled and who wished to listen. He introduced us to *Larkrise to Candleford, Memoirs of a Foxhunter* and Turgenev's *Sportsman's Sketches.* After Tin Can died, he became The-Man-About-The-School. He cajoled us into teams, ever willing to lug chairs from all quarters of the school to be arranged in rows under the cedar tree for plays or to clean and tidy classrooms for the parents days' displays. He supervised estate management and was brilliant at 'dealing with fathers'. Mine thoroughly enjoyed his company. It was mutual. He was the best teacher I was to have, ever.

The reason Mrs Canning needed only the tiniest *Louis Quinze* console table for her paperwork was because Mrs Sharp did everything in the office, single handed. Before the days of word processors let alone computers or iPads, she administered all aspects of the school from accounts to catering. Her very neat italic writing in blue ink, crafted with an Osmiroid pen, mirrored her posture and poise. It was everywhere. She had an enormous sense of fun behind that stitched-up façade and was particularly amused when told that one new girl had thought she was called Mrs Shark. When Mrs Canning retired and handed the school to Sarah, the Sharps joined her in the headship, giving her the confidence and back-up that she needed.

Health and Safety was dictated by Mrs Canning's common sense. When Daddy and Granny went to look at the school the first sound they heard had been the chirruping of little girls, like starlings, high in the cedar tree. My father told me later that was why they had chosen it.

"All heads describe their schools as happy, at Hanford you could hear it." There were three 'cubbies' in the cedar tree by the house, whence main branches fanned out. Those brave enough would sit in the top one, high above the world, level with the roof, watching comings and goings. We all played tag, running along the branches without holding on to anything. Provided we had enough experience or guts, we rode ponies flat out over the forts of Hod and Hambledon Hills, flying the gorse bushes, whooping as we went. In summer the rides were before breakfast and horseflies. If we helped in the stables and the Portman hounds met nearby, we were rewarded with a day's hunting. There was not a lot more frightening than trying to stay on a determined pony, head between its knees, gathering speed down one of the steep Dorset hills, with hounds in full cry and shouts from behind:

"Don't go in front of the master!" More peerless Hanford training.
During most terms at least one of us ended up in plaster but it was part of learning to look after ourselves and by others' mistakes. The post and rail fencing that ran down the drive was taken down to be replaced. The discarded planks still full of six-inch nails were lying in the long grass waiting to be picked up and we were told not to go near. I took no notice and ran across managing to tread on an exposed nail that pierced my foot and gumboot from sole through to arch. Luckily, I was running so fast that I was off it in one

stride. A visit to the cottage hospital for a tetanus jab, a request for a new pair of wellies from home and a, "We don't tell you not to do things for our own amusement!" was the result.

Until the Ingrams, who owned the surrounding land and hills, generously allowed us to use their pool, a half mile's walk across the fields, we swam in the ornamental lily pond. The excitement when we saw the gardeners clean it of a winter's rotten leaves and the baby frogs tempered the reservation we had about the coldness of the water. It was fed by an underground spring from Hambledon Hill. After swimming we ran naked, down to the house on the narrow strip of close-mown grass, and back, to get blood circulating again, before towelling off. The sight of dozens of goose-pimpled little girls running naked never seemed to raise the eyebrows of visitors. Now it would have been another shock horror for Child Protection and the school would have been put into 'measures'.

The food was hit and miss, usually miss and frequently disgusting. The hits were the wonderful fresh vegetables that were brought in daily in large wooden trugs from the three high walled kitchen gardens (Grade II Listed). Victoria plums ripened on the warm red brick. Lemons for our pancakes on Shrove Tuesday were from a cutting from the lemon tree in Michael Sharp's family glasshouses in Eire. It was a treat to spend summer evenings sitting with Mrs Canning, in the setting sun on the west facing garden hall steps overlooking the box gardens, shelling peas for the school's next lunch. She smiled, pretending reproach, about those we ate raw.

We were weighed and measured at the beginning and end of every term. I always lost weight. All those who did so were given a gloopy spoon of Radio Malt in break every day which was a wonderful, sugary treat. The mother of one girl, whom she took to the family doctor at the start of the holidays, was told that her daughter was suffering from malnutrition. She must have been cleverer at avoiding the food than I was. We ate in the hall at the refectory tables with a member of staff at each end to supervise manners, dole out food and make sure that we left nothing. Boiled caterpillars were rich in protein apparently and a floor cloth left bubbling in the porridge overnight would do us no harm as it had boiled. I have often wondered whether an Old Hanfordian worked on *I'm a Celebrity Get Me Out of Here*.

Mrs Canning habitually rescued the less fortunate. Lottie, an East German refugee, was the school cook who walked over the fields from Shillingstone every single morning, whatever the weather, fording the river Stour on her way. She did not show equal determination to master English. More than once she confused the hessian sacks of washing soda crystals with those of salt. The results were frothy but not *mousseline*. There were two short tables on either side of what had been the front door when the hall was a courtyard. If one sat at those one could usually slip gristle and fat through the fretwork of the panelling where it became biltong on the concealed radiators before it was eaten by rodents. Offloading food when sitting at the refectory tables was more challenging and depended on one's ability to flick it unnoticed under one's arm into the waiting jaws of one of the long dogs. Their rescue depended on how many of one's peers had got to them first. Failing to accomplish offload meant that one had to sit there until one had finished everything even if it meant missing games and still being there at tea. A lesson quickly learned was that it slipped down easier when warm than when trying to swallow it at tea-time after having looked at the congealed, grey mess for hours, when the mere idea made one gag.

Thirty years later I was with a group staying for an unavoidable night at the 'coming' Mount Pamir Hotel in Tashgourgan, on the Karakoram Highway mid-way between Gilgit and Kashgar.[7] Only two of us could stomach the boiled chicken that earlier we had watched scavenging the long drop.

"How can you eat that stuff?" we were asked.

"Hanford!" came the synchronised response despite our times at Hanford not having coincided. Hanford was perfect training for adventure travel in many ways especially when needing to chew appreciatively the choice cut of something very dubious. On reflection it is strange that we ate such shockingly bad food as Mrs Canning was a wonderful cook and always cooked Sunday lunch in the holidays. I still use her recipe for bread sauce.

The Canning's were painters, and their work was hung throughout the school. Mrs Canning had made lots of friends at The Slade and subsequently those in the Euston Group. Tin Can had supported (Sir) Anthony Blunt when he was a boy at Marlborough.[8] When the Cannings' friends visited they sat at the refectory tables and ate lunch with us. It was not unusual to find oneself sitting next to Sir William Coldstream, whom Tin Can had offered the job of art master at Canford (which he declined); or Anthony Blunt or (Sir) Lawrence Gowing. This meant that not only were we entertained by

---

7   *So described on the construction board fixed to its gateposts – building work had ground to a halt. Although described in one posh tour company's brochure as having 'en-suite bathrooms' they were locked. Ablution was possible thanks to water left in chrome dustbins on the landing.*

8   *Anthony Blunt and Mrs Canning maintained a correspondence for life. Sarah Canning burned all their letters after Mrs Canning died.*

fascinating people but were surrounded by wonderful paintings of that era. The Cannings' collection of Coldstream's was unrivalled. There were portraits of both Cannings; the 'View of the Arno' was hung above the upright piano in the hall – a welcome distraction when it was one's turn to play 'Fight the Good Fight' during morning prayers; Sergeant Major Bellani was hung in the garden hall where one had to line up before lunch to have one's hands inspected for cleanliness; 'Still Life with a Statue' was hung in the drawing room as was a Ben Nicholson and the Utrillo.

Among others that Mrs Canning 'rescued' was Bill Underwood, the gardener, who had been wounded in the war and still walked with a roll and terrible limp. Besides growing all the fruit and vegetables, his glasshouses were full of delicate pot plants that he loaded into his wheelbarrow and brought in weekly to fill fireplaces. In the summer they were replaced with agapanthus, lilies, and iris. dahlias, cyclamen, azaleas and chrysanthemums were grown for the tables. He enjoyed following the tradition of the 18th-century naturalist and horticulturist, Henry Seymer, and his son, also Henry, who were widely known for the exotic fruits grown in the same gardens and glasshouses. It was impossible not to be affected by the colour and beauty.

Sunday services, initially conducted by Tin Can and then shared by Mrs Canning and Michael Sharp, were held in the tiny Georgian chapel of St Michael and All Angels (Grade II*), that sat on a little mound in front of the house. Some of the Seymers lay underneath in the crypt, approached by a rusty locked gate on the north wall. Steep, unused steps sprouting ferns led to a heavily cobwebbed and moss-covered door. We gave that area a miss in case the Seymers popped out at us. Jane Seymer was rumoured to walk the dormitories at night. In the Summer term of 1956, there was a flurry of excitement and cleaning when the Bishop of Salisbury came to dedicate it. Visiting preachers were often bishops, always interesting. They made us think far more than the visiting public-school headmistresses who seemed humour-free and irrelevant. Little did we know.

As Hanford's congregation grew the pews were replaced by specially commissioned small chairs, copies of those that had been made for Coventry Cathedral by Dick Russel. Later a gallery was built at the back of the chapel. The head girl always read one lesson. This was great training for public speaking as one's peers and teachers were far more frightening than any public. Owing to my father's involvement with Hulton Press, that by then was publishing four children's weekly comics.[9] I read the lesson three times, from the age of eleven, in the children's Carol Services at St Paul's Cathedral. My experience reading at Hanford meant that I only had to worry about all the ceremonial bowing to the vergers who bid one to and from the St Paul's lectern. By the third year, when I was thirteen, despite the positioning of a big hassock for me to stand on so that I could be seen over the huge golden eagle, I had become cocky. I was by then at public school and thought I knew it all. I said that Mary had had her first son, a child, rather than her first child, a son. Hearing my mistake relayed by loudspeakers to over three thousand people, the length and breadth of St Paul's Cathedral, was another lesson learned.

The choir tuned by Mrs Bridgeman sang hearty descants. Sometimes we were asked to sing at weddings for which we received bags of sweets. It was worth shivering in our best dresses in unheated rural churches as we were only allowed four sweets a week, counted out by Mrs Sharp after lunch on Fridays. Jessie, a Scottish spinster friend of Granny's devised a clever way of smuggling more to me. Parcel post was opened in front of matron in her sitting room. Most parcels contained replacement socks or Cash's woven nametapes. I would receive a box of large paper handkerchiefs about three times a term. Jessie had steamed open the end of the tissue box, removed the bottom layers of tissues, filled the void with sweets and reglued the end of the box. Crunchie bars worked best because they could be tightly packed, so didn't rattle, and were light. No one remarked that I used so many tissues in a term, and I'm sure I wasn't devious enough to pretend to blow my nose. I never split on Jessie, it was our secret, and she earned my lifelong admiration and affection.

One of Mrs Canning's inspired decisions was to entrust the walking of the annual couple of Portman hound puppies to the two most energetic and mischievous girls. Mucking them out, hounds win all the prizes for the foulest excreta, and feeding them kept us busy when otherwise we might have been up to no good. It gave us privileged access to the kitchens for their food and if one timed it right Lottie slipped us cupcakes or slabs of treacle brittle. We also were given the afternoon off in the summer term and taken to the Portman Puppy

---

9   *Eagle, Girl, Swift* and *Robin* were very successful. A fifth, *Wren,* pitched for the age group between *Robin* and *Swift* never made it further than the cod copies. Besides the Carol Services there were very successful children's exhibitions held at Olympia.

Show to collect our silver spoons.[10] I still have one. After Sir Peter Farquhar retired from the mastership of the Portman, he and Lady Farquhar stabled their horses at Hanford. The Farquhars, always elegant and very friendly, sometimes allowed us to carry their tack or lead their beautiful horses, and they always filled us in on their day's hunting. Fifteen years after I left Hanford, I was asked whether I would walk a couple of VWH (Vale of the White House) puppies.

"Of course!" I replied.

"You do realise what you are taking on?" asked Peter Hudson, master of the VWH Monday country. "Have you walked puppies before?"

"I walked three couple of Portman puppies when I was at prep school."

"That must have been Hanford; a typically useful education!"

Before the need for marketing or Open Days, parents were friends of parents, and we tended to come from colonies in places such as Oxfordshire, Gloucestershire, London, and Scotland. Although we only went home once in the Winter and Summer terms and never in the Easter term, what with seeing our parents' friends and the Cannings' friends, Hanford felt like an extension to grandparents' houses. By the time I left in 1959 our numbers had grown from 80 to 130 of whom all but four were boarders. A committee (prefects) was selected by Mrs Canning to keep a ground eye on the school. Every Thursday evening after prep we had a committee meeting with her. In winter it took place in front of the open fire in the drawing room fuelled by the supper she had cooked for us. In summer she would bundle us and a picnic into the elderly Landrover and take us off to the hills such as Win Green or Bulbarrow where, with a bird's eye view of vale life, and the sounds of tractors and livestock returning home for the evening, we discussed new ideas for the school or reasons that a particular child might not be happy and what we could do about her. Sometimes we would lug the picnic across the meadows from the school to the river Stour but, however lovely and warm the evening was, we were not allowed to swim in the waters, in case we contracted polio. Eight thousand children were being paralysed in Britain each year, of whom ten per cent died when their heart muscles became paralysed. The first vaccine had only just been introduced.

---

10 *Every hunt holds an annual puppy show. The puppies - in fact the previous year's puppies - are judged for conformation. The walkers of those puppies receive prizes, and each walker receives a silver spoon with the puppy's name engraved on it. There is often a prize for the Best Working Hound, i.e. a hound that has already had a season or two hunting. It is awarded not on looks but on handsome is as handsome has done. After the judging there is a magnificent afternoon tea party provided by the masters - an afternoon enjoyed by all in the interim between haymaking and harvest.*

We slept in every available corner. A dormitory and bathroom were made above the stables for the committee; in summer four girls slept in the open fronted summer house in the Box Garden, coming inside to sleep on the floor of the garden hall if rain was driving in on them. Any cupboard that could take a bed was used and Mrs Sharp kept a waiting list for places that never became available.

To spend five years surrounded by such wonderful paintings; to be taught by the inspired, and to be cared for by the witty and wise in a school at the peak of its success, was an unique privilege. I loved it. We all cried when we left; we couldn't imagine that life would ever be the same again. It wasn't, but it prepared us to hold on to the best on offer with every digit, and to step over any breeze blocks chucked in our paths with determination and pragmatism. I was unbelievably lucky to have been there at all, let alone when I was.

EIGHT

ALBANY

1955–1956

If you stand with your back to Fortnum and Mason's or Hatchards bookshop, and look across Piccadilly, you will see a quiet courtyard with an 18th-century house at the back of it. The current house was built for the 1st Lord Melbourne by Sir William Chambers. Melbourne ran out of money thanks to his wife's expensive habits, and he had to sell it, although not before their son, the prime minister, was born there. The freehold of the property was subject to various mortgage charges involving among others, the Dukes of Marlborough and Bedford, Coutts Bank and Farrers the lawyers. All wanted their pounds of flesh, or to be rid of their debts which led to many 'interests' in the freehold. An early idea was to convert it into a hotel, but the idea of bachelor sets won, with many of the interested parties being given freeholds. It explains the current shared ownerships, trusts, and committee management.

The courtyard to be seen from Piccadilly, now offices, housed service buildings. The long rear garden reached what is now Burlington Gardens and parallel rows of sets were built on either side, linked by a covered way known as The Rope Walk, with arms to each staircase of sets. It ended in a back entrance giving access to Burlington Gardens and Saville Row. In between were courtyard gardens.

After Mummy died my father offloaded their flat in North Audley Street and moved to A12, a set on the top floor at the back of the main building. The accommodation was modest but the view from the elegant, dirty-green panelled sitting room, through two full-height sash windows, looking down the Rope Walk to Saville Row, was exceptional. There was a main bedroom, a bathroom, and two little halls with ample cupboards, doubtless necessary for the gentlemen's cloaks and coats. Very steep stairs led up to the kitchen and a bedroom for the gentleman's gentleman, in the eaves. Their tiny windows only gave views of clouds and vapour trails. Granny and I shared the main bedroom and Daddy slept as staff. Blackbirds always nested in the little garden below our windows and Mr Blackbird's song was a cheerful reminder of life beyond the metropolis.

It was to Albany that I returned after my first term at Hanford. Children are not allowed to live there but the trustees must have felt sympathy towards my widowed father and decided that as I was spending eight months of the year at boarding school, I was not a resident but a guest. I believe I am the only child who has lived there.

Granny was standing beside Daddy on the platform when the London train from Gillingham pulled into Waterloo. We went straight to the Café Royal Grill Room for what my father called 'a spot of lunch'. The Grill Room, assembled in 1865, was an exuberantly over-the-top Rococo room with gilded, garlanded caryatids, and wall to wall mirrors from the back of the plush, red velour banquettes to the moulded, painted ceiling. It was described by Sir Cecil Beaton as the 'most beautiful room in London' and now is renamed the Oscar Wilde Suite (a favourite haunt), where tourists take tea at little round tables. It had become my father's favourite place for lunch, and he always was given the 'best' table in the inside corner, only once jocked off it by Sir Charles Forte who had bought the place in 1954. Amusingly for my father, Sir Charles' guest was an old friend, Tony Gray,[1] Treasurer of Christ Church College, Oxford, who was not only being given lunch but a large donation towards the cost of creating the gallery for the priceless old master drawings that belonged to the college.

We ate perfectly pink rack of Spring lamb with new potatoes followed by warm *zabaglione*. My father and Granny splashed through a bottle of rosé, I

---

1   Later Secretary and Keeper of the Records of the Duchy of Cornwall – Sir Anthony Gray KCVO.

drank Shloer apple juice, and we all laughed. It was the perfect palate-cleanser after the disgusting Hanford food.

Daddy never took enough exercise to work up a good appetite, but he was particular about food. All but well-travelled Brits. were yet to be introduced to European food by Elizabeth David. David's seminal book *Mediterranean Food* was not published until 1950; her *Italian Food* in 1954. Olive oil came in tiny bottles from Boots to be used for loosening earwax; cheese was limited to Cheddar or Stilton, unless those returning from a grown-up holiday in Antibes or Cap Ferrat brought some back, thereby stinking out their car for weeks. Garlic simply wasn't. Although there had been Oriental and Asian trail blazers in the relevant 'ghettos' their restaurants had not erupted all over the UK, now difficult to imagine. Options for excellent dining-out in London were limited. Daddy rang the changes from the Café Royal with outings to Scott's, on the first floor above the shops in Coventry Street looking down Haymarket; Simpson's in the Strand (for beef); Madame Prunier's in St James's (for fish) and Bentley's (for oysters). When not *en famille* he dined with his friends, sometimes in the United Universities Club but mostly in The Travellers Club with its civilised surroundings, augmented by the good food and cellar.

Granny was nearly ninety, and it says everything about her imagination, her humour, and her attitude to the young, that she spent the next few school holidays managing not only to entertain an energetic, under-exercised little girl who had grown up out at grass, but to do so successfully enough to stop her presence in the hallowed confines of Albany being remarked on by other tenants.

Initially I forgot life on the farm and revelled in the buzz of central London. Shortly after Daddy had left for Fleet Street, Miss Hill let herself into the set. A humour-free spinster, I imagine that she had little in her life to laugh about. By the time she reached Piccadilly she probably had travelled a fair distance on public transport, probably with changes and waits, from a little flat in a dull suburb, to dust and vacuum in one of the most select addresses in London, a grating reminder of social inequality. It was obvious she liked my grandmother and didn't like me, which was hardly surprising. She had been engaged by my father who was meticulously tidy and ate out when alone, and unexpectedly she found herself confronted by an exuberant, until recently feral girl. She was not amused, and I suspect only stuck around because, like the Albany trustees, she knew that it was only for four months of the year. I can imagine her counting the weekdays on her fingers as she travelled home; 'Another day done. Only another three weeks and two days. That's seventeen days. I can make it.'

As soon as Granny and she had discussed the time of day, Granny fixed her hat onto her head with the pins, a performance I never ceased to find fascinating; draped a brace of foxes that looked as though they had been run over, their brushes hanging down her back like a Davy Crocket hat, their masks and front pads in front, and off we set to leave Miss Hill in peace. I clattered down the stone stairs as fast as I could run, to meet Granny when the grindingly slow lift, that must have been one of the first in London, reached the ground floor. Mr Mercer, the head porter, would ask her how she was and Harry his junior enquired after my manifestly robust health, with his broad smile. As I grew out of my clothes Granny gave them to Harry for his annually augmented litter of children.

With my hand in hers we crossed Piccadilly to Fortnum's where we had elevenses. Granny drank stewed milky coffee from a Cona machine and ate a couple of Nice biscuits and I ate a large triangular wedge of sponge, sparingly wiped with jam, and held together with an inch of whipped cream. Fortified, we did chores. My father had accounts with Fortnum's for daily groceries and Jacksons of Piccadilly for things more esoteric.[2] Cheese came from Paxton and Whitfield, wine from Berry Brothers and Rudd. We would jinx up Swallow Street to Regent Street and visit The Needlewoman where Granny bought thread or wool for whatever handiwork she had on the go. I was fascinated by the range of colours displayed on spindles, reels and in skeins. Sometimes we diverted home via Berwick Street Market in Soho, her favourite place for vegetables. I suspect she enjoyed the ambiance.

Granny scanned the entertainments column of the evening paper and in the afternoon we would either go to the cinema, films changed weekly, a museum, or the zoo. This involved bus rides and we always sat on the top deck. How sure-footed a ninety-year-old she must have been to negotiate the stairs. I loved looking down on people scurrying around below us. Sometimes she took me to lunch in the Monseigneur News Theatre on Piccadilly Circus,[3] where we sat in a raised box looking at newsreels and travelogues, like Peter

---

2   *Jacksons of Piccadilly is now a branch of Richoux pâtissiers, the self-proclaimed place to 'sip and be seen' before or after matinées.*

3   *The Monseigneur News Theatre had an auditorium for fewer than 300 and in the '60s switched to screening 'adult' films. In 2007 it became a nightclub.*

Sellers' brilliant spoof *Balham – Gateway to the South*. Our plates were barely lit by a tiny bulb in a red velour shade on a faux candlestick in the middle of the table. As the choice was lamb cutlets and boiled potatoes it didn't matter that we could not see what we were eating.

Granny was becoming more easily tired, and I now know was succumbing to some variety of gut cancer, so after the Monseigneur we'd go to a feature film a bus-ride away in New Oxford Street or Fulham. Once we did three cinemas in one afternoon.

"Now don't tell your father."

It was our secret. She hadn't wanted to worry him about her health or the pressure that looking after me was starting to take on her.

Once I had learned my way around the area, I was sent off to do errands. On Sunday mornings I walked down Piccadilly to buy the papers from the man who hawked them on Piccadilly Circus. All shops were closed all of Sundays.[4] There were few people about and little traffic. The nine-year-old was proud to be trusted to return with the right papers and correct change. Granny sometimes sent me off to the big post office in Lower Regent Street to buy stamps.

"Be careful Hinnie, look before you cross the street."

Evenings dragged especially in the dark winter. Granny tatted, mended, or played patience. I fidgeted. Once Daddy was home, she finished cooking supper. We ate early together, played a few hands of rummy or donkey and I went to sleep listening to Solomon's recordings of Rachmaninov's piano concertos that Granny played on the Pye Black Box that Daddy had given her for Christmas.[5] Years before I saw Celia Johnson and Trevor Howard having their brief encounters I would hum along familiarly to the Rach. Two.

One evening in 1956 Daddy returned with a small, square, black and white television set, our first. He, the Hultons and the other directors were agonising about the future of *Picture Post*.[6] A television to keep up with the news had been deemed essential. I was not remotely interested in news, or having to remain silent while Daddy watched it, but I did find the early evening antics of *Champion the Wonder Horse* and *The Lone Ranger* welcome distractions before his return from the office.

---

4   *The Sunday Trading Act, allowing all shops to open, was enacted in 1994.*

5   *The Pye Black Box, the ultimate Hi Fi Gramophone record player, became available in 1955.*

6   *Picture Post 1938–1957 was famous for its photojournalism and anti-fascism. At its height it sold over one and a half million copies each week. Eventually superseded by television where many of its journalists ended up working.*

Even before we had left Aynho, Daddy had been looking for somewhere in the country to become home, but nothing had risen to the surface. Much spare time was spent looking at the advertisements in *The Times* and *Country Life* and making appointments to visit hopefuls. Every Saturday the three of us would pile into the car and go to the country to look at short-listed houses for him to buy, to enable our escape from life in town. The brief was an eight bedroomed house with a sitting room for Granny spacious enough to take her piano; a service cottage; a good garden for Granny; stables and about twenty-five acres, within commuting distance of Fleet Street. The budget was £25,000.[7] We were shown round houses with moats in Essex; pristine Regency manors in Buckinghamshire; crumbling rectories in Kent and Tudor wannabes in Surrey. Besides finding it fascinating to see how other people lived, it was the perfect introduction to English domestic architecture and when Osbert Lancaster's *Here of All Places'* was published in the late '50s it was hilariously familiar.[8]

Nothing worked out before Granny's illness became too serious to hide and one cold, January weekend, while she was in The London Clinic, Daddy and I went to Hertfordshire to look at a house available to rent on the Brocket Estate. Bert Hardy, the legendary photographer attached to *Picture Post*, came with us to take photographs for Granny's approval. Although not for sale, it ticked the other boxes and was empty so we could move in immediately. Granny would be able to leave hospital and be reunited with her piano and she would have a lovely garden in which to keep an interest.

---

7   *Under £700,000 in 2022 money.*
8   *ISBN 10 – 1125214090 / ISBN 13 – 978-1125214091*

NINE

WATER END

Pantechnicons converged on Water End House, near Wheathampstead in Hertfordshire bringing my grandmother's furniture, including her beloved piano, from Northumberland; my father's furniture from Albany and all the stuff from Aynho that had been in store. Much of it stored by Pickford's had been bought by my mother and it must have been difficult for Daddy to see it again. My grandmother had left her beloved Northumberland for ever after ninety years and had moved three hundred miles away from Andy, her eldest surviving son. It would have been difficult for her too. For me it was heaven and I was like a bird released. The ponies including a recently bought little dun called Teddy, that had been with Captain Stannard while we were in London, arrived. We were on the edge of the Brocket Estate over which Lord Brocket had given permission for me to ride.[1] Teddy was the ideal pony. He took no notice of my riding capabilities or lack of them and looked after us both. Inspired by Red Indians in cowboy films, I rode bareback which had the advantage of my

---

1   *Brocket Hall now is an events and wedding venue, and the park has two golf courses. Built for Lord Melbourne's father in 1760 it was designed by Thomas Paine and is Listed Grade I.*

not having to brush his hairs from the wool bottom of my saddle with a dandy brush. Mick, the latest dachshund, came everywhere with us. Before we cantered, I would stop Teddy, Mick would put his paws on Teddy's knees, and I would pull him onto Teddy's withers. At the end of the canter, I put him back down.

London had opened new doors and introduced new distractions, but they had started to wear a bit thin and being woken by the chorus of garden birds and the corvids' caws was better than the distant honking of taxis. I wallowed in the big outdoors as the days became longer and the sun warmer.

Water End is a Grade II* Listed, red-brick E shaped house believed to have been built in 1601 for the Jennings family. Charcoal scribblings on the wall above the large stone fireplace in the main bedroom recorded Sarah Jennings's birth in the room, fifty years after the house was built. Sarah became the first Duchess of Marlborough. The scribblings are dated 1692 so perhaps they waited until Marlborough was released from The Tower before they risked celebrating such association.[2] Sarah was the greatest friend and confidante of Queen Anne until they fell out in 1711. She was tough, energetic, and opinionated. She argued with many including George II, Robert Walpole and Vanbrugh, when he was working on Blenheim Palace. Water End was for years a farmhouse, and it is impressive that she had such self-confidence and mastery of political intrigue having come from somewhere that would have fitted into a tiny corner of the contemporaneous Burghley or Hatfield. For the Duchess of Marlborough, Princess of Mindelheim and Countess of Nellenberg it had been a modest beginning.

The house is on the side of a hill beside a narrow lane that forded the fast-flowing River Lea. Three storeys high on three sides and four storeys on the other it appeared bigger than it was because of its position on the hill. The three vast chimney stacks disappeared out of sight in valley mists. It was surrounded by wonderful gardens created where stock yards and barns had been, and their foundations remained.[3] The garden had been created by the wife of a previous tenant Lucie Marie Ludovika Anastasia Adelheid Karola

---

2   Marlborough was thought to have signed letters, later discredited as forgeries, in support of James II and was incarcerated in the Tower of London for five weeks in mid-summer 1692.

3   A barn on the lower garden was removed in 1938 because it obscured the view to the river and beyond across the valley. It was reassembled in St Peter's Street, St Albans and is now a Weatherspoon pub.

Hedwig, Comtesse Haugwitz-Hardenberg-Reventlow of Denmark. She had further print footage of German ancestry in the Almanach de Gotha. She had married a Lieutenant Colonel Walker and had happened on his garden implement business Rolcut Secateurs. The Countess Reventlow, as she was known, not Mrs Walker, had needed a location to photograph the implements to be advertised and doubtless her accountant enabled the garden's creation almost as helpfully as the German prisoner of war who had done the heavy work, under the hands-on supervision of her gardener Mr Wyman. When we arrived, he was still the head gardener, and there was no doubt that it was his garden that we were privileged to enjoy.

So, Granny had a garden and as importantly someone as knowledgeable and as interested as herself with whom she could discuss gardening and plants. She had one wing of the 'E' that included a sunny sitting room with ample room for her piano, always covered with her small sepia prints of Greig, Brahms and Schumann. A door led directly to the flagged terrace that faced southeast and overlooked a rectangular sunken lawn retained by the old stockyard flinted walls and wonderful herbaceous borders. Roses edged a lawned path above the walls and their scent wafted across at nose level.

The other wing of the 'E' housed what the estate agents' particulars imaginatively described as, 'Kitchen and Staff Quarters'. There was certainly a smallish kitchen and a butler's pantry, each with one wall of glass fronted cupboards. The staff sitting room was cramped with a high ceiling and a fireplace large enough to roast an ox. Staff sleeping arrangements were up to the tenants. My father gave them rooms with us in the centre of the house.

I can see Granny sitting on the terrace outside her open door in a rounded wicker chair enjoying afternoon tea, out of the wind, in the sun and of course wearing one of her big-brimmed linen hats. It is a bittersweet memory. Her cancer, if that is what it was, had taken hold and she returned to The London Clinic. She didn't stay there long but when she returned, she needed twenty-four-hour nursing care. An agency nurse 'did' the days and one of Granny's medically trained cousins 'did' the nights. The day nurse thoroughly upset things in the kitchen. Mollie, the cook, was furious. Not only was she told that my grandmother found her food indigestible, which was highly unlikely, but she was elbowed away from the Aga just as she was trying to cook for me and Daddy. I didn't like her because she tried to make Granny's bedroom off-limits for me and Mick. We would sneak in when she was in the kitchen or the evenings, to Granny's evident delight.

"Oh Hinny, how lovely of you to come and see me," and she'd pat the bed beside her. "Come and sit here," and Mick would jump up and join us.

I think Daddy only put up with the nurse on a needs-must basis.

Granny died aged ninety-two at Water End in July 1957, six weeks after I had last seen her while home for half term. I was told that Mrs Canning wanted to see me in the drawing room. When I opened the door sneaky Ferne lay on the sofa under the window and didn't even lift her head. Mrs Canning sat me beside her on the sofa by the fire and told me. I adored Granny. We always had such fun; we were partners in crime, and we shared secrets. I knew Daddy adored her too. They made each other laugh, enjoyed each other's company and he valued her advice. I had never overheard a disagreement. I didn't cry because I didn't want Daddy to worry about me and I worried about him, but it was nearly the end of term and soon he and I would be together again. Everything would be alright.

Whenever I hear Chopin's Impromptu No 1 in E Flat Major, (later I learned what it is) I see Granny's smiling eyes in that wise, gentle old face, as her head, slightly inclined, followed her right hand's fingers skimming up and down the keys.

Water End was unexpectedly cheerful when I returned. There was no nurse wandering proprietarily through the house and Mollie was smiling. Warner, the butler, whistled as he polished each fork and spoon, while laying the table for two instead of three. Daddy and I had become a gang of two. He was fifty-six, I was eleven.

He left for the office at nine o'clock and returned, on an easy day, by seven. On Wednesdays he had to put the paper to bed at the Sun Printers in Watford and returned after midnight. Although I was always encouraged to have schoolfriends to stay, and Daddy made it attractive by my always having a spare pony for them to ride, without Granny I spent most daylight hours having to amuse myself. Thus began my life spent badgering Daddy's staff.

Mr Wyman was target one. I would find him, wherever he was working, and try to engage him in conversation. For that I mean that I would quiz him about everything. He had lied about his age to fight for King and Country and had found himself in the trenches in WWI when barely fifteen. Frustratingly he would not tell me anything about it. He did tell me about creating the gardens and he tried to teach me how to do things that he regarded as essential and lamented I was not being taught them at school. He told me repeatedly how water rats and bullfinches were the bane of every gardener's life, especially his. Bullfinches had the temerity and foolishness to eat the blossom of the apricot trees that grew against the warm, south-facing brick walls of the house. Water rats ate the sweet corn that for some reason he always planted in the second kitchen garden next to the river. He was a dead shot with an air rifle and many a time I saw one of the pellets send Ratty, who inoffensively had been nibbling the grass bank, into the middle of the river. He bobbed away downstream past the azalea garden, never having known what happened. One day, having given me yet another lesson with his airgun, I was taking aim at a bullfinch when an imperious voice shouted at me:

"What on earth do you think you are doing, girl?"

It was evident that this was not concern about ricochet from the brick wall supporting the apricot trees. Within minutes I overheard the countess, who had returned to visit Mr Wyman, chastising him for encouraging the culling of bullfinches, although I am sure she had enjoyed the apricots he had brought to the back door in one of his wooden trugs.

He failed to teach me to skin warm, just deceased rabbits. Mr Wyman had a pruning knife, that he absentmindedly sharpened to a razor on a whetstone every morning when drinking his flask of tea.

"Start here," as he would cut round the hocks of a rabbit lying on his workbench, "then pull the skin from one leg, then the other, as hard as you can down its body, towards its head as if you were taking off a tight jersey, a pullover." It did look just like a lovely, furry pullover. It stuck at its head that he then cut off with a crack and a slice and chucked the head and redundant pullover into the wooden wheelbarrow.

"Now your turn." I would silently count to three: it became ten, fifteen, twenty and still I failed to insert the knife. There was something so Benjamin Bunny, something about the way the eyes yet to glaze over, watched. I just couldn't do it, despite wanting to show Mr Wyman I was up for anything he thought important I should know.

Two events heralded the end of the long summer holidays.[4] One was being allowed to help Mollie stir the Christmas pudding and the other was the apple harvest. There were two fruit orchards and lush grass grew under the trees. Teddy loved the opportunity to graze it and wandered very slowly, head down munching as he went. By standing barefoot on his quarters I could reach the

---

4   *Our Summer holidays ended in the third week of September. There was no long half-term in October.*

apples beyond reach of those on ladders. Once the wheelbarrows were heaped, I was sent into the low-roofed apple loft and the filled buckets were passed up to me. I had to arrange the apples on racks making sure that none touched in case one had been bruised and would rot those next to it during the winter.

Tom, although older than Mr Wyman, was the assistant gardener and as the junior was referred to only by his Christian name. He must once have had Cary Grant good looks. In his late sixties, he still had a guardsman's bearing, and cycled from Wheathampstead three days a week. I looked forward to his days. Probably because, as he was badgered by me less often, he gave the impression that he liked me to be with him. I don't remember his trying to teach me anything, but it was he who explained the reason that Mr Wyman sometimes must have been cross with my intrusive questioning. It was Tom who told me a bit about life in the trenches.

"Grown men were never the same again and he was only a child."

It was difficult to imagine Mr Wyman any younger than he was, let alone as a child, but I always believed Tom knew what he was talking about.

Mollie and Warner were in their fifties and unmarried when they arrived. Mollie was Irish and had a face so worn and sad that she herself might have just come through the potato famine. They had met working together in a Yorkshire stately home. Mollie confided in Granny that Warner was an alcoholic. Together they tackled the problem, locked away the drink and were successful. As though it was part of the deal Mollie agreed to marry Warner. Mr Wyman gave Mollie away. They had the Saturday evening off but didn't 'bother' with a honeymoon.

After Granny died, I had weekday lunches on a tray in the library, but on Daddy's Watford evenings, Mollie invited me to have supper with them. The first thing Daddy had bought when we moved to Water End was the latest enormous television, almost as deep as it was wide. He gave Mollie and Warner the one we had had in Albany. It looked even smaller, lost in the middle of the large brick fireplace but the three of us would sit, with supper trays on our knees, and watch Double Your Money with Hughie Green.[5] It never occurred to me, in the days before the National Lottery, that unless lucky on the horses, the programme was the only chance many people had to dream of doubling their money.

Mollie became her version of happy after marrying and amazingly was not cross when I returned from Hanford one Easter holiday with a jam jar of recently hatched, wriggling tadpoles. Lottie had given us the jam jars and Mrs

---

5   Double Your Money was a television quiz show that ran from the mid-50s to the late 60s.

Canning had let us keep the spawn on the mantle in our dormitory (North) after we had scooped them from the lily pond. Each evening when she walked round at night to say goodnight, she had checked their progress as they changed from black blobs to wriggling micro-tadpoles surrounded by jelly. We had attracted attention at Waterloo station when a handful of us descended the London train with our night cases in one hand and the slopping jam-jars in another, but Mollie even gave me a large fruit preserving jar to give them more space to grow. They lost their appeal when, fully limbed and having been released to the edge of the rockery pond, frogs started hopping back across the terrace, through the opened door, into the garden hall.

I was less popular when I went to stay with a Hanford friend near Inverness and left ginger beer brewing in the airing cupboard. While I was away the two dozen two-pint glass bottles exploded scattering shards of brown glass and drenching every single sheet, pillowcase, tablecloth, napkin, and towel. Everything had to be boxed up, listed in the book, and sent to the laundry. The cupboard walls and ceiling, and all the wooden slats were covered in sticky gingery liquid that had to be laboriously washed. I didn't receive the 'Welcome Home' I'd anticipated.

Mollie and Warner left after five years, thinking that if they didn't move, they would be too old to find another job. By then the socially acceptable married couple, they went to Lord Howard de Walden near Hungerford.[6] Mr and Mrs Easton, who replaced them, had arrived for their interview with an elegant French green and gold oven-proof dish that they presented to my father. In it, to prove her brilliance as a cook, were the casseroled breasts of some of their current employer's pheasants, no doubt marinated in their brandy and cooked with their cream. We never liked each other. Doubtless I was a bumptious mid-teenager and the 'staff' car soon had 'L' plates tied to the bumpers. At weekends Daddy would take me off for a practice drive and they no longer had first use of it. The writing was on the wall.

Lord Brocket must have decided that my father was good company and, when invited to Brocket Hall for estate and staff parties, he, and by association I, would be treated like family rather than tenants. Well not quite like family, he was horrible to his heir and had nothing to do with him, or the next

---

6   *In the late 1960s Daddy and I bumped into Mollie and Warner in Hungerford. They begged to return to work for him '…it was our greatest mistake.' By then things had changed. We lived in a house too small to accommodate staff and, armed with Bee Nilsen's Penguin Cookery Book, had worked out how to look after ourselves.*

generation who reputedly had been despatched, out of sight, across the Irish Sea.[7] Sometimes His Lordship would drop by for a generous glass or two of Daddy's sherry. One time he asked whether we could give houseroom to a vast late 16th-century oak four-poster bed, hitherto in Bramshill House.[8] The two main bedrooms already had four-posters, but I had moved into a larger bedroom, and it was decided that I could have the bed. I spent the next few years sleeping in this vast oak construction, a contemporary of the Great Bed of Ware,[9] that Lord Brocket thought and hoped (I imagine so he could sell it for sums even greater than the cube it occupied) had also been made by Jonas Fosbrooke. It was fun having the niche, carved for a candle, where I could put a book. I spent hours looking up at the carved tester, studying the faces, acanthus leaves and strapwork. It was a ridiculously large bed for a small teenager even if I did share it with, by then, two dachshunds.

On another occasion he arrived to ask my suggestion for a name of his latest racehorse.

"You are our little horse expert!"

Not coming from a racing family, I had no idea that thoroughbreds usually were registered under names that connect, however tenuously, with the names of the sire and dam. I thought horses were called Fred or Beauty. He was thinking more along the lines of Hyperion, a Greek sun god, out of Selene a moon goddess, or Blenheim by Blandford. He had no concept that anyone might not know.

His friendliness had limits. When after seven years the rent came up for review his agents, Cluttons, sent my father a letter saying that the rent would be increased by four hundred per cent. The house and gardens were exceptional, but they were not worth it and the cost of living there was not the rent but the upkeep. The partial central heating had been installed between the wars and the boiler, that guzzled oil, was big enough to drive a transatlantic steamer. There were staff wages. Mr Wyman managed to keep on top of the gardens,

---

7   *Lord Brocket died in 1967. He had been pre-deceased by his son in 1961 and was succeeded by his grandson who was still at Eton. He later made himself rather too famous for an incident involving fast cars and an insurance claim.*

8   *Bramshill House, one of the largest Jacobean houses in England, was sold by Lord Brocket in 1952. Brocket Hall was built in 1760. Lord Brocket was right when he said that the bed was better suited to a Jacobean than Georgian house but it was a tight fit in Water End's modest room.*

9   *The Great Bed of Ware was thought to have been made circa 1590 as an 'attraction' for an inn in Ware, Hertfordshire. It was mentioned by Shakespeare in 'Twelfth Night' (Sir Toby Belch) and Ben Johnson in 'Epoceone' and is now in the Victoria and Albert Museum.*

just, with Tom's help, but it was only because it was his garden, and he chose to put in many more hours than he was paid to. It needed more gardeners. The house would not have accommodated a traditional family as well as the domestics needed to keep the spiders at bay. All was added to the fact that we had only moved there to give Granny somewhere to end her days. Daddy surrendered the lease.

Whether or not it is true that adolescent girls attract, or are more aware of the supernatural, I had decided that Water End was haunted. I had become frightened of sleeping there. Doors would open and shut in the night; the dogs would jump off my bed or jump up from their favourite place in front of the Aga. They would get halfway up the staircase only to yelp and rush back down as though they had been kicked. The cellar at the bottom of the stairs, by the kitchen, had been sealed off and internal walls did not correspond to those outside. I had wondered whether I had simply become frightened of the dark or whether there was something there. It may only have been a fertile imagination but once germinated it had kept growing. I had loved Water End but was delighted to leave and to discover after all that I was not frightened of the dark.

TEN

CRICHEL

1959–1962

In the Autumn term of 1958 those of us at Hanford who were entered for Cranborne Chase School had to be interviewed by Miss Galton, the headmistress, to see whether she might 'invite' us to take Common Entrance. Michael Sharp drove eight of us through the Dorset lanes in the Landrover. With a mixture of trepidation and excitement we bundled out of it and then had to sit in the passage outside her study in a mute row until it came to our turn to be interviewed. We went in one by one, alphabetically, and Betty, as she was known behind her back, saw one out as she held the door open for the next. There was no opportunity to be primed by those nearer the beginning of the alphabet. I was twelve years old and had no idea what to expect.

"Just be yourselves... polite... enthusiastic."

Her study at the front of the house from which she kept watch over comings and goings, seemed a dark room. After motioning me to a chair in front of her desk she sat behind it with her back to the window. With the light behind her I could not see her facial expression and I had no idea what reaction I was causing. A favourite trick of hers I was to discover. She seemed unresponsive and humourless, especially after the teachers whom we had taken for granted at Hanford. Her eyes, when one could see them, scrutinised in a raptor's way.

I wondered whether I really wanted to spend any more time in her orbit, but she had our futures in her grasp. Hanford had done its job because by some miracle I must have said the right things or not too many of the wrong ones. Betty ticked us all off on her list. I know that in my case she came to regret it. We never did see the point of each other.

Mrs Canning's report at the end of term commented on the change in me following the interview. I became hardworking. I was moved up a form. This may have had something to do with the fact that Daddy had threatened me with Cheltenham Ladies College if I failed the Twelve Plus to Cranborne. When he had done the rounds of public schools he had been most taken with Miss Popham, the Cheltenham Head. She had been the only head to offer him a glass of sherry and it had been a generous glass of dry sherry at that. None of that medium sweet stuff that he associated with women of that age and occupation. I had met some Cheltenham girls and was determined never to wear their grim green tweed uniform. Also, the majority of Hanford's 'bright' went to either Sherborne Girls or Cranborne Chase and it would have been too shaming had my peers got in and I had not. I was not academic, but I somehow managed to drift just above the middle of any form.

Fast-forward eighteen months and Daddy delivered me to another lovely house Listed Grade I with '…some of the most spectacular 18th century rooms in Dorset… possibly by Wyatt.' (Pevsner).

Everyone was very cool. We, new girls, were not. The clothes list stipulated that we should be sent back with white or grey knee socks. All the girls who were not new wore opaque black tights. White knee socks felt very silly, and we were branded. Although there was no uniform the clothes list also stated that we should wear pale- or medium-grey clothes. Again nobody else did, they ligged around in pencil-thin skirts and baggy jumpers, in deepest charcoal as nearly black as could be found. As soon as I had left Hanford, I had persuaded Daddy to let me have my pigtails cut off. He must have consulted the wives of friends and I was dropped off at an ultra-chic salon in Hay Hill and I had been expensively coiffed. Nobody at Crichel, we quickly learned to call the school Crichel not Cranborne, had coiffed hair. Everyone had long straight hair hung over faces like half drawn curtains. Ears were used as tiebacks if ever it was necessary to see out.

We found ourselves in the situation that hundreds find themselves every year. They've left their prep schools at the top, respected, trusted and in my case head girl and overnight they have become irrelevant squirts. We were incorrectly dressed, and I was immature, not even needing a bra. It was one of the few times that I wished I had had a mother. She would have made sure that I wore a bra even if there was nothing to put in the AAA cups.

Often it felt as though Betty, an uncamouflaged snob, had chosen her girls because of their parents. She had preference for the famous and titled.[1] Practically everybody's parents fitted the parameter and as Crichel had become the thinking-parents school, most were interesting, famous, extraordinarily intelligent, fun, and unfailingly friendly. The girls with parents like Lord Rothschild, Sir Solly Zuckerman, Sir Fred Hoyle, Sir Henry Moore, Dame Celia Johnson, and Peter Fleming added to a smattering of girls whose parents' names were the same as their castles and telephone exchanges. Despite the parental roll call, top boarding school education was not as financially excluding as it is today. Annual fees were about four hundred and fifty pounds a year, eleven thousand pounds in 2022 money. A similar school in 2022 costs four times as much.

We had our Hanford friends and as we had been very well taught, we were put together in the top form for our intake. It turned out that Sarah Canning had taught us Latin so well that we were ahead of the rest and a special form was made for five of us – four from Hanford. Corinna Robinson, who had just come down from Oxbridge came to teach us. Her parents had bought Stepleton House when the Cannings did not, and one Sunday afternoon she took us out to tea, and we boated on the Stepleton Lake, a very civilised escape.

Crichel House had been leased by Mary Anna and Toby Marten to the newly founded Cranborne Chase School in 1946. During most of the school's tenure (1946–1960) the Martens had been fighting the government for the return of land that had been compulsorily purchased during WWII. There was a Public Enquiry, resulting in the Martens' favour. It was scorchingly critical of the government and led to the resignation of the Secretary of State for Agriculture, Sir Thomas Dugdale. The Martens got back their land and the episode was a milestone in attitudes to ministerial responsibility. The Crichel Down Affair is still talked about. Although the Martens lived nearby, we rarely saw them as they were far too busy to bother with us, so we treated the place as ours.

---

1   *Fourteen years later Betty must have been keeping up with critical news in the Court Circular and noticed I had married and gained a minor handle. She tracked us down, telephoned out of the blue and invited herself to lunch. She could not hide her disappointment that lunch took place in the kitchen, a couple of chickens walked through, the elbows in George's jersey had gone and we didn't have a portico.*

Senior girls had one of the 'spectacular 18th-century rooms' that led to the portico with westerly views across the lake and down the valley. Our place was in the semi basement. If we stood on tiptoes, we could just see the lawns flowing down towards the lake and in the middle of them the chapel built in the mid-19th century. Lord Alington, Mary Anna's antecedent, had set out to make it 'the most ambitious chancel in Dorset...' (Pevsner again). After the Georgian simplicity of Hanford's chapel, it simply got in the way like a sore Victorian thumb. We had two common rooms off a passage that led to a door and steps up to the lawns. In winter one of the rooms was heated with a coal fire which at least meant we could cook chestnuts and marshmallows. In the other direction it led to the domestic science kitchen, the science laboratories, and the cloakrooms. In the cloakrooms we had wire cages in which to put games shoes and any fruit that our parents sent us. My father had a standing order with Fortnum's and once a fortnight I received exotic fruits, not available elsewhere. Pomegranates and kiwi fruit looked rather Dali shoved into plimsoles and lacrosse boots. We discovered an overgrown orchard over a high wall beyond the kitchen wing. We decided to harvest it, we always wanted more fruit. Taking our laundry bags with us, we climbed over and filled them with apples that we then sold to augment our pocket money. It was the first foray into free enterprise and a lot more lucrative than those in later life.

The lacrosse pitches were on a flat field on top of an exposed hill, a good walk beyond the lake. I have no recollection of having played a single game there, just of the walk in driving cold rain to be avoided at all possible costs. Crichel quickly became a life of avoidance, of dodging and weaving. Chemistry and physics, in the cellars, did not inspire us so we set about deceiving the teacher. Someone had a wig that she wore on alternate lessons pretending to be two different pupils. She adopted a family name –Forrester. Briony Forrester was ill once a fortnight. Romayne returned to class. Romayne was away but Briony was better. It worked for the best part of a term.

The first term of domestic science was spent learning how to clean, using salt, lemon juice and wire wool. Quite why our teacher, Miss Gregson, known as Dregs, thought this a useful way to spend the fees our parents shelled out I am unsure. We were privileged girls from privileged families, unlikely to have to clean the numbered ranks of coroneted copper saucepans or swooping mahogany bannisters. Perhaps it was so that we could supervise staff when we married those wonderfully titled men; perhaps it was so that if we didn't marry the wonderfully titled, we could hold our heads high when our friends who had done so, came to stay. By the time December came and we knew how to clean, we learned how to make rock cakes. Whose mothers ever served rock cakes? What use was that going to be? They were perfect for indoor lacrosse in the cloakrooms. Shrove Tuesday pancakes stuck to the ceiling most satisfactorily.

Music at Crichel was important, and at the end of one lunch (welcomely good food after Hanford) when school announcements were made, Christopher Irby, the lead cellist with the Bournemouth Symphony Orchestra asked for more cellists and bass players. The school orchestra would become unbalanced when the older girls left in the summer. He was charismatic and pleasing on the eye and straight away there were as many aspiring cellists as he could possibly teach. I was one. Anyone who played two musical instruments was let off one afternoon of sport so that they had time to practice both. In a school of one hundred and thirty, there were two school orchestras. We were lousy at sport and rarely could field a team for inter-school matches. All that running around, the blue thighs and chilblains, so uncool.

None of us were aware when we arrived, although presumably our parents had been told and assured that nothing would change, that we would only have one year at Crichel. The lease was coming to its end as the Martens wanted their home back.[2] They probably also wanted to see their invaluable furniture and paintings that had been locked away in a central room for decades.

The school governors had cleverly managed to buy New Wardour Castle – another stunning house – to which the school would move. Already everything had started to change and as things turned out the governors had not been all that clever. Well, clever in finding another glorious house for us in which to pass eight months of the year but less clever in vastly underestimating the costs of turning an empty historic house into a building fit for a school, albeit a trendy school.

The immediate change was that some of the staff had decided to take the opportunity to move on. Some had left, others planned to do so at the end of the year. The most critical to go was the Director of Studies and Classics teacher Anthony Brackenbury, 'Bracks.' He had already returned to Bryanston by the time I pitched up, but his reputation was legendary and within three years had been appointed the first head of the Yehudi Menuhin School. His successor, Mr Cameron, was not big enough to replace his laces let alone fill

---

2 *In 1996 Crichel was used for some of the filming of 'Emma' with Gwyneth Paltrow. The Marten's five children sold Crichel with 400 acres in 2013 to an American hedge fund billionaire.*

his shoes. Crichel had been founded as a sister school to Bryanston and Bracks and Betty, who had taught geography, had been drafted-in as founder staff. Without Bracks, Betty floundered.

Another to leave was my tutor P F Davidson, who went off to Tasmania to be head up a boys' school, a very kind and interesting history teacher who introduced us to the Incas. They were so romantic and much more exciting than those Saxons. It was the first time most of us had learned any history of 'abroad'.

As we supposedly were bright, we would be bound for Oxbridge. The school had a tutor system to prepare us for the experience. We had assignments each week in each subject, the marks for which were put on a card. Every Friday after lunch we lined up to see our tutor with our countersigned cards. We were applauded for good marks, had to justify less than adequate marks and, in my case, explain any blanks for the assignments not presented therefore not marked. Mrs Canning had written in a report eighteen months before I went to Crichel, "If she gets out of the habit of working, she will find it hard to acquire again, they have an easy first year, but the next year is *real* work." She was prescient as always. We had been brilliantly taught at Hanford and I cruised for a year. I don't think I did any *real* work again until after I married.

Escape from tedium took three forms. The first was enabled by the Martens' agent who still had two daughters at Hanford. He must have persuaded Betty to let two of us, old Hanfordians, ride the daughters' ponies at weekends so that they would be fit-ish for hunting in the Christmas holidays. During that autumn we spent many happy Saturday afternoons cantering round the Crichel Estate. The second escape was cycling to Witchampton, a small village about a mile and a half away, with a village shop that enabled replenishment of fruit and chocolate stocks. The third, initially mind-boggling diversion, was the Tuesday evening arrival of a coachload of boys from Bryanston. We were far too young to be included in what was called 'joint activities'. Joint activities were mostly music based and revolved round senior girls singing madrigals with the Bri-Boys. Cannabis had yet to make its mark. We peered at them from behind glass. As they descended the coach steps, black lace-up shoes grey socks and hairy knees preceded those grey corduroy shorts that the Bri-Boys had to wear. Some of the boys did not have acne but the spectacle did not make us want to take up unaccompanied singing. That said, all those of us who wished were bussed over to Bryanston once a week to rehearse for the joint production of Handel's *Acis and Galatea*. (Dame) Janet Baker appeared from London to sing Galatea on the day. The next year it was Gilbert and Sullivan's *Iolanthe*.

The short Easter terms always seemed the longest with grim weather and neither Christmas nor summer in the offing. Our first Easter term was always going to be a let-down especially as any illusion that life at public school existed on some sunny upland had evaporated. By the first weekend we were bored; by the second we needed to get out. For some reason we no longer had access to the Seymour's ponies and Crichel's woodland. We were allowed out if we signed the Going Out Book, stating direction and timings. One Sunday we signed out as cycling to Moor Crichel, a little village about two miles away, and that is what we had planned but once there, we decided to pedal on and go back to Hanford to see how they all were. It was only another eleven miles.

Spinning the gravel as we went down the drive it felt like the next best thing to returning home. Mrs Canning must have seen us from the drawing room and came out to greet us. We told her what we had done.

"Oh, you are going to be in such trouble. Miss Galton will be furious!" She smiled.

Mr Sharp turned up with the Landrover. We bundled our bikes in and as we clambered over them, Mrs Canning filled our hands with some of Lottie's cupcakes. Dropped out of sight of Betty's study, we cycled merrily the last few hundred yards and signed in, but someone must have seen us on the Blandford road and we were soon in Betty's study. As usual she sat with her back to the light, and we couldn't see her face but there was no doubt that she was not smiling. The three of us were gated until the end of term. Had we gone missing they would not have known where to look for us, a fact she did not mention. Instead, she tried to make us feel like immature worms unworthy of the school we attended. It struck me that she was simply a sad, jealous woman. Jealous of Mrs Canning and jealous of Hanford. Respect for her began its downward spiral and the shortest term became even longer.

During the summer term the entire school was bussed the twenty-odd miles to see New Wardour Castle so that we could become excited about The Move. Wardour was completed in 1776. Regarded as one of James Paine's masterpieces it has additions by Quarenghi, Catherine the Great's court architect who was responsible for much of St Petersburg including the Alexander Palace. It is sited on a gentle hill, surrounded by earth moved under the direction of Capability Brown, and is just over a mile from 'Old' Wardour Castle, trashed during the Civil War.

For nearly four hundred years the Arundells lived at Wardour, Old and New, the last Lord Arundell dying of tuberculosis in WWII. The 1st Lord

Arundell had been made a Count of the Holy Roman Empire, the 3rd was incarcerated in The Tower having been implicated in Titus Oates' Popish Plot, the 13th was to become a priest. A devout Roman Catholic family, it was a given that they needed their own chapel, so Paine incorporated one into the house. That, and the magnificent sweeping rotunda staircase with its forty-five-foot diameter and sixty-foot dome – '…the most glorious Georgian staircase in England…' (Pevsner), made Wardour the most fabulous building.[3]

We should have been over the moon to be moving there but somehow, after decades of being uninhabited and an unsympathetic conversion to a school, cats-cradled in scaffolding, it failed to inspire as it should. By the end of the Summer term we were sad. We spent a lot of time lazing in the sun on the lawn outside our subterranean common room looking up at Crichel's Portland stone façade and down across the grass to the lake with its chattering waterfowl. We would miss Crichel, miss the building, miss the place. We would even miss some of the teachers.

I don't think that the staff were deserting the sinking ship, but we hadn't been at Wardour long when we began to suspect rats. Much of the teaching had dipped. With lessons less interesting and the increased self-confidence of second year girls, now with the correct clothes, increasingly wayward hair, and another year before our having to apply ourselves for 'O' levels, we looked for distraction. We weren't allowed to use the house chapel as one parent had said that if his daughter prayed in a Holy Roman church, he would remove her. All Saints Chapel in Wardour (Listed Grade I*), designed by Soane is exquisite with acoustics described by Julian Bream, who lived nearby, as 'pleasantly resonant'. He recorded in the chapel more than once. Pevsner described it as 'grand in its decoration' and there was a lovely Virgin and Child marble relief by Monnot from the very early 18th century, but we never got to walk past it or were even allowed to see the paintings, altar, or stained glass. Instead, every Sunday morning, because of one parent's religious prejudice, we had to arm ourselves with adequately generous coins so that we didn't 'let down' the school in the eyes of local parishioners, and after Matron's inspection we were bussed to St John Baptist in Tisbury. It is a nice old church, but it was not the same, and the little community of Jesuit nuns who continued to live in a bleak house near New Wardour, could well have done with our contributions. Perhaps to assuage guilt we were encouraged to support their Church Fête. Willingly we

---

3   *Used as the location in the film* Billy Elliot *as the Royal Ballet School.*

went with our pocket money to buy raffle and tombola tickets. For the only time in my life, I won a bottle of gin as well as a bottle of whisky. Smuggled back we hid both bottles under leaves between the roots of a tall conifer a few hundred yards from the house.

The landing of this bounty coincided with the arrival of one Countess Zamoyska to help teach us French. Rumour had it that she had been the head of another girls' school where the governors had hoped the queen would send Princess Anne. They worried that HMQ would think a divorcée, therefore the school, unsuitable for her daughter. Countess Zamoyska graciously stepped down and came to us. This ruffled feathers, not only Betty's, who I think found her difficult as she was not only titled, albeit Polish and as Betty probably told herself, all those surviving grand Eastern Europeans had titles, but she also had an informed view of how to run a girls' school. The other trouble in the coop was with our existing French teacher, Cynthia Pettiward. CP had been in the SOE in the war and dropped behind enemy lines. She was a woman of stature and *avoir du poids*. It didn't occur to me that she must have been at least two stone lighter as a 'girl' and the thought of her floating down through the clouds, dangling from a parachute, was hilarious. She was an excellent teacher and having been trained to handle the Gestapo, was not fazed by adolescent girls. To keep a semblance of calm in the staff room Betty allocated French language to CP and French literature to the countess. She decided that the best way to make us learn the ins and outs and every single word of Molière's *L'Avare* was for us to perform it. I also suspect that in an act of defiance, in the hope that Betty was watching from her study that overlooked the Temple folly,[4] where we rehearsed, she made those cast as males carry cheroots.

"They're cigars, not handbags!"

She never collected them at the end of rehearsals so we would retire with the cheroots and a box of matches to the tree where the spirits were hidden, and a half hour of coughing and spluttering followed. The tiny shop on the lane didn't stock tonic water. I suppose the nuns, the main customer base, had no need of it. Neat gin was not the treat we had hoped. Inevitably Betty found out and I was summoned to her study. I took certain delight in pleading guilty and declining to name names but asked Betty to give my father the half-empty bottles at the end of term. She had already given them to Mr Cameron which I regarded as theft and any vestige of respect for her vanished.

---

4   Listed Grade II. Originally the Dairy, designed by either Soane or Paine and built circa 1794.

One summer term someone in charge decided to test us for tuberculosis. I was one of seven who tested positive. Grave faces accompanied us to Wimborne Cottage Hospital to have our lungs X-rayed. All of us were fine. We had parents who had herds and having drunk unpasteurised milk we had developed natural immunity. TB vaccination scabs had to be kept dry until they dropped off. As the only ones who didn't have to be vaccinated, we were the only ones who cycled through the leafy lanes of the Nadder Valley to a large private pool that had been made available to the whole school. Vaccinations could have been done at any time. Had the powers that be not noticed swimming things on the clothes list? It was difficult to take all but a few of the staff seriously.

It was about this time that a couple of ducklings made it into our dormitory. Both Kate and Lucy Fleming's birthdays were in May and Emma Rothschild persuaded her parents to bring a couple of ducklings for birthday presents. They were kept in a box under a bed, and we would take them outside whenever an opportunity arose. I think they were discovered just before half-term when they were taken 'home' to Nettlebed.

One August, to our unbridled delight, it made the front page of the Daily Express that a 'Leading Girls Public School' was facing bankruptcy. Owing to the original cost of the move to Wardour and the under-estimated renovation costs of a massive Palladian mansion, money had run out. Our parents received letters saying that unless they came up with a donation equivalent to a term's fees there wouldn't be another term and they would have to find other schools.[5] With under a month to find alternatives it was perfectly calculated blackmail. Disappointed, we ended the holidays back at Waterloo heading for Tisbury.

My year was described as the worst there had ever been. For a school of academically and socially selected girls that hyped itself as encouraging individuality, it was a badge to be proud of. We rose to it. Bored, we again cycled to Hanford. As it was about sixteen miles, again we were spotted again and again gated for another term. When not gated we frequented the coffee bar in Tisbury and fed the juke box. Pippa Lewis and Mary Moore managed to get to Salisbury. Spotted by the police they were mistaken for two girls who had absconded from a Wiltshire borstal. Before the days of faxes or e-mail there was no way of checking facial likenesses with the borstal, and they were taken

---

5   £150–£3,700 in 2022 money

to the police station. Asked for their home addresses they gave Bournemouth and Hertfordshire. Wondering why they were together in Salisbury, clutching cigarettes and gin, a detective probed:

"Next, you'll tell me that your father is a famous sculptor?"

They fessed up and were brought back in a squad car. On their way up to Betty, they chucked us their contraband for safekeeping. Betty suspended them but it made Fleet Street and soon the 'Famous Sculptor's Daughter and Friend' (an architect's daughter) were reinstated. Betty hated being made to look foolish in the press.

The debating society operated intermittently. Open to everyone it provoked lively debate and a lot of people, having listened to their parents, knew what they were talking about. A proposal to abolish public schools was carried with a comprehensive majority, possibly because Betty came into the room halfway through and we knew it would irritate her. Another hotly debated topic was nuclear disarmament. Bertrand Russell and Canon Collins had been instrumental in establishing the Campaign for Nuclear Disarmament in 1957. Several high-profile parents had expressed public support. There cannot have been anyone unaffected by the appalling photographs from Hiroshima and Nagasaki and there was no doubt they should never be used again but it also had the reputation of being left wing, which suited our rebellious streaks.

Soon a handful of us were wearing the eponymous CND badge everywhere we went. Over Easter weekend in 1958 the first Aldermaston March, from The Atomic Weapons Research Station to Trafalgar Square, took place. After a few years The March had become a well-oiled machine. I and a Crichel friend, who happened to live about eight miles apart, registered to join the other tens of thousands and spend Easter walking the fifty miles. We sent off the few pounds required to cover our overnight stops in church halls and refreshment along the way and looked forward to getting street cred for carrying banners and doing something positive to prevent a nuclear winter.

As Easter weekend drew nearer the weather forecast started to make it look less like spring and more like winter. Our respective parents, who at no time had tried to dissuade us, had made clear that it was up to us to get ourselves to Aldermaston. They had theatrically loud telephone conversations about plans for delicious picnics for point-to-points and general jollities.

"What a pity you won't be with us."

Neither of us clocked, until years later, as we had never seen our parents at a point-to-point and it was highly unlikely they were planning anything of the sort. By Maundy Thursday, the prospect of trains from St Albans to Newbury via Paddington, then the walk up the hill from Newbury to Aldermaston in sleet, even before four days walking to London sleeping (wet) on church-hall floors, while everyone else was having fun, looked very unappealing. There was a limit to how much we could do to save the world. We agreed to bottle out. On Good Friday our parents asked us whether we really wanted to go to a point-to-point in such hideous weather. That seemed unappealing too. Our parents had performed a master stroke. No confrontation with rebellious girls and a satisfactory result without their even having to dust off a picnic basket.

In the Summer terms one of the tennis coaches from Wimbledon came down to help us grasp rackets correctly and understand the tricks of tennis. He was a twinkly old man with thick white hair and matching whites. His sun-leathered face beamed friendliness, enthusiasm and fun and Thursday afternoons became something to look forward to. Tennis, unlike lacrosse, was cool as some parents had grass courts, not to mention Etonian sons, and it was useful to be able to play reasonably competently if invited to do so in the holidays. In our third year, if we had shown an interest in tennis, and by then apparently mature enough to cope with joint activities, we were bussed over to Bryanston to play mixed doubles. The tennis playing seventeen-year-old Bri-Boys in white shorts with chiselled, tanned legs, turned out to be a different breed to those who had signed up for madrigals. After the masters had made sure we were on the right courts with the right height nets and enough balls, they retreated to supervise something less challenging. We casually sauntered off to The Hangings, the woods on the banks of the river Stour, with alcohol and cigarettes of which there appeared to be a limitless supply.

We didn't bother with 'O' levels in the subjects we were to do at 'A' level, the idea being that we took 'A' levels the year after 'O' and would only have to spend one more year at school. I was to do Classics and initially enjoyed Greek. I loved the alphabet and the way the vocabulary often fitted with ours. *Hippos* = horse; *potamos* = water = Hippopotamus. It was like the monkey's gravestone at Hanford commemorating 'Homunculus'. It made Classics almost relevant. But there were only two of us in our year doing Classics, the other being Emma Rothschild,[6] eighteen months younger than me, who at the age of fifteen became

---

6   *Emma Rothschild CMG, Economics Historian, Fellow Magdalene College, Cambridge.*

the youngest person to gain a place at Somerville. Fabulously clever, she only had to look at a page and she knew it. Within days she was pages ahead of me; chapters in months; books in terms. It was too discouraging. I had no one with whom to discuss prep. I lost interest and as our lessons were conducted beside the organ in the rotunda, I spent most of them scrutinising the reliefs of musical instruments around the ceiling and the little iron flowers in the bannisters. It was understandable that Mr Cameron concentrated on his star and wrote me off.

I spent as much time as I could in the art room. It was located out of everyone's way up new concrete stairs high above what had been the kitchens and were to become the gymnasium, if ever the governors found enough money. Some space had been allocated to sound-insulated cubicles for practising our many musical instruments. I only had to tuck my cello under my arm to avoid suspicion and made increasingly spurious excuses to my tutor for only having French assignment marks on my card.

Our art teacher was the Dorset painter Anthony Brown. A civilised, pipe-smoking man who never asked us whether we should have been attending academic lessons. He and his wife had no children, but he seemed to understand us, was non-judgemental and provided a haven. As the art room stairs were near a side entrance he managed to slip in and out without becoming embroiled in the staff common room and its politics. He was often joined by our new assistant director of music, later director of music, Harrison Birtwistle then in his mid-twenties.[7] Mr Birtwistle taught some woodwind, Theory of Music 'O' level and sometimes even composed for us. Being in their presence made the art room far the most interesting place to be, but the hours I spent there did nothing for my academic achievement. I took eleven 'O' levels and passed one – French, thanks to my fear of CP.

In three years, I had gone from my prep-school headmistress saying that she and the school would miss me when I left, to my public-school headmistress hardly waiting to get rid of me. Some of it could be put down to adolescent belligerence but the rest must have been mishandling. I'm sure that without Bracks, Betty found it difficult to cope. The wonderfully named Thorold Coade, headmaster of Bryanston, had been Betty's head when she was Bryanston's geography teacher, and it was said that it was he who had persuaded her to become Cranborne's first headmistress. He visited her weekly until he died in 1963.

---

7   *Sir Harrison Birtwistle CH.*

D. H. Lawrence's *Lady Chatterley's Lover* had just been published by
Penguin Books after six days in the High Court when an Old Bailey jury had
found it not to be obscene. We'd managed to get hold of a copy that we loaned
out for a small fee, another successful venture into free enterprise. Preoccupied
as we were with love and sex, some girls thought Betty and Mr Coade were
lovers, but the only manifestation we saw of Betty's ability to be affectionate
was with Rupert, her rather gross dachshund. I think Mr Coade drove over the
hills once a week simply to give her much needed moral support.

One day Betty summoned me to her study. An elegant small drawing room
off the rotunda, it had a pretty fireplace, a high ceiling with fine mouldings and
a big sash window against which she sat, of course. In an attempted put-down[8]
Betty told me that as I was contributing nothing to the school it would be
best if I left at the end of term. With what must have been infuriating teenage
gall I agreed with her. I responded that I thought the school was contributing
nothing to me either. What she must have planned as a castigating interview
was over almost before it had started. Reckoning that we had a draw I decided
to leave it and her at that, thanked her for seeing me (her choice not mine) and
let myself out through one of the elegantly bowed, cornice-height satinwood
double doors. Why anyone would choose to be the headmistress of a boarding
school full of bright, under-exercised teenage girls incarcerated in rural
Wiltshire in the '60s I cannot imagine. I was not the only one who must have
been dementing.

---

8   *The school was closed in 1990 and the building sold in 1991. Betty's study, originally 'the
boudoir', was described in the sale particulars as "probably one of the most attractive rooms in
Wardour Castle." The fireplace was made of fleur de peche marble inlaid with onyx and lapis.
The three ovals on the ceiling had been painted to designs by Soane. Nigel Tuersley bought the
building. John Pawson converted it into flats. Betty's study became a bathroom.*

ELEVEN

MONTREUX – LONDON – MARSEILLE

1962–1964

It was all very well having scored one over Betty but then I had to fess up to my father. I pressed button A and heard the coin clunk to the bottom of the tin box in the hardboard phone booth. I always longed to hear his voice but was apprehensive. He was pragmatic. I suppose that having lost the love of his life only a little over a decade earlier kept everything in perspective, and it cannot have come as a great surprise as my school reports had been *au point* for a while.

What on earth was he going to do with a rebellious 16-year-old who had spent most of the previous three years bucking school authority and who had shown little interest in anything other than painting and music? My interest in music came with a rider. It was a nice notion, but I rarely practised either the cello or piano and the cello's spike was most often extended when used to help carve a path through crowds at Waterloo station.

Daddy talked to everyone to see whether they had any ideas. An acquaintance, who had worked at the Milk Marketing Board, was then employed by Nestlé outside Lausanne. His wife worked part-time in an international boarding school for girls near Montreux. At the start of the school holidays the two of us were off to Montreux. Bleu Léman, named after the *lac*, had a very convincing colour prospectus that would not look dated now. The headmistress assured my father that it was not a 'finishing' school; 'her' girls already had excellent manners, knew how to lay a table, and sit with crossed ankles. She said I would be able to continue learning the cello and the piano; lessons would be conducted in French and that I could start learning German. There would be frequent visits to the opera house in Lausanne and once the snow fell the entire school would decamp to the mountains where we would do lessons in the mornings, ski in the afternoons and learn to make a traditional Swiss fondue. A few years previously a rebellious girl had 'foolishly' drunk chilled white wine (not allowed) and the cheese had balled in her stomach. She had to be rushed to hospital for an operation which saved her just in time. That would not happen again. I did wonder whether she was worried that my father might have heard rumours or even had the inclination to scour back issues of *24 Heures*. With Lausanne Opéra and skiing the omens were good. I was positive and welcomed the opportunity to clear the slate and make a fresh start after my disastrous 'O' levels. I had let Daddy down. It would be a chance to show him that the three years at Crichel had been only a blip.

The building perched on a cliff a few hundred yards from the lake, was a square block of three storeys with a semi basement. Each elevation had two floors with about a dozen French windows with Venetian shutters that opened onto the narrow balconies that encircled the building. At the corners were substantial stone balconies. There were three lozenge windows under a Chinese pagoda roof with a spire on top. Below the lozenges *Bleu Léman* in tiles was framed in relief. A black and white photograph taken in the early sixties, makes it look like a sanatorium for the tuberculoid or insane.

On my first morning I woke to find that I was lying under a blanket of smoke floating six inches above my bed. My roommate satisfied her need for nicotine by smoking an entire packet of Marlboroughs first thing every morning, before the pastoral staff patrolled. The French windows were left open while we breakfasted. Had anyone outside looked up to see the smoke billowing out, they would have thought that the room was on fire. My suggestion that we might sleep with the window open lasted one night as not only the lake's north shore road, but the main railway line ran underneath the cliff on which Bleu Léman was perched. Hot-rodders tested their machines in the small hours and at regular intervals the building vibrated, the noise reached a crescendo and a train sped by towards Milan or the Valais ski region.

When not smoking my roommate spent her time repainting her nails and spreading out her jewellery across the bed to be admired. When told we were off to the Lausanne Opéra to see the Cossacks from Moscow, her concern was the dilemma of diamonds or pearls. Allowed out on Saturday she invited me to join her. I suggested a visit to the 16th-century Château de Chillon jutting into the lake. From a distance it looked as romantic as Byron had described it, but I was told that it was terribly dull. We spent three hours in Villeneuve, trailing from shop to shop in search of make-up and more nail varnish. She was thrilled to be at the school while her parents toured Europe.

"Oh my God, am I relieved they didn't drag me to Paris and Florence! They send me cards from all over. I've stopped reading them. Europe is so boring. All those Madonnas and it sounds as though Vienna is full of churches and choirs singing songs for the dead."

She added that her father had helped finance President Kennedy's election campaign. Had I taken more interest in American politics, I would have realised he was a Democrat. Interesting.

It became clear that most of the things the headmistress had promised my father had, to put it generously, slipped her mind and the stark reality of the result of my absurd rebelliousness began to nag. Ninety per cent of the girls were American, dumped as their parents toured Europe, and none had studied French so lessons were in English. No arrangements had been made for me to see either a piano or cello closer than the orchestra pit of Lausanne's opera house and in the one German lesson I had learned that Germans spoke in the subjunctive. I had exchanged my place in possibly the most academically, musically, and artistically privileged school in the UK, full of interesting contemporaries, for an educational mirage. To ram it home I hadn't managed to find anyone to commiserate with. As the days accumulated the enormity of my having failed virtually all my 'O' levels, kept me awake between the revving of engines and rattling of trains. A term, let alone a year, spent in the place was going to be an irksome waste of time.

After days of mounting regret, I admitted to myself that I needed to return to England for retakes. I contemplated running away but my passport was locked in the headmistress's safe. Daddy advised that I gave it another week. If nothing improved, he would telephone and tell them to release my passport. A week later my passport was shoved at me, and I was told to "Get out!"

My safety was no longer relevant to the headmistress. Until the earliest flight a couple of days later I was free to do as I pleased, not even having to return for meals. I explored Montreux and stumbled on the arms quarter. I resisted buying a revolver, but I did buy a lethal flick-knife with a bone handle that I smuggled home and used for decades as a letter opener – the only tangible memento of my stay beside that beautiful blue lake.[1] After I left, the headmistress assembled the school and told them:

"Suzanne was not representative of the English people. Forget you ever knew her." She was right and I'm sure they did. I had lasted three weeks.

I was enrolled at Davies, Laing and Dick, the crammer in Notting Hill Gate. Within a month I had taken and passed six of the 'O' levels I had failed. Most of the students were boys who had disappointed their parents and headmasters in a spectrum of ways and, like me, were being given a second chance. Hitherto, my knowledge of London was limited to within about two tube stops of Piccadilly. Notting Hill, yet to be discovered, was an edgy new world. The ice-cream-cake houses that now are sold for multimillions to the glitterati, housed families of Caribbean and African families crammed together in undisguised poverty and boredom. The men would sit side by side on the steps blocking the way to battered front doors, with locks that had been replaced multiple times. They watched everything with unblinking eyes and held rolled cigarettes between thumbs and index fingers, ready to be sucked. Our lunch hours were spent in one of the two trattorias. The choice was between spaghetti and minestrone, dependant on how much 'monthly allowance' we had left. Daddy found digs for me with two retired actors who lived in reduced circumstances above the Wimpy Bar in Queensway. Four nights a week I fed the gas ring in the fireplace of my bedroom with coins and fried fish fingers in a tiny milk saucepan. On Friday nights I went home for comfort and food. When walking back to Queensway in the evenings I stuck to well-lit streets. One evening I watched from a discreet distance as the back of an American station waggon was lifted and a brown bear let out. It was led by a chain attached to its collar and ambled behind its owner across the pavement and up the steps into a nearby house. Another evening I found police barring my way to the flat. Someone had been shot dead on the pavement. I didn't tell my father. I already had caused him enough worry.

I wasn't the reformed character that was hoped. The success with which I passed the exams before Christmas gave me the confidence to relax before my shot at the final handful scheduled for the summer, and I became part of a group that played poker in the ladies' loo – all our tutors were men. Nobody came in for some weeks but overconfident we stopped being so quiet and

---

1   *Before the days of air terrorism neither cabin nor hold luggage went through X-ray machines.*

were busted. As I was the only girl, the blame fell on me, and I was removed to Davies's in Holland Park. It was less pressured. My Classics tutor was a delightful old boy, and we spent most lessons in the sunshine in the leafy garden at the back of the building identifying birds by their song. Granny had been fascinating about birds and I had missed her knowledge and enthusiasm. I failed Latin and Greek, but thanks to the Kensington High Street branch of the British School of Motoring I passed my driving test first go. Daddy still wondered what on earth to do with his un-employable daughter. We had joked at Wardour that if one had passed one 'O' level, one was overqualified to gain a job as a lavatory attendant.

In the sixties most parents of middle-class girls sent their daughters to Paris to learn French. It wasn't simply to Paris they went. It was to the *seizième arrondissement,* and the hosts were usually descendants of survivors of The Revolution who had managed to hold on to their heads and a mention in the *Almanach de Gotha.* They probably had lost their *Hôtels de Villes,* but they still drank from crystal, laid the exquisitely embroidered, if threadbare starched tablecloths with slightly chipped monogrammed Sèvres porcelain, and spoke correct French. There but for the Grace of God and Edmund Burke would have gone many of the antecedents of the English parents, so it was reassuringly OK to send daughters to these unknown families despite their being French. It was equally OK for the French to augment their reduced income in this way, their payees were at least of parallel stock, despite being English.

Sir Edward and Lady Hulton had built up their portfolio and Hulton Press attracted several Oxbridge graduates, among them one who had recently married the daughter of an English shipping agent in Marseille. He suggested that I was sent to stay with his in-laws who missed their daughter. There was a good art *atelier* that I could attend while doing something that I appeared to enjoy, and I could hone my French. A term there would see me through to my 18th birthday when options might be easier to spot.

I landed at Marignane airport at about the same time as four hundred and fifty thousand *pieds noirs,*[2] fleeing the Algerian war, were disembarking from any ship that they had been able to board. OAS[3] was daubed in white paint over advertising billboards and across any blank wall. Marseille was also the main embarkation port for the heroin and cocaine trafficked to America,

---

2   *Pieds Noirs were Algerians of European, mostly French, descent from the time of the French rule of Algeria 1830-1962.*
3   *Organisation Armée Secrète.*

The French Connection. It is estimated that five thousand pounds of heroin were shipped annually from Marseille. Police were often to be seen making a circle round a corpse lying on the curb, blood trickling between the old cobblestones towards the Vieux Port. It was a million miles from the safe and respectable *seizième*, and the frisson was exciting. Even had Madame Fenton not made it abundantly clear that I was lucky to be there, and she expected me to play her game, by her rules, of which she would be the only arbiter, I no longer felt the need to rebel. Simply being in Marseille in the '60s was individual enough. I knew I was going to love it from the moment the aircraft doors had been opened and I had been met by the warm air, heady with garlic, thyme and Gauloises. The *National Geographic* magazine lights the fuse for colour but nothing had prepared me for the scent of travel. I was determined to make it work.

Margit Fenton was the daughter of an erstwhile Swedish Consul General to Marseille. She was ramrod straight, had her hair done once a week, permed every six; wore crippling high heeled shoes so already had painful bunions. She ran the *Association France-Grande Bretagne*, and played bridge with club members every Tuesday evening. Her husband, John, a tall, elegant man whose clothes hung loose, kept a thin cheroot, between his fingers on which he frequently pulled as if anguished. Every autumn he made a detailed and accurate drawing of a sailing ship that was turned into the Christmas card.

The house, on a steep hill above the Corniche, housed Swedish yellow and blue souvenirs. The pink, velvet curtains were embellished with gold brocade trim, ropes, and tassels. A collection of Copenhagen Christmas plates was added to annually and symmetrically rearranged on the wall. Furniture, upholstered in pale blue velour, was reproduction Louis XVI for perching on, rather than sitting in. Positioned below the road on the side of the hill, the front door was at bedroom level and a carved wooden staircase swirled down to the living room. It took up the width of the house and overlooked the lawned terrace and on east to the hills and the *Sommet Ouest de l'Homme Mort*. The little port of Cassis, where we often went for Sunday lunch, was over the horizon. The bedroom balconies above supported luxuriant bougainvillea and sweet-smelling jasmine. The house and terrace occupied the whole plot except for a slim strip from the back gate for dustbins and the dog, that had a bare concrete shelter under the steps. Ourlé, never taken for a walk, was the unfortunate German Shepherd who spent his life pacing up and down the concrete like a bear in an east European zoo. Fed on boiled white rice, sometimes livened with leftovers, I think the theory was that he would attack burglars, anything for some meat. Years later I learned that the immediate neighbour on one side was head of the Marseille Mafia which explains the big black cars with blacked out windows, always attended by men with arms that proverbially hung away from their shoulders like gorillas. As a result, the avenue was a haven of tranquillity and the least likely place in Marseille to be burgled.

M & Mme Fenton were at the heart of the diplomatic community and were invited to all the parties. When the British Navy sailed into port, whether Marseille or Toulon about sixty miles away, they were invited on board. I tagged along as family on all occasions. I understood the captain's puffed out pride as I watched the band of the Royal Marines beat the retreat along the quay, to signal the end of each reception. The *Fusiliers Marins* couldn't hold a candle to 'our boys'. When *France-Grande Bretagne* held their annual Christmas dinner, I was placed on the top table. We started with *les cailles* (quail). The white beaded eyes were not the only ones that watched me as I steeled myself to eat, bones and all. *Le Roti de Dindon* was followed by *Le Christmas Pudding au beurre de cognac*. I wished that we had represented our kitchens better with something like potted shrimps, rack of lamb and cold pear soufflé instead of endorsing the French prejudice of English food.

When a ship carrying one of M Fenton's cargoes docked, the captain, purser and first officer were invited to lunch at home. Mme Fenton spent the day before preparing an exquisite meal. She would take me with her to buy fish from the market for the *quenelles*; ready whipped *Chantilly* cream from the *laiterie*; and flowers from the *fleuriste*. She would place a large arrangement in the niche halfway down the stairs and tiny saucers with floating buds on the pink and a gold brocade runner, that matched the curtains. Everything had to be, and was, perfect. The Fentons' main shipping line was the NYK (Nippon Yusen Kabushiki Kaisha) and it was very rare that the officers spoke more than a few words of English, let alone French or even Swedish. Conversation, if any, dried up very quickly and as it would have been rude to talk between ourselves, the meals took place in almost total silence only punctuated by the forks on the Limoges plates and the '*arigato gozaimasu!*' with much bowing of heads after each course.

Madame Marguerite Allar was a senior and respected professor at Les Beaux Arts de Marseille and accepted twenty students to her own *atelier* every year. Housed at the top one of the original warehouses on the south side of the Vieux Port,[4] it was approached by the straight, near vertical brick stairs, the treads held in place by wooden strips. Plaster casts of every type, from death masks of various popes, to Michelangelo's hand and foot of David, and Corinthian capitols were hung on the unpainted pink plastered walls. The flue of an ancient stove, as though designed by Heath Robinson, snaked to the uninsulated tiled roof twenty feet above. The unevenly worn concave red-brick floor was witness to over two hundred years of moving and storing freight from the eighteen thousand ships that once had used the port each year.

We spent mornings drawing one of the plaster casts in charcoal: twenty-four hours each week on a single cast chosen by Mme Allar. I found drawing in charcoal challenging. To achieve a dark line, one needs to apply pressure. As often as not the pressure snaps the charcoal which then marks and scatters tiny black specks. Try to remove the mark and you make a smudge. A careless cuff makes a smudge; a correction makes a smudge. Nearly everything makes a smudge and trying to remove said smudge makes more smudges. Mme Allar circulated behind us pointing out our errors: gaps between nostril and lip too short; thumbs at wrong angles; acanthus leaves too long. One had to rub out a lot and start again. It was exasperating but marvellous training.

We had two hours off in the middle of the day that I spent with the Fentons at La Pelle, the posh beach and yachting club. We swam and sunbathed and enjoyed steak, *salade*s and *frites*. The first time I gingerly walked into the sea I expected it to take my breath away like the North Sea at Bamburgh. I couldn't believe how pleasant swimming in a sea could be. Back at the *atelier* until six o'clock we studied architecture, graphic design, perspective, and Mme Allar dictated *l'histoire de l'art* in clear, rasping, correct French that must have been audible through the open windows, above the incessant angry exclamations of the *klaxons*. She rolled her 'R's so they sounded like the boys' cycles as they raced down the shallow stone steps from Notre Dame de la Garde.

Anthony, the Fentons' twenty-five-year-old son, returned from a few years learning the family business in various European ports. There was little doubt that, after the independence of bachelor pads with a girl in every harbour, he found living with his parents, under his mother's beady eye, restrictive. It can't have been helped by their expecting him to make my stay more interesting. He was persuaded to drop me off at Mme Allar's on his

---

4   *The blocks of warehouses on the North side of the Vieux Port had been surrounded and dynamited in 1943 by the Gestapo to flush out members of the résistance. 40,000 people were displaced or shot.*

way to work and made it clear that having a lumpy teenager in the passenger seat of his Triumph sports cars (TRs 3 & 4) hadn't been the plan and did nothing for his street-cred. As if to prove to any onlooker that he was cool, at traffic lights he would put his arm over the low driver's door and stub out his cigarette on the tarmac. If ever he was cajoled into giving me a lift to anything social, and he had a chick in tow, he would make me lie on the parcel shelf. The already ungainly *Anglaise* never did manage to extricate herself with any semblance of elegance and felt even more gauche when observed pityingly by the blondes who having simply swung their long, tanned legs from the passenger seat, chucked their golden hair over their shoulders and eased their way across pavements.

Sometimes he relented. A stage of the Monte Carlo Rally was to go through Marseille. Roads were closed but Anthony knew the back streets.

"Come on, let's see whether we can join in!" We did. Screeching round corners and roaring up straights as the police held back traffic and spectators.

On the 22nd of November 1963 he took me to the cinema to watch Steve McQueen escape from *Stalag Luft* III.[5] Without warning the film froze and the soundtrack went silent. A thunderstorm raged outside, and we could hear the rain bashing against the corrugated iron roof. We thought the projector had broken down and there were jeers from the stalls. An announcement was made. The thirty-eighth president of the United States had been shot. It was almost exactly a year since the Cuban Missile Crisis and the stunningly charismatic, protector of the world JFK was dead.[6]

Possibly thinking that I might be homesick for my pony, Anthony persuaded one of his friends to invite me to spend a Sunday on the family ranch in the Camargue. It may have had more to do with his wanting to see his friend's gorgeous sister. The *Camargais gardians* are thought to be the antecedents of American cowboys. They used saddles made from cork from which western saddles were copied. It was obvious that I was to be the morning's entertainment and they could hardly wait to see *l'Anglaise* try to do rising trot in one of their saddles, but having ridden bareback for years I was perfectly comfortable. Despite the absence of the anticipated joke, I was welcomed with broad smiles, and they taught me their game of galloping with a flower held high while others tried to snatch it. The one who still held

---

5   *The film The Great Escape had just been released.*
6   *John Fitzgerald Kennedy, president of the USA January 1961 – November 1963.*

it when others had run out of puff would be the next to marry. They asked me to help complete an outward facing mounted circle to protect one of them as he dismounted to check a sickly calf while its mother, an evil looking cow, pawed the ground in frustration at being unable to protect it. Cow (not bull) fighting regularly happened in the Roman amphitheatres in nearby Arles and Nîmes and was equally dangerous, cows being nimbler than bulls. We cantered back to the farmstead as a team and twenty of us sat down at a single table and polished off a sheep that had been cooking on a spit over the open fire.

Although I had studied French to 'A' level, Molière-speak hadn't cut it. To begin with I managed to get by without engaging in conversation, remaining uncharacteristically silent, then after a few weeks I dared to chip in. From that moment I was no longer *l'Anglaise* but 'Soo'. As term neared its end my fellows asked whether I really was going home.

"Tu n'est pas sérieuse, vraiment?"

It was a sad thought. I felt that I was learning to draw and to speak useful French and was becoming quite good at both. I had broken the stream of failure, was achieving something at last and loving it all. That evening I broached the possibility of staying with the Fentons. Telephone calls were made. It was agreed. I would go home for Christmas but would be back for the remainder of the academic year.

As the year went on, and I became the Fentons' genuinely surrogate daughter, they revealed that their business was in serious trouble. My presence was helping to diffuse the angst, a bit. Monsieur Fenton was the epitome of integrity. A profoundly honest man he was reluctant to believe what Anthony had been telling him since his return, that their business partner was working against them. Long evenings were spent in the office after hours, in unlit rooms going through files by torchlight. The offices were on the first floor above a restaurant and looked the length of the Vieux Port to the Louis XIV Fort St Jean. A peerless view for a shipping agent but it meant that anyone on the Quai des Belges could see what was going on inside. The truth was worse than even Anthony had suspected and the Fentons had to go to Japan to try to retrieve the situation.

While they were away, I went to stay with their friends, Gustave and Lise Villameur. In their early sixties, they were the most fascinating, attractive, and *soigné* couple – even by Parisian standards. Gustave, an excellent painter, had carved a very comfortable life as an interior decorator specialising in luxury yachts. Lise, modest about her history, had been in the SOE and was the first woman to be parachuted into France. Codenamed Odile she had set up resistance groups round Poitiers. In 1943, rumbled by the Gestapo, she was evacuated by a Lysander aircraft. The next year she was back in France, this time dropped in Normandy. She cycled everywhere, including to Paris, carrying messages, and organising sabotage. She, and her brother Claude de Baissac, are credited with crucially delaying German re-enforcements to Normandy before the Allied Landings. She was awarded the Chevalier de la Légion d'Honneur Croix de Guerre avec Palme. She never let on. Gustave had converted the warehouse, next to Madame Allar's atelier, into a wonderful flat full of treasures. They weekended in St Tropez where he had made another charming flat overlooking the little harbour. Gustave loved the girls and kept his telescope in the sitting room, trained on the afterdecks of the yachts moored below. I hadn't known until then that some old men's lust never dies. While the Fentons had a worrying and sadly unsuccessful time in Japan, I had a treat living with this remarkable couple, in fabulous surroundings, commuting between Marseille and St Tropez.

Mme Allar always referred to me as *La Petite Anglaise* although when I arrived there had been nothing *petite* about me as I had spent the London months cramming carbs more enthusiastically than facts. Every pound showed. After two months of running up and down the *atelier* stairs coupled with Mme Fenton's strict *régime*, I had lost two stone. I was in a different shape mentally and physically. After nearly two years I could speak fluently with either Parisian or Marseille accents, switching at will, and had a portfolio of work. Marseille had become a much-loved home.

Grandfather

Andy, Walter and Malcolm

Granny at Bamburgh

Mummy

At the University of Maine After
Addressing the "Farm and Home Week" 1943

With Howard Watching the Horses Being
Prepared For Hertfordshire County Show

Talking Farming with Daddy

Talking Farming with Teddy

First Tractor Lesson

Two Ragamuffins:
With Howard at Aynho

The Relaxed Parent

Granny and Daddy

Already the Best of Friends

The Editor

Lord Apsley in the Shack's Kitchen, Australia 1925

*Lady Apsley Outside the
Shack, Australia 1925*

*Lord & Lady Apsley
George and Henry*

George

… Another Cup

*With Joe and Betty at the
Boxing Day Meet of the
Vale of Aylesbury, 1948*

*Jonny - 1st Competitive
Ride, Astrop Park 1953*

*Beamish – 2nd and
Last Competitive Ride,
Stowell Park 1981*

*In the Chilean Andes,
2012*

TWELVE

LONDON – HUNGERFORD

1964–1972

Fritz Wegner had done a lot of illustrating for Mummy and was by then teaching illustration at St Martin's School of Art in Charing Cross Road. He suggested I apply there, and I was one of 70 from 700 applicants to be given a place on the pre-diploma course. Despite appreciating my luck at being at my first-choice London art school, I was rather narked that two years being taught by Mme Allar wasn't counted as pre-dip. but I soon realised the difference in curriculum as well as the range of facilities. Instead of spending every morning drawing plaster casts we spent every morning life drawing. In the afternoons we had access to the photographic darkrooms and etching plates and presses. We did fashion drawing; oil painting; and what might have been described as 'sculpture' but was more like advanced Blue Peter 3D creativity. One afternoon a week we lugged our boards and paper around London. Although by then I had enjoyed access to a lot of London, I discovered new places like the Transport Museum and the Chelsea Physic Garden. Learning to draw flesh, plants, and the great wheels of steam engines in perspective, was as exciting as it was frustrating.

The painting school was at the west end of Soho. It proved a fun backyard: less dangerous than Marseille but interestingly edgy. We discovered the Italian cafés and delis. The school dining room served heavily subsidised food and the ketchup, decanted into chipped glass Coca-Cola bottles, made good camouflage, but the coffee was beyond disguise.

Many of the Soho hookers spent the mornings as our life models. One of them brought her tiny daughter. The two-barred fire kept them both warmish for a few hours and saved the grandmother leaving her Berwick Street Market stall to baby sit. They were wonderful to draw. Before long we attracted cheery calls from those who propped up doorjambs, hoping for lunchtime trade.

"Finished my boobs yet darling?" hailed across Old Compton Street dropped jaws in those tourists who had strayed from theatre land.

A lesson learned immediately was to keep dumb about one's background. All but five of us had ground their way through the state system. This quickly manifested itself as we were older than the others. They had come straight from school; most had never been away from home, let alone to London. We had been able to take our time, all of us had travelled, one had been in the army, and I wasn't the only one who had taken up art having failed to apply diligently enough to aspire to academia. It wasn't that we were any less talented than them, we had all been accepted anonymously on our portfolios, but we had had it easier. Unwittingly we coalesced into a group that shared pencil sharpeners, teaspoons, and cigarettes.

I continued to have it very easy. While most of my fellows lived on restricted budgets in less than cosy accommodation, I lived in great comfort with my father in Holland Park. By the time the tube had whooshed and clacketed through the seven stops of the Central Line to Tottenham Court Road I had metamorphosed from ultra-privileged to unremarkable. It was not difficult. In my pre-Marseille days, I had rarely removed jeans or the sloppy jersey with the CND badge strategically positioned, and until a few near misses with toes on escalators, I had spent weeks crossing London barefoot. By the mid-sixties there were the more committed and successful rebels than me and my Marseille makeover had stuck. I had learned that conforming opened doors that otherwise would remain closed.

Once a month I walked to Mayfair to have my hair cut for free by Vidal Sassoon who used my head to help train the staff he had selected to open his first salon in Los Angeles. Sometimes I hitched a lift towards school in my father's car, but I was dropped in Piccadilly so as not to be seen and I walked through Soho. If I'd run my monthly allowance short and couldn't afford lunch, I'd rack up smoked salmon on my father's account at Jacksons and eat it with my fingers in the street.

Friends of my father's, aware of what they knew to be gaps in his interests and therefore of my experience, took it upon themselves to remedy the situation. George, the advertising manager of *Farmers Weekly*, was one of my father's favourite companions. They often lunched together and kept a jointly owned bottle of cognac under the counter in the Café Royal Grill Room. The one who finished the bottle bought the next. The fizz had long gone out of George's marriage, but he went home to somewhere in the Home Counties every weekend to be with his children and spent the time writing pocketbooks on antiques. His passions were music and art about which he was knowledgeable and discriminating, and he divided the week's evenings between Sadler's Wells, Covent Garden and Private Views in State and private art galleries. If I was around, he took me with him. If he thought the music wasn't up to scratch, he'd leave an opera after the first act. In art galleries, after peering at what was on the walls, between shoulders of jaw-droppingly bejewelled women, who spent more time focussing their beady eyes on the exquisitely tailored men and their cheque books than the art, he would suddenly say:

"Come on. Let's get out of here, and you drive. Let's go down East."

'Down East' meant the Isle of Dogs. Although it was nearly twenty-five years since the last bombs had fallen on the East End,[1] it was still out of property developers' comfort zones. Buddleia flourished in the roofless warehouses and the fractured basement walls of bomb craters. The Kray twins had just been arrested and 'gangland' was regrouping. It was as dodgy as anything I had experienced in Marseille and not somewhere to be ventured alone.

George was the son of an East End publican. In the early '20s aged fourteen, he had stowed away on a ship and by the time he was discovered, it was too far out at sea to turn back. He was 'adopted' by the ship's company. The sailors would take him ashore, wherever they docked, and he had a fund of hilarious tales, many on the lines of their escaping gangsters in red-light districts. In Cape Town, a fight had broken out between a madame and a pimp

---

[1] *Operation Steinbeck, known as the Baby Blitz, lasted from January to May in 1944. In January, Greenland, Canada and Surrey docks were bombed; at the beginning of February Victoria docks were hit and then at the end of February an operation codenamed 'Hamburg' was intended to finish off docklands and guiding flares were dropped on the Isle of Dogs.*

in which they'd got involved and were losing. George was thrown into the bottom of a handsome cab, and the sailors jumped in after him, to escape. The cab was so old that their combined weight made the floor collapse and George, underneath the sailors, had had to run, with his elbows partially supporting him on the remaining floor, as the horse was whipped back to the quay with the opposition in hot pursuit.

We'd head to Tubby Isaac's in Goulston Street and eat jellied eels out of card beakers or go to The Grapes pub in Limehouse for a few beers and then, with a bottle under his arm, we'd amble, he walked with a roll as though still at sea, across the road to the unlicenced Good Friends Chinese restaurant. The food was delicious. The round tables, covered by unlaundered white cloths, were large enough to accommodate extended Chinese families, but mostly were used by groups of men, who spoke their unintelligible language in undertones, and looked sinister enough to be Triads. George was the best possible passport to real life.

My Parisian-educated friends got me invited to 'deb' dances. Debutante, from the French '*debut*' beginning; girls' lives beginning when they were Presented at Court. It had started in the 16th century when aristocrats presented their daughters to Queen Elizabeth I in the hope she would choose them as her ladies-in-waiting. By the 20th century it was more of a marketing project to ensure that blue blood was not diluted by marriage, or increasingly, for others to gain a purple tinge. HM Queen Elizabeth II stopped presentations in 1958 as presumably she already had enough friends whose company she enjoyed and who were happy to help handle her correspondence and carry the bouquets she was given on walkabouts. However, the gravy train kept rolling under the beady eyes of the 20th-century uber-snob – Betty Kenward who, for forty-six years, was social editor of the glossiest women's magazines.[2]

Early in the year mothers had lunch together. If they didn't know enough other suitable mothers, or own a thumbed copy of Debrett's, Ms Kenward came to the rescue with a list. The list included suitable young men because, before the days of mixed-sex public schools, unless you had an older brother or two, your access to them depended on friends of parents' having sons the right age. Mothers gave tea parties for their daughters who shared their address books. Mothers consulted Ms Kenward to make sure that their proposed

---

2   *Tatler, Queen, then Harpers and Queen.*

dates didn't clash with those higher up the pecking order. Dates synchronised, parents hosted The Cocktail Party. The Season was interspersed with such social imperatives as Henley Royal Regatta, Royal Ascot, Wimbledon, and Queen Charlotte's Ball. In 1780 George III threw a ball to celebrate Queen Charlotte's birthday and ordered a huge cake, beside which the royal couple stood as the girls curtseyed to them. Now they curtsey to a vast cake that looks as though Dame Edna Everage might explode from it.

It all drum-rolled to a crescendo – The Dance. Dances in the country were fun and often necessitated spending short weekends in house-parties in charming manor houses or converted rectories. It was astonishing to be able to scrutinise and marvel at the Canalettos, van Dycks, and Seymours still on the walls of some parents' drawing rooms. Those girls unlucky enough not to have a relative with a stately home, were given dances in posh London hotels where mega-bucks were spent on vast flower arrangements cascading from pedestals, in a futile attempt to make the places feel less anodyne. With no art on walls or ceilings to look at, we played poker in the loo until we could leave, without seeming rude, and go off to a nightclub. We went to the Ad Lib, a nightclub off Leicester Square, frequented by the Beatles and Stones, whose eyes we tried to catch, and to Annabel's in Berkeley Square,[3] patronised by friends' fathers, whose eyes we tried to avoid as they often danced closely with other people's mothers.

By the end of the season many were bored, some exhausted, and mothers were either delighted that their daughters had caught a targeted eye or were hoping loneliness in grouse butts would make hearts grow fonder.

I hunted other people's horses when not weekending in stately homes for shoots or camping under leaking canvas (before nylon or flysheets) in the Atlantic gales on north Cornish cliffs.[4] It was such another world, but I managed to return to Charing Cross Road undetected.

Towards the end of the pre-dip. year I wanted to earn money. I had loved the three years of learning to look and draw but I was never going to make it as a painter and although I was mildly interested in graphic design, I wasn't keen enough to think it fair to keep milking my father's generosity for another three years to gain a diploma.

---

3   Annabel's was the 'grown-ups' private members nightclub in Berkeley Square. It was started to provide somewhere to go after an evening's gambling and was the 'smartest' nightclub in the world.

4   The pheasant shooting season runs from October 1st – January 31st. Many estates were shot over once a fortnight.

My first foray into employment was working for *soi-disant* aristocratic Yugoslavs, who owned a Brompton Road boutique called The Carrot on Wheels. Its moment of fame came when a crochet dress, totally transparent from shoulder to mid-thigh, was taken up by fashion editors. Those who had good enough legs and a body stocking, flocked to the tiny shop. I learned which way to face coat hangers and could answer the telephone politely to the rudest, but being neither blonde, leggy, nor chic, and with no interest as a *vendeuse*, I was soon released.

While at St Martin's I had been lent a Rolleiflex camera by one of *Farmers Weekly*'s staff photographers, Gordon Cradock. He and Barry Spikings, then a *Farmers Weekly* reporter, later more famous as producer of *The Deer Hunter*,[5] had persuaded my father that *Farmers Weekly* should have its own film unit. Barry had moved on to wider screens and Gordon invited me to join him as a general dogsbody. He was the only person who knew that I was my father's. I worked under an assumed name. The deal was that the unit would finance itself and agricultural films by hiring itself out as a freelance crew. I spent the next two years as the clapper-girl, grip, factotum and doing the accounts. I did not reveal that I had not been thought competent enough to sit maths 'O' level, but I got away with it. We filmed a medical series including thirteen months on *The Birth of Your Baby* for the BBC (unappetisingly transmitted just before Sunday lunch); we worked for *Tomorrow's World*; for the ORTF (French); for CBS (Canadian) and a theatre series for ITV. It was hard work, strange hours, varied, and hugely entertaining. Michael Caine was fun, as was Judy Dench, both totally unspoiled. He suggested camera angles; she helped me carry the heavy tripods. Disappointingly, females weren't allowed on the crew to spend a week with Omar Sharif, hearts still raced after seeing Doctor Zhivago in that sledge with Julie Christie. Paid eight pounds an hour I have never again been so well off.[6] I bought a long-loved suede coat. One of only two made; the other had been bought by Leslie Caron, so said the talented King's Road *vendeuse*. After a while Gordon let me direct some of the agricultural filming as he moved to more interesting work. He was a very good lighting cameraman and another who taught me how to look.

*

---

5   *The Deer Hunter – 1978 Vietnam War film, nominated for 9 and winner of 5 Academy Awards.*

6   *£8.00 – about £150 in 2022 money.*

By the mid 1950s Hulton Press had spread over four buildings and the Hultons had bought a site in Fleet Street and had an office block built for them that they called Hulton House with door handles in the shape of an H. Nika Hulton's office was on the third floor and had a balcony reached by French windows. I don't think that she ever managed to wave to her public from there, but on that chill January day in 1965 it gave my father and me an exceptional private grandstand view of Sir Winston Churchill's cortège. The building was on the slight curve in Fleet Street, and we were able to see everything as it passed, all the way from St Clement Danes Church until it disappeared under the railway bridge at Ludgate Circus towards St Paul's.[7] The spectacle was well documented, but it was the unrelenting sound of hooves and wheels and the slow-marching boots that has never left me.

Nika, (Princess Nika Youriévitch) was the daughter of a Russian sculptor. She was attractive and exuberant. Sir Edward Hulton financed her interests and her amazing parties, but she was the engine. They lived in splendour, surrounded by valuable art in Hyde Park Gate and on one occasion a themed Indian party was brightened by caparisoned live elephants. When they went abroad on business trips, they took my father with them. One evening after dinner in New York, Nika wanted to go dancing and 'Teddy' did not. Daddy's early nightclub partners had included Adèle Astaire and Tallulah Bankhead. He was legendarily nimble on the dance floor, and Nika expected him to take her.

"I can't take you out like that! We'll be hit over the head!" he said. She was dripping diamonds that she promptly unclipped and dropped into his dinner jacket pockets. He spent the night checking the pockets.

My father helped them make a lot of money, and they appreciated what he did for them as well as his company. He declined a pay rise as almost as much would have gone to Her Majesty's Revenue and Customs as into his pocket, so they paid my school fees. They also gave him a gleaming black Bentley: ODA 900. I saw it being driven along Aldwych about thirty years later and felt rather silly having waved at it.

*

An interpreter, due to accompany an official tour of Texan and Australian cattle breeders round the notable Charolais herds in France, fell ill and the

---

7   *The Ludgate Bridge became redundant in 1925 and was demolished in 1990.*

British Charolais Society, that had organised the trip to culminate in the Royal Show and a tour of the English herds, contacted *Farmers Weekly* in search of a last-minute replacement. Whoever answered the telephone remembered I had been in France. The next day I received a sheet of technical agricultural vocabulary to learn by the weekend.

My father, with Princesse Mimi de Croÿ,[8] had been instrumental in bringing the first Charolais to the UK, against considerable opposition from British beef breeders. Mimi had established one of the premier herds in France, with over two hundred head of prize-winning cattle, and was the only woman to be accorded the *Chevalier de l'Ordre du Mérite Agricole*. During the war the de Croÿs enabled dozens of allied airmen to escape. Those temporarily holed-up in the de Croÿs' Parisian *hôtel de ville* were fed on produce smuggled up from the estate. Eggs were transported in dozens, hard-boiled. On one occasion fifteen-year-old Mimi, enrolled at a Parisian convent, arrived to see the Gestapo searching all the houses in the street. She veered off unnoticed, sat on park bench, and ate the lot to avoid suspicion, with predictable aftereffects. When silently escorting escapees through the moonlit Nivernais countryside, with the flick of a finger to those behind, Mimi would scramble through the hedge to rejoin the lane a hundred yards further on. She was kept informed of German tripwires by estate staff. Not one escapee was caught. Later she drove a Red Cross ambulance with concentration camp survivors.

The first time my father stayed with her, he joined her parents to brush storm water from the chequered marble hall floor of the leaking mid-18th-century Château d'Azy.[9] It swooshed through the impressively tall front doors to the top of the broad stone steps and cascaded down to the weedy gravel. Maintaining their pack of boar hounds took priority over buildings. I still regret failing to take them up on their invitation to hunt.

I stayed in Mimi's *manoir* 'Valotte', before linking up with the cattle breeders. Built in the 15th century it looked like a small château with views down its own valley with woodland on either hill side. I slept, fully clothed, in the dampest of beds and was extremely disappointed she no longer had the once orphaned, fully grown, wild boar living at the end of

---

8   *Marie Dorothée de Croÿ-Solre*
9   *After a decade of renovations, it is now a wedding venue with 50 guest bedrooms.*

her bed. Those, who had stayed before, warned me of the noise his hooves made as he racketed down the uncarpeted, spiral stairs in the middle of the night. I don't know whether she and my father were lovers. They would have had fun, but I suspect a wild boar in the bedroom might have put my father off his stroke. Mimi was a free spirit, like her sister Rose, who kept a white rat in her chignon, whence his beady pink eyes peeped through her back-combed hair to the astonishment of many aspiring suitors at Parisian cocktail parties. Sometimes referred to as 'La Princesse aux pieds nus' Mimi created a music studio in the 1980s, made famous by Julian Lennon who recorded there and named the first track of his debut album 'Valotte' as a tribute to her and the place.

Over the fortnight I assimilated the finer points of Charolais cattle in both languages and I learned that the breed had been improved by imported Herefords. I met French herdsmen with English surnames – descendants of those who had crossed the channel with their animals during the 18th century. I could tell a well-muscled bull from an over-muscled one and I had whispered, inside information on which animals were changing hands to be shipped across the oceans.

I also received my first, and last, tip. Paray Le Monial is home to about nine thousand people in the Charolles district. It became a pilgrimage town in the 17th century after Jesus, with His heart, repeatedly appeared to a nun.[10] Critically, for us it meant that, out of the pilgrimage season, there were enough beds in this small town in the middle of rural France to accommodate so many under one roof. I went down early one morning. The hall, until then a cavern only lit by the neon virgins and crucifixes on sale, was unexpectedly busy. During the night one of the Texans had had a terminal heart attack. His body had to be got to a nearby private airfield, thence Paris Orly and back to Deaf Smith County. Mercifully by the time I arrived the hotel manager and the croques-morts[11] had matters in hand. After the hearse had snailed out of sight his brother-in-law pressed a note into my hand to thank me for all that I had done. Never having been briefed on how to receive a tip, I pushed it in a pocket, commiserated, thanked him effusively and waited until the cortège had disappeared before rushing to the loo to see how much it was worth. One dollar. He had tipped

---

10   Margaret Mary Alacoque was beatified in 1864 and canonised by Pope Benedict XV in 1920.
11   Undertakers' assistants – so called because of the old habit of breaking a skull to make sure the person was dead.

me one dollar for 'all that I had done'. Was it irony? Probably as I had done nothing other than share a few laughs with this well-fed stereotype. He had joked with me that he came from a town called Hereford but wanted to breed Charolais. I wonder whether the old boy's plan to have a white, instead of brown and white, emblem bull over the gateway to his ranch was ever realised.

"It would be one between the eyes for the Hereford boys, Susie!"

*

By now my father had relinquished the lease on the Holland Park flat and had retreated to the rented Georgian farmhouse outside Hungerford. To keep a toe in swinging London I had rented a room in a first-floor flat in Jay Mews behind the Albert Hall. A bachelors' bonking base, my room had a tiny leaking skylight, a large double bed and a Victorian fireplace with a grate that caught the drips when it rained. When the wind got up it sounded as though someone had left a mouth organ in the chimney. I paid three pounds a week, discounted rent as I was responsible for clearing up, washing up, and vacuuming.[12] If I was away for a week the guys bought more glasses and mugs and shoved the dirty ones under the sofa with its retired springs, there to grow *îles flottantes*. Water shot from a gas geezer high on the wall and splashed, depending which way its arm was swung, into the shallow enamel sink or the stained bath. It was so scalding hot that it would have skinned a rhinoceros. The bonuses of living there, besides the minimal rent, were the good collection of watercolours by Edward Lear belonging to one of the guys, and an early colour television, bought by the other guy, to attract girlfriends to watch the first colour transmission of Wimbledon. Diana Ross and the Supremes blasting from the record player helped energise cleaning duties. Not yet sexy enough to be noticed I was welcomed to watch Wimbledon with them, from the back row, and I observed comings and goings from the skirting boards. It was a useful experience for a girl without brothers.

There was a wonderful summer and as I spent more time enjoying the country the mugs mushroomed. I decided to give up my room in Jay Mews and move back in with my father. I accepted a job as a dogsbody on a nearby large farm. I revelled being back on the land. I had loved metropolitan life

---

12   £3 – about £50 in 2022 money.

but as soon as I was helping on a farm, I realised how much I had missed it. It was over twenty years since we left Aynho. I enjoyed the office work: doing accounts; keeping records; working out profitability and collecting cash from the bank to fill the little brown envelopes to pay the men after lunch every Friday. I even enjoyed the challenge of transition to decimalisation.

Bizarrely, I enjoyed climbing on hands and knees to the back of farrowing pens to stitch up irascible sows that had prolapsed; was fascinated helping those who were calving cows. I liked walking round the barns at night to see which were bulling and looking into milk yield records to tell the AI[13] centre whether we wanted our own bull's semen, specified semen or 'bull-of-the-day'.[14] I enjoyed walking the fields to check on crops and learn about fungal diseases and weed control. I loved helping with lambing in the Spring; rolling the fleeces at shearing and helping push the ewes through the race to be dipped. It was glorious to hear the skylarks as they fluttered high above the downs, the owls at dusk as they worked the headlands, and the plovers even when I was dive bombed when too near their chicks. I felt I had achieved something when I had mastered driving the corn cart so that the moving combine emptied its load without spilling it on the stubble or the tractor's bonnet and once I had learned to drive the combine harvester and no longer worried that it was going to run away with me, down the steep Berkshire downs, when I was helping with the night shift I enjoyed spotting the foraging foxes picked up in the headlights. There was something immensely satisfying about shutting down the corn dryer when the last load of a full day's harvest had gone through the system, and then driving home in the dawn.

It all felt like going back to where I belonged. I earned money; bought a sports car with a sound system that throbbed louder than the engine. I fell in love, and failed to fall in love, and when not in the pit of unrequited love, life was huge fun.

*

---

13 *Artificial Insemination.*

14 *To save farmers the trouble/expense of keeping their own bulls, and for the benefits of preventing inbreeding/improving the private and national herds, the Milk Marketing Board (1939–1994) kept its own selected bulls (both beef and dairy) from which they collected semen. Every time a cow was 'bulling' the farmer could telephone the MMB and could order selected semen from a named bull, or semen from Bull-of-the-Day, usually young or unproven. Semen from the farmer's own bull could also be collected, stored and used.*

One Saturday morning my father answered the phone.

"… for you…"

"Who is it?"

"George."

"George who?"

"Your uncle George."

Mummy's brother had tracked down my father through *Farmers Weekly*. The last time I had seen or spoken to him was when, to celebrate my tenth birthday, he had taken me to see Gregory Peck as Captain Ahab, trying to get the better of *Moby Dick* in John Huston's film.

Strangers, uncle and niece, briefly exchanged pleasantries. Then he told me that Derick had died and that I was a beneficiary of his will. I expressed regret… surprise. I wondered 'Who was Derick?' Uncle asked whether I could meet him and Betty, his and my mother's half-sister, at Derick's flat. The last time I had seen Betty was when she had come to stay for a weekend when Mummy was alive. Together they had made a felt rug for my bathroom with appliqué star fishes and seahorses. Thereafter the seahorse tank in aquariums had been the first port of call. While Mummy had cooked supper, Betty had painted fairground horses on a parchment lampshade for my nursery. I had kept both rug and lampshade until they fell to bits, but I would not have recognised Betty had we passed in the street.

I asked Daddy who Derick was.

"Oh, has he died? He was Mary's youngest brother."

"You knew about him?"

Later I learned that Derick had been an editor of PHS, *The Times*' diary column. Daddy and he must have known each other; bumped into each other on Fleet Street or at the bar in El Vino's. I still wonder why he was never mentioned.

The next Sunday morning I drove to London. Derick had lived in one room in the semi-basement of a 1950s block of flats in a quiet, tree-lined road near Primrose Hill. We perched in a row, on the edge of his single bed like birds on a telegraph wire about to take flight. The bed was rammed into the corner against the outside wall under the window with its unlined, drab beige curtains that for years had been collecting black specs of smoggy London soot. Next to the bedside table, with its Anglepoise lamp, and a tiny three-drawer chest that had doubled as a dressing table, there was a large chest for architects' drawings. It took up more space than the bed. There was barely room for the three of us to stand simultaneously on the threadbare carpet.

It felt weird. I had had no connection with my uncle and aunt during the years in which I had evolved from being frightened by Moby Dick to being entertained and energised by Hair's dawning of Aquarius.[15] I had sat on the edges of beds in friends' digs when there had not been enough chairs or orange boxes. There had been Andy Warhol posters of Marylyn Monroe and photographs of The Beatles stuck to the walls to cheer the gloom of basements. We had eaten Chilli Con Carne, and baked camembert topped with tinned mandarin oranges washed down with copious amounts of Algerian wine, and we had kidded ourselves that we were grown up, and everything was delicious. There was nothing like that in Derick's basement. Nothing to relieve the walls, painted that pale green colour once popular for lavatory paper; there was not even sight of a kettle or a mug. Was this a grown-up bachelor's *pied à terre*? I hoped his *pied au ciel* was cheerier.

Uncle and Betty scrutinised me in an unnerving way.

"You look so like your mother." George said with quivering lips, as though he was about to cry and it was Mummy who had died earlier in the month. I didn't know how to respond. Apologise? Be flattered? Burst into tears? I knew there was a strong resemblance because of the battered photograph my father kept on his dressing mirror, but Mummy had been dead for twenty years. I felt they should have got used to it. We had.

Betty was silent. It was obvious that her brother's death had hit her terribly hard. Uncle did the talking. He said that the flat was rented but Derick's architects' chest contained an important collection of Japanese art that had to be kept in the dark. I tried to imagine this uncle, who had died of a heart attack in his forties, drawing the curtains so no one could see his treasure and decide whether to steal it. I thought of his opening the drawers, perhaps a different one each night of the week, to inspect his collection. There were six drawers so if he had started at the top on Monday, the next Monday would be the second drawer. I hoped he had gone out to supper sometimes.

Uncle, who kept pausing as he took another look at me, my mother's ghost, said Derick had wished the collection to go to the Ashmolean Museum. Would I be happy with that? Of course, I was. Had it been a collection of Impressionists I would have been more interested but Japanese art, too valuable to see the light of day, didn't light a bulb in my head. I hadn't known Derick existed; had expected

---

15 *Hair was the 1967 rock musical by Ragni, Rado and MacDermot. Its staging in London had to be delayed until after the 1968 Theatres Act because it was stacked full of profanity, nudity, and references to fun sex and the Kama Sutra.*

nothing; would miss nothing. It went to the Ashmolean. On the way home I realised I had no idea where either of them lived, nor did I have their telephone numbers. I heard nothing more from them. I had assumed that my father never had anything to do with Mummy's family after her death because they were dull. That Sunday did nothing to disabuse me of the idea.

*

One Saturday evening in 1968, while enjoying hunting tea in the kitchen one of my owners, I was told that 'my' horse was in Lambourn Woodlands, and I should buy it. A week later my father and I went to look at it. For the two hundred pounds that was weighing heavy in my bank account,[16] I could become the owner of an unbroken two-year-old grey gelding with a big Tetrarch spot on his hind quarter.[17] The horse was named Beamish. For a further fifty pounds the vendor, Noel Blatchley, said he would break me in as well.

"You girls think you can ride but you haven't got a clue!"

My father immediately anti-ed up the additional fifty. Instead of thanking him on the way home, I rather churlishly told him that we should have tried to knock down the price. I had never bought a horse, but I thought one bartered with horse dealers.

"But that is a very good horse at a very good price." he replied. My father might not have been a horseman in the traditional sense, but he had a very good eye for a 'beast'. He had been right. Four months after buying Beamish, the Canadian three-day-event team managers offered me five times what I had paid, but typical girl I had fallen in love with him.

Noel was not a dealer. Described by Anthony Shaffer as 'The Lambourn Horse Psychiatrist' he made almost enough of a living breaking-in horses.[18] The core of them were colts bought by Lambourn trainers for owners who wished to appear in the winners' enclosures of Newmarket and Epsom. Quite often the horses had proved impossible to break but having shelled out vast sums of the owners' money at the yearling sales, they could not admit that they couldn't even get a saddle on these crown jewels, let alone get them onto the gallops. In desperation the colts would be sent out of prying eyes (and

---

16 *About £4,000 in 2022.*

17 *The Tetrarch was grey covered with white spots. He was unbeaten from 7 starts (ridden by Steve Donohue) and voted the Best British Trained Two-Year-Old of the 20thC.*

18 *Anthony Shaffer, twin brother of Peter Shaffer, was also an author and playwright.*

gossip) to Noel, to see whether he could save reputations. He always did. Horses trusted him. Even when his Parkinson's disease had become so bad that his hands shook the tea from a mug, he could approach a horse to bridle it without its flaring a nostril or twitching an ear. Once he had long reined the horses round the lanes, he would back them inside the stable. After a year or so of breaking in me (alongside Beamish) he used me to be legged on top, with the warning,

"If you so much as move a muscle, what he does to you will be as nothing compared to what I do."

The possibility of being fired through the corrugated iron sheeting a few inches above my head seemed the best option. As Noel led the colt round the loose box, one way and then the other, I kept determinedly relaxed. We successfully backed three Derby hopefuls without mishap in one month.

In 2017 ten of us, five English and five Kyrgyz with fifteen stallions (five packhorses),[19] were riding down the no-go zone between Kyrgyzstan and China and had to cross very unstable scree on vertiginous mountain sides, hundreds of feet above rocky ravines. Had any horse altered its balance or misplaced any foot, the scree would have given way, avalanched, and at least one horse and rider would have followed the tumbling shards into the swirling rivers of the snowmelt crashing over the rocks below us, that we could hear but not see. Noel's words were still in my head nearly fifty years on:

"RELAX and don't move a muscle!"

After one particularly unstable and frightening stretch, we reached the anchoring roots of sparse vegetation and I shouted to the others, "I've always said I'd rather die in Kyrgyzstan than in an oldies' home in England, but I hadn't planned on it being today."

"But you ride like a Kyrgyz, no worries!" laughed Marat, bringing up the rear. The best compliment one could receive from a Kyrgyz.

Noel had rescued Beamish as a yearling from some disused calf-pens where he had been chained without water, in a failed attempt to get the better of him. The dairy farmer readily accepted twenty-five pounds to be 'rid of the bugger'.[20] Noel gave the yearling a drink and then walked him the nine miles home, by which time he was halter broken. He had spent the following twelve months explaining quietly and patiently to Beamish what he required

---

19 *The Kyrgyz very rarely ride mares – they are kept for breeding. The males are not castrated.*
20 *£25 – less than £500 in 2022. Knacker money.*

of him and restoring his confidence in mankind. Noel wanted a good home for him and knew if he broke us together, he could be sure that Beamish would continue to be treated as he wished.

Noel lived with one of the two most dauntingly imperious women I have met. Diana B-P, the hyphenated names of two ducal families, had not so much fallen on hard times as was living in reduced circumstances. It was unclear the cause of their reduction, an unnamed absent husband lurked in history, but she required to be treated as though nothing had changed. How she and Noel got together was never revealed. They were both in their sixties, she older than he. By the time I met them they had been together for decades and despite her predisposition to treat him, often in public, like an irritating adolescent younger sibling, I'm sure she loved him: she certainly depended on him. He treated her affectionately with amusement, as though she was one of the horses with terrible stable manners that he had been sent to sort out, but with habits too entrenched to change; the type of horse whose ears, teeth, and heels one watches like a hawk.

Noel's earlier life was never revealed either. His brother owned the milk round in Lambourn, but he was rarely mentioned by Noel, and never by Diana. Noel had the physique of a whippet. Not one of those tucked-up shiverers that wears a blanket for eight months of the year, but a Romany's hare hound, with every ounce of flesh converted to muscle. His main interests, besides the horses, were classical music and well written books. He also collected 19th-century cavalry manuals, that he took down from the shelves, and used to back-up his instructions on how to school a horse. Dressage in his view, had developed not for tittupping across mown grass, but for sidestepping oncoming lances at full gallop or weaving between fallen comrades, and jumping brooks, ditches, and abandoned canons on the battlefield.

"It's not about marks, it's about obedience and precise positioning."

If he thought that our attempts at turns on the haunches or breaking into a canter from a standing start were too sluggish, he would laugh

"Well, it's lucky you aren't a *rejoneador!*"[21]

His weakness, if it was one, was Guinness. Diana thought it was and spent a lot of time making sure that he didn't have access to any and she kept the bottle openers hidden. Noel spent as much time circumnavigating her manoeuvres and long since had mastered the art of opening bottles on the

---

21 *Rejoneo is the Portuguese version of bullfighting where the horse is more critical and endangered than that of a Spanish picador.*

hinges of doors.[22] The car belonged to Diana, and she only let him have the keys when he needed to buy feed for the horses. As it was his only opportunity to buy Guinness, it fell to those who kept horses with him, which for four years was largely me, to smuggle replenishments. These were secreted around the stables, between bales of hay and in the bran tub. Once he was confident that Beamish and I would do what he asked, at the very moment he asked, he used us as schoolmasters for young horses. On the way home from exercise, we would stop off at the Hare and Hounds, a pub with a lean-to coach house partially filled with beer kegs. The first time he told me to dismount and lead Beamish and his horse inside, I wondered what was planned. The point of stopping at the pub was obvious but going into a dark shed was not. Two headcollars had been left dangling from metal rings in the wall.

"This is an essential part of every horse's education," he said, "learning to stand peacefully, tied up." He smiled and winked, "And of course if Diana drives by, she won't know we're here!"

When we went hunting together, he always reminded me to bring a flask. In good time for The Meet, we would stop at a pub *en route* for a sharpener, leaving the horses in the trailer. I was told to lean back with my shoulders against the bar and the back of my head on it. He would hold the flask above my open mouth and fill it with two shots of whisky and one of ginger wine. The flask was just too small. What didn't overflow into my mouth I learned to catch with my tongue before it reached my hunting tie.

Very occasionally Noel did overdo it. He was a benign and very amusing drunk, but Diana never saw the jokes and assumed the role of a castigating judge. If she'd had a black cap she would have worn it and he had to wait patiently, sometimes for days, for sentence to be commuted.[23]

Twice a year Diana dressed as though off to lunch with royalty, caught a succession of trains from Newbury to somewhere east of Greenwich where she owned 'a street'. The rents from her properties kept the roof on the house and food on the table, which she mentioned from time to time, as though to remind Noel that his income from the horses did not. Somehow, they had managed to buy a farmer's derelict *almacén*, on a terrace in the hills above Pollensa, in Mallorca. Every summer off they'd go, down through France on a scooter, to Barcelona and the ferry. I never witnessed this and still find it

---

22 *Draft Guinness in cans did not become available until 1988.*
23 *Before condemning a man to death, a judge put on a square of black cloth known as a 'black cap'.*

impossible to imagine. While Noel converted the little *almacén* into a *cabaña*, Diana perfected her pitch-perfect Spanish as she rescued island cats and harangued those who didn't look after them as she thought they should. When they became too old for the scooter and had more money, they took the car and Diana became adept at smuggling sedated strays in her hand baggage. Before the days of 'terrorism' and 'immigrants' one could smuggle most things, and unless one looked like an international gangster, usually get away with it. One kitten turned out to be a genuinely wild cat,[24] sweet when a kitten but ferocious once mature. Unless 'Tigre' was out killing rabbits, it passed the day in the house terrorising visitors. Its favourite pastime was flying round the room at head height, to land on one's shoulders and sink its claws and teeth into anything it fancied. Invitations to lunch became a matter of weighing up the prospect of Diana's delicious food with that of having to feign enjoyment of the pain. Diana was proud of its wildness but often had terrible wounds on her hands.

"Oh, naughty Tigre!"

I was to spend four years being educated by Noel, and in different ways by Diana. Neither brooked excuses. Thanks to Sarah Canning's riding reports, I had spent years thinking my 'shape' prevented my becoming a decent rider. Early one autumn morning Noel, fed up with my using the shortness of my legs as an excuse for my shortcomings as a rider, told me to jump in the car and drive him down to Lambourn. As we watched the strings return from the gallops, he pointed out that all the jockeys were short.

"… and they manage to win races! No more excuses!"

He told me I wasn't to put Beamish at a jump higher than three feet during his first season's hunting.[25] "After that he will never stop. You will have built up his confidence."

"How will I know what three feet is?"

"Come here," he sighed, picking up the horse measuring stick and standing it against me. With his thumb at nine hands (thirty-six inches), he prodded my stomach with his index finger. "There," he said. "Is that your stomach button? Well now you know what three feet is."

"But if I am on top, how will I know that a fence is the same height as my tummy button?"

---

24 *El gato montés.*

25 *Beamish never did stop. I was asked to give many MFHs a lead and he never let me down, whatever the obstacle or take-off.*

"Oh, for goodness' sake! Get off, walk up to the fence, find out. You could of course learn what three feet looks like."

Diana unwittingly taught me not to be frightened of people like her. She was *au fond* one of the kindest people, rescuing many animals besides the cats. She landed me with two abandoned dogs and if she heard of anyone in trouble, she was there for them. Once or twice, when they were in Mallorca, I horse-sat for them and noticed that there were two five-foot oxygen cylinders in her bedroom. She had been near death a few times and I think her manner was to disguise incipient fear. I began to wonder whether her almost freakish attempts to control Noel were because she needed him, and not only to manhandle the heavy oxygen canisters. I wondered whether her general mien was a warning to the world at large: her life was to be on her terms, and she wasn't going anywhere quietly. As years went by, I noticed the haughtiest of those in the hunting field were the most frightened.

What I learned from Noel about looking after and training horses, formed the basis of all my future dealings with them, as well as with dogs, and children. I have found they are much the same. Beamish carried me behind hounds for the next twenty years. I owe him and Noel for a lot of the best fun I have had, and despite both having been dead for over thirty years, there are few weeks that go by that I don't smile to myself and thank them both.

*

At a staff Christmas party in Daily Mirror House in the mid 1960s, Cecil King, chairman of IPC (International Publishing Group), that by then owned *Farmers Weekly* and the other magazines for which my father had been given responsibility, beckoned Daddy away from what he called 'the mob' into his inner sanctum where they chewed the fat sitting in quiet, well-fuelled comfort. My father had always liked Cecil King as much as he had disliked Hugh Cudlipp, who later became chairman of IPC. King told my father that while it was IPC policy to retire employees at sixty-five, he had decided that he and Daddy would both remain until they were seventy.

As it happened King was sacked, aged sixty-seven, by the IPC board in 1968 after he worked on an unrealised plan, with Lord Mountbatten to oust Harold Wilson's government. Mountbatten had fancied becoming Prime Minister. My father continued to be on IPC's payroll until he was seventy.

They did not prove to be happy last few years. Under my father's editorship, *Farmers Weekly* had become the most successful trade journal in the world with a worldwide weekly circulation of more than one hundred thousand. When on a ferry ploughing along a far-north Norwegian fjord the captain invited us onto the bridge. He asked what my father did and was overjoyed. Throughout The Occupation *Farmers Weekly*, somehow had made its way past the Germans, and kept them in touch with the outside world.

My father's act would be difficult to follow and the job was thought to be a poisoned chalice. None of the first-choice successors would take it on. The reins eventually fell into the safe hands of someone already on the staff, a man with whom my father had entrusted the jobs he personally did not want, like running the *Farmers Weekly* farms and the estate at Salperton in Gloucestershire that he had found for the Hultons. The idea had been that my father would spend the last few years as consultant editor. Whether to get back at him because they had never shared a glass of Scotch, or whether because he lacked the self-confidence to ask for help, but for two years Daddy waited to be consulted and never was. He had been dropped.

It was a kick in the guts for the man who had been so respected by all the big guns in the agricultural world. His brain remained sharper than most of those of half his age, and he still had a lot of ideas. While renting from Lord Brocket, house prices had spiralled, and he had dropped off the property ladder. He could no longer afford to buy the sort of house he wanted. To say that he was depressed in the current idiom of mental illness would be overstating it, it was more a case of dejection. He had a lot of reading to catch up on, stacks of Stuart history and philosophy. He had taken out massive insurance in case he died while I was a child, happily had not died, and as a result had a good pension, but he was not as happy as I thought he should be.

In 1972 I saw his-sort-of-house advertised to rent near Cirencester. I persuaded him that we should have a look. He agreed, while 'not holding out much hope' on the proviso that we visited Paul Weller's bookshop in the town. He knew its reputation including the soft armchairs into which customers could drop and dip. He would give me a pub lunch. It was up to me to find the pub and to drive.

THIRTEEN

TARLTON

1972

A few months later my father was sitting in his high-backed, tulip shaped, Georgian chair beside the fire, with a large box on the floor between his knees. He carefully unwound the newspaper in which was wrapped the blue Meissen dinner service that Mummy had found in a favourite junk shop in Edgeware Road. She was always buying part services of beautiful porcelain; nine of this pattern; eleven of that; a soup tureen big enough to fill a dozen bowls of which there were only five. He hadn't seen any of them since they went into storage when he left London. His happiness to be reunited with the familiar plates kept a smile on his face. Now, twenty years after Mummy's death, he could smile when reminded of specific occasions; of the time when she had asked him to help her carry them into the house.

"Do we need more plates?!" He had shared the enjoyment she always had when returning with beautiful things.

The house was one of three, almost identical, built in the mid-19th century as rather pretentious farmhouses. The one my father rented in Tarlton had been altered internally which gave him two high, light reception rooms at the cost of an unprepossessing front hall and staircase and a third room with a sink that was imaginatively described as the kitchen. We bought an electric cooker. Although larger than a widower needed, it gave wall space to hang his collection of early 19th-century engravings of bovines that he had bought in an attack of patriotism after the war when they were to be sold to Texas. More importantly there was room for all his books. The gardens, largely ignored by the outgoing tenants, had been created thirty years earlier by a plants' woman, and a lot had survived. There was a large kitchen garden, a small paddock, and some stables.

"You have a wonderful horse; this is some of the best hunting in England. Make the most of it."

I took no persuading. Beamish and I had had two careful seasons in the cloying mud of the Old Berkshire Hunt country. The thought of better going over Cotswold brash and vale, on a horse keen to take a straight line and jump anything that got in the way, was exciting. I spent the summer helping sort out packing cases, painting the house and getting Beamish really fit for the upcoming season. I poured over Ordnance Survey maps and realised we had landed with direct access to Cirencester Park, arguably the most glorious, landscaped woodland in the world, now Listed Grade I.

Beamish and I started to explore. We crossed the Stroud road and, encouraged by a notice welcoming those on foot and horse, set off up a wide ride with great beech trees over one hundred feet tall on either side. Halfway up the incline Beamish stopped in his tracks. Pheasants he was used to; raptors he was not. A buzzard swooped down from a top branch. Still persecuted by keepers, buzzards were rare in southern England, and it was the first either of us had seen.

The land levelled off and we reached an open space from which ten rides fanned out. To our right, we had a spectacular view of Cirencester Abbey's church tower. This was Ten Rides, and we were midway down the Broad Ride that runs from Cirencester to Sapperton, about five miles, possibly the longest avenue in the world. The park was laid out in the mid-18th century by the first Earl Bathurst, with input from his friend the poet Alexander Pope and the garden designer Stephen Switzer. When planted it was theoretically possible to see a church tower or spire down each of the ten rides: Rodmarton or Tetbury (Bath Ride); Tarlton (Hailey Ride); Coates or Kemble (Coates Ride); South Cerney (Wiltshire Ride); Cirencester (Broad Ride); Barnsley (Barnsley Ride); Daglingworth (Woodhouse Ride); Duntisbourne (Overley Ride); Miserden (Park Corner Ride) and Oakridge (Broad Ride).

Imagine what it must have been like three hundred years ago. Allen Bathurst and Alexander Pope riding along, with a couple of grooms at a discreet distance behind with a few longdogs, and their stopping to look over the Wolds. Still over a hundred years to go before the General Enclosure Act,[1] there would have been a few single trees: clumps of gorse and brambles; single Breughel birds flying across the sky; a shepherd calling to his dog to keep the roaming flock tight; neither the sound of an engine, a plane, nor even a cock pheasant.[2]

"Bathurst, do you see, if we stand here, on this spot, we can see ten church spires? I think we should have ten avenues fanning out from here, to focus the eye."

"Splendid! Let's do it."

I wondered which ride to take, and as we set off, I speculated whether the grooms had overheard and were pleased there would be work for their cousins for years to come. How long it did take to plant all those avenues? How many saplings did deer eat off – some would have escaped the Deer Park?

We found ourselves among ancient yews beside the crumbling Alfred's Hall. Listed Grade II* it is thought to be the first purpose-built (1721–32) Gothick 'ruin' in England and had been used for shooting lunches until becoming too unstable. Now genuinely ruined it was protected by looping, rusting barbed wire and threatening notices. We chucked a right and found ourselves back in the Broad Ride by the Horse Guards (Grade II), copies of Kent's Horse Guards in London. Crossing the Broad Ride, we went down Lady Georgina's Drive to Three Mile Bottom and ended up back where we had entered the park. I could not believe the beauty of the place. It was Arcadia.

The blights in what I otherwise remember as a wonderful summer of discovery, of sunny days and woodpigeons' cooing, was when Sarah Canning and Peggy came to stay.[3] Sarah was competing in a dressage competition; Peggy was riding shotgun and they brought their dogs and two horses. Walking up the garden from morning stables, Peggy's dog went berserk, screaming, convulsing, turning herself inside out and rushing in ever more demented circles in excruciating pain. She died in agony on the vet's doorstep twenty minutes later. The vet diagnosed strychnine poisoning. She hadn't left our

---

1   *The first parliamentary enclosure act had been in 1604, others followed. The General Enclosure Act was passed in 1801.*

2   *The Normans brought pheasants to Britain in the 11thC but they more or less died out and were re-introduced by the Victorians as game.*

3   *Peggy Michell was another of Mrs Canning's rescues. She had started working as second matron at Hanford in the mid-50s, hated it and took it out on us. It was she who screamed at me one day "You're Messy by name and messy by nature!" (She was right), Mrs Canning soon transferred her to the stables to help with the ponies. Once happy, she became benign. Over the years she became Sarah's factotum. She died at Hanford after sixty-five years.*

property and the only explanation was that a corvid flying over, had dropped some baited meat left for foxes by the local keeper.

A few weeks later Beamish pricked his ears at a patch of brush and brambles. Something was in there and I got off to have a look. It was a live fox that had been caught in a snare that it had pulled out of the ground. The snare had cut through its belly and its intestines were visible. A fortnight later I smelled something dreadful before I came across a very sick fox. It had been wounded when shot in the leg (they are difficult to shoot clean) and it was dying of gangrene poisoning. Like most people, I always hoped that a hunted fox would get away but after that summer I had no doubt that a fox meeting its end when the lead hound snaps its neck has the indisputably more humane end.

As I was to discover, Cirencester Park keeps on giving. There are ten follies in Oakley Wood, all Grade II Listed, half of them listed with asterisks. It is a unique place, curated by one family for over three hundred years and always open to 'the town' for their enjoyment. In practice few members of the public ventured west of the Mile Posts, a mile from the town. Some made it to Ivy Lodge polo ground, but it was unusual to see other than estate staff west of Rough Hills. The Cirencester to Stroud road, that once had followed a similar path from Cecily Hill, at the Cirencester end of the park to Hermit's Hill, had been diverted by Act of Parliament in 1818. On days when there was polo, strings of ponies would be led down the Broad Ride from Sapperton to the grounds and back. The only other horses were hunters on exercise and very occasionally John Oaksey,[4] who could be seen giving one of his thoroughbreds a pipe-opener up the Broad Ride before a race. Other riders were always friendly, we fell into conversation and rode alongside for a mile or two. It meant that by the time cubbing started I knew a few people.[5]

Inevitably one of those was our neighbour who lived the other side of the no through lane in Tarlton. We shared the quickest tarmac-free route to the

---

4 *Lord Oaksey was George's exact contemporary and schoolfriend. It was George who encouraged him to ride when they were up at Oxford together. Lady Apsley gave him his early rides on her racehorses. Besides being a highly respected journalist, he was a seriously successful amateur rider and nearly won the Grand National in 1963 only beaten by the outsider Ayala. He massively supported the Injured Jockey's Fund and the rehabilitation centre in Lambourn is named after him.*

5 *The hunting season starts on the first Saturday in November. Cubbing started at different times across the country in late summer/early autumn when the standing crops had been harvested. It was the time when the previous year's puppies were entered into the pack and learned to hunt with older hounds, learning not to riot and to obey the huntsman. Traditionally mounted followers only attended by invitation of the masters.*

park. Questioning of my father's dailies revealed him to be Lord Bathurst's younger bachelor brother, George. He quickly worked out that I had horse transport which he did not. Soon I was giving him, and his horses, lifts to the meets that were beyond hacking distance. His sister-in-law, Judy, did not intend to spend her failing years being responsible for both Bathurst brothers,[6] and, spotting an opportunity to offload one of them, she started inviting me to join them for hunting teas, provided by Nanny, in the nursery. Daddy and I were invited to Christmas lunch. George was absentmindedly good with animals and very interested in and kind to his nephews and niece – a promising sign.

The following spring George invited me skiing. For the previous seven years the parents of a one-time boyfriend had invited me to ski with them. It was *grande-luxe*, and I had already accepted to go again. I supposed I could make it: all of March spent skiing while the UK would be spent in the grip of biting winds. It was an invitation too good to resist. After a fortnight in Méribel, I hired a car and left the butler, cook, gourmet food, exquisite wines and longstanding friends of two generations, and I drove across France via Marseille, to meet George in Toulouse. We were to ski in Andorra where I had never been.

What he had not revealed was that he had chosen Andorra not only because it was terribly cheap, he had honed the younger-son poverty mantle, but because he thought he could swing it across Her Majesty's Revenue and Customs as being halfway between Malta and Cirencester for his company's AGM. The other directors of his company were Harvey who lived in Malta and Madge and Steve who lived in Cirencester. I later discovered that failing to divulge The Whole Story was one of George's amusements. Living with him became like dealing with the arithmetic teacher who put me off maths.

"If Janet has six apples and Robert has five pears how many bananas must Mary buy?"

"Please, why does Mary need bananas?"

"That is for you to work out Susan."

George always kept back critical information. The chill in Toulouse was far worse than it would have been in Gloucestershire. Madge and Steve knew George's once-girlfriend, whom he hadn't treated well, and made it plain that they had no intention of befriending her replacement. Neither did they like

---

6   *Judy and Henry were divorced in 1976 so she didn't look after either brother in old age. She died of Leukaemia in 2001.*

abroad, especially France, or foreign food and there was absolutely no way they were going to risk strapping skis to their feet and slipping on snow. Harvey never left Malta.

The *pension* selected for the mythical AGM was owned by a couple who had fled Blighty to escape their respective spouses. They were good cooks, operated a generous honesty bar but had nothing spare to spend on maintenance. The bedrooms were arctic, the bedclothes damp. Every time one pulled the chain, dangling from the high-level cistern, chilled water jetted into the small of the back or waist. With his inculcated idea of responsibility George set about repairing the split lead pipe and wrapped it with the strips of Elastoplast he had packed for blisters. Thereafter water seeped down and across the uneven linoleum floor to pool near the shower. My reckless enthusiasm for piste-bashing was tempered when the rescue team let go of the blood waggon and it careered past us down the mountain, eventually wrapping around a conifer that remained firmly rooted. The occupant, initially suffering with a dislocated knee, went to hospital with a broken back.

On the return journey through France Madge and Steve sat in the back of George's car in total silence. My Pollyanna attempt at conversation had withered before we had descended the Pyrenees. We jinxed to Carcassonne. George loved Medieval fortifications. We found a celebrated restaurant within the walls that served cassoulet and risqué cabaret. In the intervals waiters wove between tables in time to plucked Spanish guitars. Madge and Steve didn't like garlic or saucisson; duck was too rich, and beans had a gaseous effect on their digestion. Nor did they understand French. George and I laughed a lot. The situation degenerated the following day when George and I ran out of cash. Banks had closed for the weekend and Madge and Steve refused to lend us as much as ten francs for a couple of mugs of coffee.[7] We were told that we shouldn't have wasted what we had on THAT meal. We limped back to Cirencester on a diet of private jokes.

Despite Henry's lack of enthusiasm, George, and their mother Lady Apsley, had restarted Cirencester Park Polo Club in the early 1950s. The famous Ivy Lodge Polo Ground, claimed to be the best all-weather polo ground in England, had been ploughed for potatoes during the war and was reseeded. George spent the summer playing polo and I accompanied him to the Argentinian *asados* that happened most evenings. We lived on warmed sheep

---

7   *ATM machines did not become widely available for another twenty years.*

meat spiced up by BBQ sauce and washed down with generous quantities of high-quality alcohol. Roberta Flack's 'Killing Me Softly', Carly Simon's 'You're So Vain' and Shirley Bassey's 'Never... Never... Never' drifted from opened windows across the Cotswold stone terraces and sylvan valleys. Any sane person would have stood back and assessed the situation, but it suited my frame of mind at the time to remind myself that no one is perfect. I found him a hilariously eccentric product of over three hundred years of selective breeding and nothing like any I had met before. Love lacked bi focals.

FOURTEEN

TARLTON

I had to decide whether I was going spend another season hunting and find a job. I would have to start getting Beamish fit. Anthony Fenton had asked me to return to Marseille and help him with a tourism company he was setting up. I told George.

"Oh well, we'd better get married, then."

Not exactly romantic, down-on-knees with an ancestral diamond but at least indication of intention. A month later, special licence from the Archbishop of Canterbury in hand, we knelt together before the altar of St Kenelm's Church in Sapperton. The irony of Kenelm having had to negotiate jealous, ambitious relatives had not struck me. The congregation consisted of my father, Henry, and Judy, their two sons taken out of pre-prep school for the morning, and Nanny Bathurst. Sir Henry Poole, one time owner of Sapperton and Sir Robert Atkyns, whose son sold it to the Bathursts in 1716, witnessed in cold marble without emotion. Nanny recorded the event with her box-brownie. My father and now four Bathursts repaired to Tory Oaksey's restaurant Pink's, in Fairford, for a delicious lunch in the eaves above the restaurant.

George had specific life interests: hunting; polo; the history of aviation; the military history and espionage of the 20th century; and aerodynamics.

148

Offered a place at Trinity College, Oxford, where an antecedent had been president for forty years in the 17th century, he had wanted to read engineering, but had been told that it was not a suitable subject for a Bathurst. He signed up for Medieval English Literature. Credit to his brain that he gained a second Class degree without appearing to read a book or attend tutorials. A contemporary said he was rarely spotted crossing Garden Quad out of riding breeches.[1] He spent most of the time playing polo and whipping-in to the Bathurst hounds.

By his mid-forties George's grey cells were preoccupied with aerodynamics. He had invented and patented a furnace that was so efficient, thanks to tangential inlets for air intake and the resultant Coanda effect, that it burned any refuse from paint solvent to rubber tyres without ash or smoke. The furnaces generated so much heat that they successfully provided hot water and heat for ships and factories. George recently had become fascinated by a new hovercraft that had just started commercial channel crossings. We spent the first night of our honeymoon in the eaves of a filthy hotel in Ramsgate to catch the first sailing the following morning. We were two of the handful who returned our complimentary brown bags unused, not having been sick on the crossing, and then we drove to Brussels. Our marriage was conveniently timed for an international pollution conference being held there throughout the week. After it we visited Waterloo. The Third Earl Bathurst had been Secretary of State for War and The Colonies and, at a dinner party in Grosvenor Square, had been the first to receive news of Wellington's victory.[2] As a concession to my interest in 'art' we tagged on a weekend in Bruges.

Early on our first morning home we woke to the sound of horses doing a steady trot along the lane from Coates. From the window we could see they were with hounds, on exercise. Peter Hudson, then still a bachelor, had thought it a good joke to disturb the newlyweds. We made a mad scramble into clothes and just managed to reach the front door with mugs of warm milk, whisky, and slightly soggy Hobnobs, as they trotted up the drive to the toot of the horn.

---

1   Partly designed by Sir Christopher Wren on President Ralph Bathurst's instructions. He was also responsible for the building of the chapel, designed by Henry Aldrich, with Wren's input. It was consecrated in 1694.

2   He was responsible for sending Napoleon to St Helena and 200 years later is still believed by some French to have ordered his poisoning. The actual cause of Napoleon's death remains debate, one theory being that he ingested arsenic from the paint used to decorate Longwood House.

The first letter of condolence to arrive after George's death, nearly forty years later, was from June Stevens, the much-respected master of the Cotswold Hunt. 'George was a true countryman,' she wrote. He was. To follow hounds with him was fascinating. He may not have been allowed to get a job, but he had been allowed to spend a year whipping-in to the Tipperary Hounds in Ireland. His family had had their own pack of hounds for nearly eighty years. Previous generations and his immediate grandfather, step-grandfather, aunt, and mother, all had been masters of hounds. He had a good idea of how foxes and hounds would behave and was a human sight hound, able to spot a fox in the far distance when others would have needed binoculars. He taught me to scan the horizon methodically; something that impressed my guide, when fifty years on, we were looking for leopards in Jawar's volcanic hills.[3] I learned to mark flustered cock pheasants and irritated jays; to register a flock of pigeons break from a field of roots and to notice which way bunching ewes pointed. Sometimes, when hounds found a fox and streamed off over the hills, with the field in steaming pursuit, George didn't move.[4]

"I'm waiting here. You go on if you like but I think he'll come back to us."

Sure enough, as often as not, twenty minutes later, a flock of corvids would flap grumpily to the sky from the recently turned plough where they had been scavenging eel worms, and moments later there Charlie was, trotting along the headland without a care in the world. Always a 'he'; always a Charlie. We'd saved our horses miles.

I had galloped behind eleven packs in England and Eire and thought that I knew about hunting but after marrying George, I realised I had only scraped the surface. I found it absorbing watching hounds work, their trying to own a line over foiled ground or on tarmac; especially when I recognised the puppies I had walked. It made even the slowest days interesting. Towards the end of one busy day, I was cantering along a tarmac lane beside the huntsman, Sidney Bailey. Hounds in full cry, were led by one of 'my' puppies. I remarked on her proudly.

"Yes Madam, but she is descended from Lord Bathurst's Laureate '37,[5] the most famous of road-hunting hounds."

---

3   *North of the Aravalli Hills in Rajasthan.*

4   *The mounted followers of a hunt are called 'the field'.*

5   *Lord Bathurst's Laureate was by the Duke of Beaufort's Pedlar '33 out of his own Lawful '32. Lawful was out of his Lavish '29. Hounds usually have names starting with the first two letters of the dam.*

I became interested in hound breeding. Urban, hill and lowland foxes are different. They evolved to suit their habitats. Similarly, hounds are bred for different conditions and terrains. Just as Salukis, evolved over centuries to hunt the farmlands of the Fertile Crescent, so Kyrgyz Taigans developed lungs that could absorb enough oxygen at very high altitudes and pads that could cross the Tien Shan Mountain's cliffs and scree without damage. Both are sight hounds and to the casual observer look vaguely similar. Hound breeding is thought by some to be as much of an art as genetic science and is as controversial. The seventh Earl Bathurst thought crossing an English hound with a 'woolly Welsh' was sacrilege, but Tim Unwin used a 'whiskery Fell' hound stallion and his bitch pack proved one of the most exhilarating to try to follow.[6]

Every year I walked a couple of puppies for Roland Shepherd (Cotswold kennel huntsman) as well as Sidney Bailey. With our own Pointer x Labradors, known as the Tarlton Hounds, my son's North Cerney Terrier, and my old Labrador, they made a scruff pack of four couple that exercised with us and the horses every day. Dogs were not allowed west of the Mile Posts in Cirencester Park and one morning we met a new keeper. Not recognising George, and why should he have done, he stopped us and told us that dogs were not allowed.

"Do you enjoy being a keeper?" George very politely asked the rather surprised keeper.

"Yes..."

"Well, I suggest you learn the difference between dogs and hounds."

This could have been seen by some as his joke (it was), and semantics, but in seven decades of living with a wide array of canines I know that hounds, whether scent or sight hounds, are poles apart from domestic dogs.

George and I divided roles. When not making models of his latest invention, George wrote incomprehensible papers to support his theories that honeybees are capitalists, and that it is possible to divide the history of the world into epochs and aeons. I was responsible for the horses, hound puppies, dogs, and food, in that order. I cleaned boots, spurs, and hunting whips. He cleaned the coats and his top hat. We competed for shine. Joan, born in the village the day WWII was declared, came in five mornings a week, and did her best to keep on top of dust and mud. In due course she became our trusted mentor on child rearing.

---

6   *Joint Master and Huntsman of the Cotswold Hounds for about thirty years.*

Evenings frequently involved dinner parties in manor houses, convened I sometimes felt, so that those who neither played polo nor hunted foxes could see exactly what the cat had brought in. I wasn't displayed, more inspected as the unpredicted answer. Some mothers had been disappointed.

Hunting followed polo followed hunting followed polo. While I became more passionate about hunting, I liked polo less. The early days of the restarted polo club had attracted royalty and maharajas. One Saturday in June 1970, the Maharaja of Jaipur, arguably one of the best polo players of the century, dropped dead midgame at Cirencester. It was critical to get his body out of the country before the Inland Revenue could impound it as hostage for tax liabilities. George, always keen to out-flank the taxman, went to fetch his plane while Juliet Worsley, one of the first female players, drove round the leafy lanes with the corpse, wrapped in a horse blanket, bumping around in the back of her muddy Peugeot estate car. George, his aeroplane fully fuelled, flew Maharaja Sawai Shri Man Singh II to France. He was well on his way back to Rajasthan before the news leaked.

Following his death, the Indians stopped coming over to play polo. It coincided with the game becoming more professional and less of a means of giving hunting grooms something to do in the summer. The Argentinians arrived. It was as though the different attitude of Hindus and Christians to animal welfare manifested itself in the polo ponies' lot. The care of some ponies became cavalier, at best, and occasionally it was worse than neglectful. I was pregnant and decided to learn to ride side-saddle. I thought I might look rather elegant in floating Laura Ashley dresses, but as the foetus grew it became apparent that 'it' did not like it. Within minutes of being on a horse I developed stomach cramps so, unable to ride-in the ponies for George, I had nothing to distract me from the pony-lines.[7] With the input of our groom, who had read Spanish at Cambridge, and was unobserved as she tended to George's ponies, we not only saw but overheard. We knew what the gauchos were up to, not always behind closed stable doors. Farmers who offered pony accommodation to teams visiting for tournaments, and a local vet, complained to George about pony welfare. We became increasingly appalled. At the end of the season, encouraged by George, who was more than happy to send me ahead out of the trench, I wrote a letter, supported by photographs, to the editor of *Horse and Hound*.

---

7   *Like all athletes, horses need to be loosened up with gentle exercise before the serious work.*

Our son chose to pitch up, bang on time, on November 11th, 1978, Remembrance Day – wouldn't he just? I was having an uncomfortable time in Cheltenham Maternity Hospital, appropriately the repurposed Cheltenham Workhouse, when George arrived on his way to the racecourse for the November meeting. Untroubled by immediate events he came to the head of my bed.

"Its IN…" he said, beaming "…It's IN!"

The obstetrician and surrounding nurses looked completely non-plussed. They had been trying to get it out.

"WHAT is in?" I asked.

"Your letter… it's the lead letter in *Horse and Hound*!"

It was. Letters in support from a wide range of polo players and some vets, preceded me home. Others wrote in support to *Horse and Hound*. The *Observer* despatched a team from their Insight desk. Vets from other polo clubs gave interviews in support. The sh*t had hit the fan. Then the owners of the major clubs closed ranks. Vets, threatened with the termination of their leases on estate premises retracted statements. The furore died down. Whether or not as a direct result, the Hurlingham Polo Association created a welfare committee that has become integral to British Polo. Hurrah.

George's inventions moved on from furnaces. A multinational company had stolen the idea and challenged him to sue, which of course he could not afford to do. He invented a dart gun, so accurate that it could be used to sedate and immobilise, rather than exterminate. Unwilling to patent it, which would release it into the public, therefore the enemy's domain, George, always the patriot, took it directly to the Ministry of Defence. It was poo-pooed. A year later it was described in the broadsheets as the MOD's latest invention. He invented a self-regulating windmill with secondary blades that would catch the slightest wind, but which would slow down the primary blades in storms. Having had his furnace patent, that had been internationally registered, broken by a multinational company he had decided patents were expensively worth nothing. He reverted to his practice of not revealing the critical elements. Understandably nobody bought his incompletely explained ideas. Our income depended on the Stock Exchange, the ups and downs of which George rode with skill, but with the birth our son expenditure increased faster than income.

I volunteered that if we farmed, we might augment income, if not in cash, at least it might be fiscally helpful. Henry let us rent one hundred and twenty acres. Sometimes it worked and had its moments. I ended up looking after and lambing three hundred ewes. George operated the corn drier.

FIFTEEN

FAMILY – LOST AND FOUND

1984

My father spent seven years in the house he had rented before downsizing to George's groom's cottage that he modernised. When our son fell foul of his parents he would cross our walled garden, climb the wrought iron gate (we put an old kitchen chair beside it so he could reach the high latch), and toddle over the field to his grandfather. We would telephone to say he was *en route*. On Sundays, having heard The Blue Danube heralding the arrival of the ice cream van from the next village, my father would stand in the lane and buy a Flake 99, sometimes two, one for his grandson's little partner in crime.

Daddy and I had seen each other at least once every day. He had shared in my happiness: the prospect of a grandchild and the birth of his grandson, whom he had helped to grow for five years and even taught to play chess. Until his last month he had only been in hospital once in his life, for a small hernia operation. Then one evening he telephoned to say he felt unwell and uncharacteristically suggested I call the doctor. The doctor came, immediately called an ambulance, and my father was taken, wrapped in tinfoil, to Cirencester Memorial Hospital. As the ambulance bounced us down the lane over the roots of the felled trees that had succumbed to Dutch

Elm Disease, a hand-written sign, hanging from the oxygen cylinder's tubes, tapped against the metal. 'Don't Use – Broken!' He didn't need oxygen, luckily. The doctor met us at the hospital and discussed the situation in hushed tones. He asked whether I wanted him blues and twos-ed to Swindon. The chances of survival would be better but slim. The prognosis? A couple of years with drugs for the cancer that had probably already started to seep through his body. Daddy had taught me not to prolong animals' lives to spare my own misery.

"Leave him quietly here, what will be will be." It was the least I could do for him.

I held the beautifully manicured hand that had held mine through thick and thin. It was cold. He seemed tired. Ready to go. Peaceful. I'm sure behind closed eyelids, he could see my mother. It was time for them to be together again. I did so hope they were. A few hours later the ghastly rattling stopped and the room was silent. I called the nurse to make sure he was dead. I couldn't risk his opening an eye and seeing me cry.

"Don't be silly…" he would have said, "I'm fine, now go on, and remember: keep laughing and splashing."

It was early morning on May 31st, 1984. The dogs' tails thudded when I entered the kitchen. The house was silent, George and the boy fast asleep. The sun's promise grew beyond the horizon; a defined semicircle rose and surprisingly quickly it was all there, backlighting the trees, floodlighting the fields, blindingly bright. A glorious sunrise heralded a perfect day. There was no point going to bed, so after a mug of tea, I whispered to the dogs and they followed me out. Beamish grazing in front of the house, looked up. I put my arms round his neck, and tears streamed down it. I felt his great jaw against my cheek, continuing to chew, he swallowed, paused, and lowered his head to snatch another mouthful of spring grass. I agreed. Enough. Had I asked for Daddy to be taken to Swindon he might still be alive, but I had done what I thought was best for him. What he would have wanted. All my adult life I had anticipated what I would do when he died, there had been forty-four years between us. It finally had happened, and I had been with him. How lucky I had been, I had had him more than twice as long as Mummy had.

The dogs and I headed across the fields. As the sun rose higher and the air warmed, the dawn chorus mellowed, and the skylarks tuned up. In the distance a tractor engine was started and could be heard heading back to the village from the dairy. The dogs disturbed a covey of partridge. Another tractor began circulating a field, mowing first-cut silage. It would wilt well today. It was a hundred years since the first silage harvest. Farming would continue; the world would spin; our five-year-old son would be asking for breakfast; the school run; smiling people.

The first person to telephone after Daddy's obituary appeared in *The Times* was Hugh, the most welcome of voices. We hadn't spoken for some time, but he was instantly recognisable, typically, cosily, supportive Hugh. Aunt Wall must have sat down Hugh and Amyas, with their fountain pens and paper when Mummy died. I had come across their letters written to Daddy. In neatest prep-school handwriting they started: 'Dear Malcolm, we are so sorry about Jill…' I was again five, straight back to the hall at Bishton with the snuffling pugs; teasing; laughter; school bell. Thirty-three years, some of them only linked by Christmas cards, but they were still there – 'my family'.

The next call was from 'George'. There were a lot of Georges in our lives, and I did not recognise the voice. I played for time which he must have sensed.

"Uncle George!" came reproachfully down the wires.

I had not heard his voice for twenty years; before that it had been ten. Unlike Hugh's his had never mattered. Here he was out of the blue; expressing sympathy; trying to be avuncular but, "…sadly, unable to be with you in person, dear." It was a relief. There was enough to handle without having to feign affection for a stranger.

I collected the death certificate and registered 'the death'. Daddy was eighty-two. Primary cause of death on the certificate was septicaemia, secondary cause, cancer of the prostate, for which he had been operated. He had contracted septicaemia while in hospital. The impersonal pro-forma released yet another corpse to yet another undertaker. I made an appointment with the undertaker who, George told me, dealt with all dead Bathursts. He sounded pleased to hear from me and the next day welcomed me effusively into the tiny front room of his premises, that shared a back yard with the society butcher. Biped and quadruped deadstock came and went through the same arch to the same back yard. I realised that he already had started conjuring plans for a large, county funeral in Cirencester's abbey church. Even if not involving black horses with plumes and reversed boots, there were bound to be cars, flowers, choirs, service sheets and a few clergy to organise. He might even have suggested to his wife that she should get brochures from the travel agent on the proceeds.

I took the proffered chair. He opened his notebook, smiled sympathetically, and promised to give my 'dear father' a wonderful service. Every time I answered his suggestion with a 'no' the corners of his mouth dipped another notch.

No to the church. No to flowers "We'll pick some from the garden."

No to a fleet of highly polished black cars "We'll drive ourselves to the crematorium but thank you very much."

No to crisp service sheets "There'll be very few of us, it'll be very short, we won't need service sheets."

"Do we have to have a vicar?" I asked.

The look on his face indicated that he was worrying how to tell his wife that a fortnight in the Swiss alps or Spanish Costa had gone out of the window. I was the one in mourning, but I felt sorry for him. I tried to bluster out explanations and apologies.

"My father was not religious…, he's to have a Service of Thanksgiving in London., in St Bride's Fleet Street…, he spent his life in Fleet Street." It fell flat. As I stood up, I had a final go at raising his spirits.

"I know that you gave my late mother-in-law, Lady Apsley, a wonderful send-off. I am only sorry that the axis of my father's life was London. That is where his friends and colleagues will find it easier to congregate, otherwise of course we would have something bigger; something here, something for you to organise."

"Would you mind taking her away?"

"Sorry?"

"Would you mind taking Lady Apsley away with you, please."

"Sorry?"

"She is on my filing cabinet. She has been there for… well it must be nearly twenty years."

If she was on his filing cabinet, she couldn't be in a coffin. It must be an urn, thank God, but why was she there?

"Lord Bathurst refused to talk to me. In fact, His Lordship would cross the market place if he saw me walking towards him. I tried to make it easy for him. I said I'd take her to The Mansion or wherever he wanted her scattered, but he'd refuse to take my calls, cut me dead. In the end I gave up."

The undertaker agreed to keep her until my father was ready. They could come home together.

I drove home trying to work out how to tell George that his mother had spent eighteen years in an urn, on a filing cabinet, in that gloomy back office. It always surprised me that George was frequently disappointed with, exasperated, and embarrassed by his brother, but was never angry with him. It was as though George was the elder and thought Henry was in some way disadvantaged and couldn't help it.[1] This time he was just desperately sad. Their mother had expressly wished that her ashes be scattered at Ten Rides. Whenever George had asked when they were going to do it Henry had said that he would let him know then one day he said that he had done it by himself, without George.

It was an ignominious interlude for a remarkable woman. Her mother was the eldest daughter of Bertha Mansell-Talbot and John Fletcher, Tenth Laird of Saltoun in East Lothian. 'Miss' Talbot's estate stretched, without much interruption, from Margam Abbey, above Port Talbot, to Oxwich point. It was said that she and her agent could travel eleven miles before leaving her land. Violet Fletcher, their eldest child, married Lt Colonel Bertram Meeking. They had two daughters Viola, who became Lady Apsley and Finola who became Lady Somers. Bertram Meeking died of dysentery in the Boer War. Violet, Viola and Finola were devoted, and when, in due course Violet married Herbert Johnson, they became devoted to him too. 'Jonny Johnson' was a friend of Edwin Lutyens who had built him a fabulous house, fit for entertaining the grandest, Marsh Court, in Hampshire. So, Viola and Finola travelled between South Wales, Scotland, Hampshire, Buckinghamshire and London, pausing along the routes to stalk deer; stand encouragingly behind grouse butts; hunt with different packs six days a week in the season, and dance the evenings away.

Their paternal grandfather, Colonel Charles Meeking had owned real estate in Buckinghamshire and Marylebone. In the way that estate ownership circulated round the landed families, the Bathursts had owned Richings Park in the 18th century.[2] Lord Bathurst had wanted an escape from Apsley House and the smoke and smells of London and had laid out the park including an avenue of chestnut trees dedicated to Pope – 'Pope's Walk'. By the mid-19th century it had been sold to the Meekings. The Meekings, of Irish descent, had owned a large shop in Holborn and they too had wanted to escape the putrid London air. Viola and Finola's grandfather consolidated the Buckinghamshire estate when he married Sophia Tower, daughter of a neighbour.

---

1   *The two brothers could not have been more different physically or intellectually, something Henry found difficult to handle. In 1945 R T Assheton wrote to Lady Apsley "...(George's) mind is cast in a different mould from Henry's: his is the curious, acquisitive, and retentive mind; and in the General Knowledge paper he came out 124th, or about 350 places higher than his elder brother!"*

2   *Viola Meeking (Apsley) sold Richings in 1922. Situated where the M4 eastbound meets the M25. Bathurst Walk is a residential road. The house was demolished in 1946. The Park is a golf course.*

As a sixty-eight-year-old widower, still mourning his son, Charles Meeking married his French companion, who ran under the name Marie Michelle Anne Sybille Dedons de Pierre-Feu, Comtesse de Coligny, and ten months later they had a daughter – Sybille Marie Anne.[3] In under four years he had died, choking on his breakfast, but not before he had altered his will, leaving the London estates, including a chunk near Oxford Street, to the comtesse, who smartly sold up and hoofed it back to France. Foul play was suspected by those who had presumed to inherit, and it was Viola who managed to persuade the authorities to exhume her grandfather's body to see whether poison could be traced. Nothing untoward was detected.

In 1924 Viola married Lord Apsley, the eldest son of the seventh Earl Bathurst. In 1917 a month after his twenty second birthday he had won a Military Cross (MC) for storming a wireless station near Damascus and showing 'splendid gallantry and marked ability to command'. By the time he was twenty-three he had added a DSO to his ribbons. Viola Apsley took three lady's maids on honeymoon, to look after her clothes. Within months she was in the outback of Australia looking after her husband, living in a wooden shack, as he grubbed tree trunks out of virgin territory with teams of eight horses. Lord Apsley was Parliamentary Private Secretary to the Under Secretary of State for the Overseas Trade Department and word had reached Westminster that conditions for the 'settlers' were not as they had been marketed so the Apsleys went out, under cover, to find out first-hand. 'Mr Bott', the name borrowed from the Bathurst stud groom, and later renamed Mrs and Mrs James, travelled on false papers arranged by the Foreign Office.[4] Both born with immense privilege they were a formidable pair without any sense of entitlement.

VA as she was known in the family, became a competitive car hill-climber, gained her pilot's licence by the time she was thirty and produced an heir, and a spare. Then disaster struck. While hunting with her father-in-law's hounds near Coln St Aldwyn, her horse stumbled on the landing side of a hedge, by a rabbit warren, and rolled on her. Her back, wedged between the stirrup and saddle, snapped. A five-barred gate was taken off its hinges and used as a stretcher to get her to the nearest road. As soon as the seriousness of her injury

---

3 *She changed her name to Annick Maeking, and married François Richepin in 1928.*
4 *Their book 'The Amateur Settlers' was published by Hodder and Stoughton in 1926.*

became clear she was taken to Edinburgh, where a new approach to back injuries was being tested. She spent the next few years almost horizontal, in a specially constructed wheelchair, in the hope that if her back was kept flat it might mend, but it didn't. She never walked again.

When it looked as though Hitler would invade, George and Henry were sent out of danger to Ridley College, Ontario. By December 1942 the threat had passed, and they returned to be 'suitably' educated at Eton. Lord Apsley, serving with the Arab Legion, was coming back on leave to see them and enjoy a family Christmas, when the Halifax DT542, that had stopped to refuel en route to Gibraltar thence home, exploded on take-off from Malta.[5] All fifteen on board perished. Nine months later Lord Bathurst died. Henry his heir, was only sixteen and VA, set about managing things for her eldest son. She settled what many thought insurmountably crippling death duties and saved Cirencester Park in its entirety. She took over her husband's seat in parliament and represented Bristol Central until defeated in the 1945 election, by Jennie Lee, wife of Aneurin Bevan.[6] She took on the mastership of the family hounds; she sat on numerous committees; organised a pageant; co-wrote two books on riding; compiled *The Foxhunter's Bedside Book*;[7] sat on the committee of the Victoria League and was women's chairman of the British Legion, all done from a wheelchair. She died in 1966, to be left on a filing cabinet.

On the day of my father's cremation, George picked some roses for the coffin, augmenting them with dog roses. Five of us crammed into the car. As we came up behind the hearse on the road to Cheltenham, George announced that we were running out of petrol. He never like having capital tied up unnecessarily. We agreed it would be unfortunate to stutter to a halt before we got there, so George floored it, and as we flew past the undertakers, their inscrutable faces flickered astonishment when they realised it was us. Daddy would have laughed. They overtook us while we were in the petrol station, and we caught up with them as the hearse cruised between the Edwardian gates

---

5   *It is thought to have been sabotage. The crew was Polish, and it was rumoured that, Wladyslaw Sikorski, Prime Minister of the Polish government-in-exile and Commander in Chief of the Polish Armed Forces was on board. He met his end six months later when his aeroplane exploded in similar circumstances, on take-off from Gibraltar.*

6   *Aneurin Bevan was the Labour Minster for Health 1945–1951. His National Health Service Act 1946 came into force in 1948.*

7   *The Foxhunter's Bedside Book published in 1949 by Eyre and Spottiswoode was illustrated by VA's family friend from Marsh Court days – Lionel Edwards with a jacket designed by Cecil Aldin. It is the ultimate hunter's anthology.*

of the crematorium. Smoke billowed from the chimney. The eleven o'clock slot was going up. George put the roses on the coffin. Daddy would have loved that he had included dog roses. Our local vicar was waiting for us. I had been persuaded that it would be easier if we had one as it would give the proceedings structure. As he led me from the waiting room along the passage to the chapel the muzak started its loop.

"Please can you get that turned off." I asked

"What? No music?"

"No music. Please." If only we could have had a Bottesini or Hummel requiem I would have flown with it, but it would have reduced me to tears. It was as well.

Considering that he knew my father was an atheist the vicar gave a convincing service. Brief. A spoken prayer. He pressed the switch. The castors squeaked as the pink velour curtains surrounded the coffin. Just before they closed, I could see the doors beyond it slide open. We went out into bright sunshine. The undertakers had already left. I thanked the vicar. That was that. I'd held it together.

"Let's go." I didn't want to see Daddy's smoke. We overtook the empty hearse on the way back to Cirencester.

*

In the autumn, when a digger was on the farm, we took delivery of two well grown pink horse-chestnut saplings. I collected the boy from school, the weekend's meat from the butcher, and popped next door to the undertaker. When I returned to the car with two cardboard boxes, our son chirruped from the back seat: "Ooooh, presents for me?"

I distracted him by pointing to a B52 flying in the sky high above the town, heading for Fairford. I did not tell him that two of his grandparents were in the boxes. George scattered my father and I scattered VA in the big holes made by the digger. The design of pinkish grey plastic urn hadn't changed in twenty years. I put her funeral sheet with her as George asked and noticed that the date had been altered in ball point pen. Presumably some secretary, or George, had corrected every service sheet before the service. Had nothing been done properly for her? We planted the trees and fetched a couple of barrows of well-rotted manure from the stable yard. We might have been terribly sad but there was something rather comforting about having them back home, in the field

161

in front of the house, with us. At the outbreak of war VA had bought the field, the house, the village and the surrounding thousand or so acres, with her own money left from the sale of Richings. She was home.

Henry went to his grave in 2011, thinking his mother was still in the undertaker's office forty-six years after he had abandoned her there, if he ever gave any of his family a second thought.

*

After my father's death Uncle decided to take up the role of Senior Relative and occasionally would write to me on an A4 sheet of lightweight paper. He used an elderly typewriter, the 'R' typed a 'P', on both sides of the paper and then corrected in ink with minuscule handwriting. There was often an apologetic postscript along the lines of 'I shouldn't bore you with this.'

Over the months I gathered threads. He gave the impression of a weak, and later in life a bitter, unforgiving person. Unsurprisingly. He had been five years old when his mother died and did not appear to have had my mother's umph or humour. Perhaps it had been squeezed out of him. On leaving The Central he had become a successful graphic designer, had worked for advertising agencies but managed to time his departure from a successful agency, where he had been well remunerated, to one that immediately went bust. 'Saved' from unemployment by WWII he ended up first as a prisoner in Changi Prison in Singapore, then transferred to Burma to help build the railroad, Death Railway. That would have been enough to destroy anyone, and did kill an estimated one hundred thousand, but he returned home to find that while he had been wracked by the Japanese, his beloved older sister, the one on whom he had relied after their mother had died, had not only been celebrating love and marriage but was enjoying the joy of a new-born. In a miscalculated effort to join in the fun he quickly married someone who everyone else knew to be a lesbian. The marriage was not consummated. They divorced. The episode made him look a fool; his disappointment with life was amplified. He married again. His second wife was a kind, restorative success and they moved to Spain to start afresh, and Uncle dropped off the radar. In that cruel way that makes one doubt the munificence of The Almighty, she soon died from cancer.

He bounced to his third wife. A widowed mother of two daughters, she taught English in Spain. They moved to Canada to be near one of the daughters. By the time he reappeared they were living in Shropshire to be near the other. Then the spiral of reducing circumstances spun them to a terrace house, in a one-street hamlet dissected by an A road in the middle of Welsh nowhere. The front door led directly onto the road (he wrote); the house shook when lorries passed; he was worried about the two cats being run over and the back garden, such as it was, rose too steeply to the mountain behind for him to be able to dig and create a vegetable patch.

"At least the roof keeps out the rain, but I am not sure that I can live through another winter like this."

I had nothing to give him, and he wasn't George's problem. I suggested that we sold Derick's Japanese stuff on loan to the Ashmoleon Museum. He and Betty could share my third. It would give him enough money to find somewhere better. He wrote back that we had donated Derick's collection to the Ashmoleon. There was no point remonstrating but no wonder he was in a pickle. Magnanimous gestures are very well if you can afford them. He could not. They moved to a mobile home on a caravan park in Devon.

In an attempt at farm diversification, we had converted a Cotswold barn for self-catering holidays and the following summer I suggested to the uncle that he brought Betty with them for a week's holiday. I had toyed with two weeks, as there was a gap in bookings, but thought better of it. A week would provide ample chance for brother and sister to be together and for me to meet my mother's family. I felt there must be more to it than the story so far. If it was a wild success they could come again.

Maud, Mrs Grigs Mk III, led them from Uncle's aged but meticulously kept car. The container carrying the bulk of their belongings had been lost overboard somewhere mid Atlantic on the way back from Canada and Uncle took great care of what was left. It was clear from the outset that Maud did not intend to be overawed by those she ridiculously thought to be patronising her by not charging for a holiday. Her ample bosom, that sailed before her like a bowsprit, stretched a white acrylic cardigan to breaking point. The heavily embroidered faux mother of pearl beads arranged as sprays of flowers rose and fell as she breathed. Even George, who had a track record of charming Conservative party subscriptions out of similar women, for his old friend Nicholas Ridley,[8] was challenged by Maud. She turned out to be a racist and a bully. Betty looked desolate in sympathy for Uncle. We soon realised a week

---

8   *Lord Ridley of Liddesdale, Conservative MP for Cirencester and Tewkesbury 1959-1992. Various cabinet posts under Margaret Thatcher.*

would be more than enough of Maud, but I wanted more time with Betty. I became less reticent about taking issue with Maud and started to argue with her about everything from whether Henry Moore could draw, she though not, to whether all the Vietnamese boat people should have been left to drown.[9] I thought not. Betty's eyes supported me.

As delighted as I was when Uncle drove his bigoted wife out of sight, I had been sad to wave goodbye to Betty. She had been directed to the back seat by her sister-in-law from which she managed an apologetic wave. In the week she rarely had been allowed to open her mouth, let alone express an opinion. I wanted to get to know her better. I invited her to stay and a few months later I drove to Oxford to collect her.

I found her pebbledash semi-detached house in a road that led only to Exeter College Sportsground and meadows bordering the Cherwell. Helianthemum and aubrieta had self-seeded and were crawling over the two concreted tracks that led to a corrugated iron sheeted garage, not big enough to take a family car. I had seen her watch me, half-hidden by the curtain in the ground floor bay window, but when she opened the door, the chain remained hooked to prevent it from opening more than a few inches. Her face peeped round.

"Ah, it's you." she said with emphasis on the you, expressing surprised delight.

"Will you come in?" Although not even a thin cat could have bent itself through the opened slit, the gap had let a blast of stale air escape into the sunshine. I couldn't face going in and pretended that we were in a hurry to get back. Betty emerged wearing a belted mackintosh and carrying a small, square, brown overnight case. She looked the parody of a child evacuated from London to escape The Blitz.

The summer light on the fields, still a month off harvest, made our drive home over The Wolds a delight. Everything looked ready for John Nash to set-up his easel. I was disappointed that she had not brought hers. It wasn't only that she could have occupied herself while we were busy on the farm, but I knew that she was an exceptionally good painter. She had been the first pupil to gain a scholarship from Northampton School of Art to the Royal College of Art. She had spent her working life as an art teacher. She belonged to the Oxford Art Group and some of her paintings, if not actually hung, were in Northampton Art Gallery's collection.

---

9   *Following the end of the Vietnam War in 1975 there was an exodus by sea of refugees that continued until the mid-1990s. It reached a crescendo 1978/1979. It is estimated that between 200,000 and 400,000 drowned.*

I started to send her postcards from every exhibition I visited; we exchanged Christmas cards; she sent birthday cards, I only learned the date of hers the year she died. Once her great nephew had started at Stowe, I would scoop her up, from time to time, and take her to watch him play rugby or cricket. She looked as happy sitting in a deck chair on the North Front watching the cricket, with one of our terriers on her lap, as much as tucking into the match teas. After my son left school, I would take her to a pub for lunch. Whenever we had her to stay, I drove us to Exmouth to see Maud and Uncle. Lunch in a pub of their choice was never fun. Uncle complained about the food and referred to his bad digestion. Maud scowled in undisguised dislike of the two siblings and their niece. On the way back we shared worries about him but not her.

Like a rescue dog, it took time to gain Betty's confidence. Over the next decade I pieced together some of her life. She let slip a little, but Uncle drip-fed snippets that made me think he was trying to put me off getting close to her. It was as though he was jealous of the time we spent together, which I understood, especially as Maud wouldn't let him invite Betty to stay. Not, as Betty told me, that she would have gone. Maud had made it too unpleasant the last time.

When Betty graduated from the Royal College, she took jobs teaching first in Northampton near her widowed mother, then in Cornwall. She didn't want to leave her but her mother pushed her off.

"I'll manage, now go, get on with your life."

Months later she was discovered dead on the kitchen floor, and it was unclear how long she had been there. It was never established what had happened, but Betty blamed herself for having left, and she had a nervous breakdown. The Cornish mental health authorities decided that a few doses of a hundred volts zapped between her temples would shock her out of it but they did not. She was diagnosed as schizophrenic, a label that was tied round her neck for the rest of her life.

She moved to Oxford where Derick worked on the *Oxford Mail*. Black and white photographs show two laughing children both in single figures, running towards the camera holding hands. Bachelor half-brother and spinster sister, only three years apart, were together again and rarely out of each other's company. When Derick moved to London to work for *The Times*, her social life stalled. In the mid-sixties she became head of the art department at St Frideswide's School and when it became Didcot Girls' School, she transferred to that. Every weekday, whatever the weather, she walked the mile and a half across the Meadows, down Beaumont Street past the Ashmoleon to Oxford station and took the train to Didcot. She took the same route back each evening. I imagine she didn't have the easiest time. She would have found the noise, smoke, and politics of a staff common room far from congenial and I doubt whether many of the teenage girls were interested in what she had to say about art, but she stuck it. I later found a reference in which the head concluded 'I cannot recall that she was ever absent, and she was always punctual'. Despite that she was retired, against her wishes, after twenty years. Education had moved on, away from her. She was in her early fifties.

SIXTEEN

TARLTON – BAGENDON

1986–1990

When our son went to boarding school, his cheerfulness left with him; the leavening had left the house and there was no longer any necessity to maintain the bravura. The endless cycle of bills, chilblains, lambing, bills, harvest, chilblains, bills, and lambing dragged on. I foolishly had manoeuvred myself into being responsible for far too much. One day a friend gave me a talking to.

"Your life does not have to be like this. God does not award you Brownie points. It's not a rehearsal."

A short time afterwards Chris, our manager at Coutts, said the same thing.

"It is not necessary for you to do all this. I could reorganise the finances. Let me see what I can do".

George thought money was not something to be talked about – doing so was vulgar. While he valued country people such as gamekeepers and huntsmen as deserving respect and affection, solicitors and bank managers were not to be trusted. He referred to them by their surnames as though they were his grandfather's footmen. To keep them in the dark he shuffled money between Coutts, The Royal Bank of Scotland, and Barclays. On the annual visit from Coutts, Chris's cufflinks became snagged in the frayed cover of the armchair, and he was tethered by his wrists, listening to details of George's latest invention. He got nowhere trying to change the subject to reorganising finances.

George had inherited the house and a couple of paddocks on his mother's death and had seen no need to change anything. Confined to her wheelchair she had never gone upstairs and one of the downstairs rooms had served as her bedroom. Seven years after her death her powder compact and silk stockings remained in her dressing table and the large cast iron bath, in one corner of the room, beneath hooks in the ceiling for the winch needed to extract her from the water, collected old magazines and spiders. The boots from which she had been cut at the time of her accident forty years earlier were still in the boot room. George had seen no need to face up to their removal. Neither had he felt the need to maintain the house. Twenty years on, the only time there was not a howling gale under the front door was when the snow had mounted into a sizeable drift in the hall. Pipes froze when the wind came from the east. Water dripped through two floors from the attic and the Persian rugs in the drawing room floated. The boiler took up most of the cellar and drank fuel faster than George paid for it. While he could spot a fox half a mile off, he didn't see flaking paint or notice that the carpets' frayed edges fluttered in the draft that came under the skirting boards. He thought it normal to have enamel bowls strategically placed on perished army groundsheets in our bedroom, to catch the drips from the split lead above the bay window.

The eccentricity of living in a decaying house was no longer amusing. One morning, after six weeks without sleep, lambing in foul weather, and having spent the night trying to persuade a bitch of a ewe to let at least one of her quadruplets suckle, George said that I would have to get a job to pay for an upcoming dentist appointment. He could not have timed it worse. I wasn't up for a job search.

Nearly four years later, Jonathan, my counsel, took me and Helen my solicitor, to lunch at Manzi's, the excellent fish restaurant off Leicester Square. Five days had been booked in court to settle things and the two of them had managed to negotiate a settlement in half a day. Jonathan hadn't told his scout so that he could have one of the four freed-up days to celebrate.

When Helen had learned which judge was to hear our case, she had been worried. He had the reputation of fixing financial settlements on whether he thought the plaintiff was re-marriageable. So, I had let my hair grow and had flattened it with spray. I had bought a pale grey suit with a slightly too long

A-line skirt and found some hideous flesh coloured seventy denier tights in the sale basket in Boots. I wore a crisply clean white shirt and old, highly polished, nearly flat shoes: I was a study in respectability and terribly dull. I felt like a noviciate. A friend dropped me off outside Somerset House, where the Court of Probate was housed, and shouted from the car window:

"Good luck! You look great, you look ghastly!"

The judge sat with his back to the window. Through the trees behind him I watched River Thames traffic as the barristers introduced themselves and their clients. A tug towed two barges of yellow waste containers towards the estuary; a police launch sped upstream. Preliminaries over, we filed out and left the judge to his piles of paper. Helen and I settled on a stone staircase. George and his solicitor found a perch down the corridor. Our counsels travelled between us, negotiating. Helen personified the instruction element of being the instructing solicitor. She was impressive. Jonathan, at least a decade her senior, would come back with a fresh suggestion.

"Sue can't possibly live on that!" she'd say sending him back to George's team for more.

After some hours we filed back into the judge's sunlit office with a proposal. Whether he thought my only chance of marriage was to God or whether he was a Bollinger Bolshevik and was appalled at this minor aristo's affidavit describing the dowdy woman before him as an adventurer was not clear but he signed off on a generous sum.

Before lunch with Jonathan and Helen, I had been to Sweeney's for The Haircut having bought champagne and orange juice en route. As Greg's scissors snipped and my hair floated to the black and white tiled floor of the Beauchamp Place cellar, we celebrated with Bucks Fizz. I met Helen walking towards Manzi's, "Thank God you didn't look like that yesterday!"

It is humiliating upending the laundry basket of one's life onto legal eagles' desks and I had had this overwhelming feeling of disloyalty to the man whose foibles had at first seemed endearing; whom I had stood behind and made excuses for; whom I had once loved. I felt a failure having not made it work; that I hadn't been up to the task; a feeling of inadequacy. I wouldn't wish divorce on anybody but after three years of affidavits and court orders I found myself on the springboard for what has proved the second half of my life. It was wonderful to celebrate with the team who enabled that. We spent a gleeful afternoon laughing and splashing. Driving back to Gloucestershire was like going off on holiday.

My life became mine. Within the parameter of school terms, I could do what I liked and could afford. I resumed friendships with those I had not seen since marriage. I went on holiday with whom I liked, wherever I was invited. I could have anyone to stay or to supper and could eat anything at any hour. I went to the opera, concerts, cinema, and art exhibitions and did not have to apologise to George if they fell short of his expectation or apologise to friends if George fell asleep in the front row of a concert hall. Alfred Brendel's beady eyes had given him a very hard look when he took the applause at the end of one recital. Best of all I was in control of my house thermostat.

*

I hadn't lived on lentils, but once George had decided to 'starve me out of the silly idea' it had been thanks to Chris at Coutts that I hadn't needed to live on the generosity of my flexible friend. Chris had been super-supportive.

"It'll all work out, Sue. Don't worry."

He had been right. Once a year he invited me to lunch in the bank. The wine cellar was as is rumoured and the food always delicious, but the real treat was to see the Chinese Room with its beautiful wallpaper illustrating tea, rice, and silk production. It had been cleverly moved from Sir George Macartney's place next door in 1905. Invitations to concerts in the atrium and sponsored events in the country rolled in. As I was swept along by the charming, solicitous men in frock coats, I thought how it would make my father laugh at how things had changed.

I had to find somewhere to live within six months or penalty clauses came into play. I thought about Dorset and Northumberland, but friends touchingly said they didn't mind my divorcing a Bathurst, but they would mind if I left Gloucestershire. They went into overdrive to find me somewhere and five months later I signed the contract for a house not yet on the market. It has been home for over thirty years.

When the economy dipped in the early '90s my generous divorce settlement's earning power dipped with it, and I ended up working part-time as personal assistant to the owner of a stately home. I was responsible for everything and all the staff that were not income generating. The 'Private' stuff. Inevitably there was crossover with the areas and staff that involved the public, who paid a not inconsiderable amount for a ticket to see what Victorians had done to a Cromwellian ruin. I quickly fell into and enjoyed being part of a team of over sixty, including gardeners, guides, cleaners, restaurant workers, an office team and a shop manager. Almost to a person they were from the local small town and were excellent at what they did, and they had unwavering loyalty to the place, if not to the owner, who had arrived by marriage. There were some wonderful paintings of international importance that I never became tired of, but otherwise there was nothing about it, or the majority of its contents that I would have wanted even had I fallen under the spell of an oligarch. The windows were high, so only the tallest could look out. While the acres of assorted garden rooms had some pleasing spaces, it was at the bottom of a hill and there were no views. I like being on top of the world not under it. I think it had the overall effect of depressing the owner, whom I liked, but it meant I could work there happily, and return home at the end of each day, content with my lot.

The owner spent midweek in London catching up on body maintenance, urban life, and being entertained by the directors of the big auction houses, each one hoping to be handed the next Old Master needing to be sold. The minute the car was spotted driving away between the gatehouses, word came across the estate walkie talkie:

"The Eagle Has Flown."

This was the cue for the chief executive to do the circuit turning off all the radiators with a satisfied flourish as he went. One could see his visualising the magical reduction in the 'Overheads' column of the spreadsheet when it was presented to the trustees at the end of the year. With the owner away he toured all department heads, who knew more about their jobs than he did, to tell them what they were doing wrong. On Friday mornings, when the owner was due back, he went round turning all the radiators on to high. It was almost possible to hear the furniture and picture frames creak uncomfortably as the damp dried and they contracted. He put an embargo on the clearing of leaves from roof gullies which proved a mistake impossible to hide when water streamed down a couple of internal walls. Asked by the owner what had gone wrong, he blamed the maintenance man.

I had never spent time in the company of army officers, but it struck me odd that one who had never had to worry about buildings or their maintenance, because the Property Services Agency did it all, should have been appointed to look after one of the great houses.[1] Equally strange that one who had spent over thirty-five years ordering people to do things, safe in the knowledge that if they did not jump-to they risked court marshall, should be put in charge of country people who will do anything if asked, but whose hackles rise and do a great deal less if not asked nicely. Inadvertently, it was a master stroke of team building because everyone came to loathe the man, but within two years all but about ten staff had left and had to be replaced or 'done without'. More savings in the 'Salaries' column.

I left after two years, partly because I knew my dislike of him was mutual and I didn't trust him not to point the finger of theft – which he did without foundation, to the next PA. When he retired the following chief executive (why do essentially rural businesses try to sound like multinationals?) persuaded me to return to help with the marketing, visitors, weddings and commercial entertainment. I worked as assistant to someone who had been hugely successful in two of the most famous historic houses in the realm. He was not only huge fun to work with but taught me a lot. He could tell you, off the top of his head, everything from how many portable loos would be needed for a gathering of the Sealed Knot, through how to maximise the speedy flow of cars for a music festival to formatting a check list for a wedding of six hundred. A traditionally true gentleman, all the staff loved him but inevitably he was offered another house. I was invited to replace him, but the hours were not reflected by pay. One cannot barter elegant work surroundings for food at the supermarket check-out. We resigned within half of an hour of each other. A year later I had set up a consultancy and managed to persuade him to join me in advising on the management and commercialisation of historic property.

Over the years divorce settlements and school fees had eaten into trust funds. Many smaller historic homeowners were opening letters from their bank managers and the reality that they were going to have to do 'something' if they wished to continue living in houses with corridors of bedrooms and their own ballrooms and chapels. Such owners wrongly believed that if the

---

1   *The PSA was a government department that managed, furnished, and maintained all government owned establishments and property 1972-1993. It superseded the Ministry of Works. Army barracks and property now are looked after for the Ministry of Defence by the Defence Estates.*

Devonshires could keep the acres of roof on Chatsworth, and still have spare to commission and invest in high value modern art, it couldn't be that difficult.

We had the privilege of going behind the green baize doors of more than a hundred historic houses in two years, and although we didn't make much money, we saw beautiful houses, many in the last throes of private ownership, and we met as many of their charming if totally bonkers owners.

There was the crescent shaped house where the owner thought a job lot of beds from a prep-school liquidation sale would be ideal for wedding guests. There was the house where the Romneys and Gainsboroughs had been sold 'to keep the rats at bay' but photographs of them had been printed on paper textured to look like canvas. The owner had bought a variety of frames from an antique shop. "No one can tell the difference." We weren't sure about that.

At the insistence of one house owner's wife, a hot tub had been installed at the end of a four-poster bed in 'Queen Victoria's Bedroom', she had stayed there once on the way North. It hadn't been used because 'it always leaked'. The wife had left but the rotted carpet remained. In another house, the bedroom we were shown, that was thought would 'do' for the bride's parents, turned out to be the eldest son's. The walls were plastered with life-sized posters of naked girls.

"It's a bit untidy but Nanny can tidy up! She hasn't got much to do now that the children have left." Nanny looked as unsteady on her feet as the elderly Labrador.

An earlier financial crisis had caused another owner to sell off the Home Farm for building and the house was surrounded by a housing estate. It felt as though the place was under siege.

"*Rus in urbe*," he laughed, "and I probably have more bedrooms than the lot of them put together!"

Perhaps, we thought, but too many kerbs for appeal. Within a few years a high-class developer would turn his house into gracious apartments for those going up or down the ladder. He was a nice old thing. Hopefully he still had a Scottish lodge with unblemished vistas of Munros across the glen if the mists ever lifted.

One owner invited us to lunch. We had driven up to tall, closed, wrought iron gates held together by earls' coronets and discreetly twisted garden wire. Dangling from a couple of the balls was a notice to keep the gates shut. The drive and gravel sweep were indicated only by indentations in what was more like a hayfield than an ancestral approach. It was the most beautiful, not dauntingly large Regency house, and as we climbed the shallow steps to the front door, a herd of about twenty horses, of every age, from foal to sway-backed old faithful, thundered round the corner to say hello.

"Ah – you've met the family!" said the owner as he opened one of the double doors.

We were given delicious dry sherry from Averys in generous, chipped, leaded crystal glasses, delicately engraved with meadow flowers. If they had been washed since last used, they hadn't seen soap. Lunch was cooked by the countess.

"We hope you don't mind; we use cook's sitting room when we're *con la famiglia.*" Lunch was dubious sausages and barely defrosted peas. I hoped my stomach still harboured the Hanford antibodies. Delicious coffee came from a restaurant grade espresso machine.

"One must keep up standards, not only our great, great, greats toured Italy!"

Somewhere in the Welsh Marches, there was a vast pile of bricks, that looked like a railway station. 'One of the old aunts', to whom we were not introduced and appeared only a few decades younger than the bricks, shadowed us muttering to herself. As we drove away, we debated whether she kept an axe under her cardigan.

"Well, it's got a lake and some good trees, might work as a film location?"

"More Vincent Price than Colin Firth."

We were shown an orangery as somewhere thought to be perfect for dances. Too much glass was missing. It might have been possible had we pitched a transparent marquee inside, but that would have detracted from the ornate iron that once supported the panes, and the roots of deceased jungle plants had raised the floor tiles into ridge and furrow. The era of the Turkey Trot had passed. It would have needed a false floor as well. That house had the added problem of the divorced octogenarian parents living in the East and West wings, separated by the main block and their son and daughter-in-law. They would not allow music after nine o'clock. The grandchildren believed they turned their hearing aids to max so they could make sure the rule was observed.

Those owners who had marked the cost of replacing miles of braid-covered electric cable against the income from the house-herd of Jersey cows, were doing well and didn't need advice but many of the owners we visited already had hit their bankers' buffers and were not about to be lent the thousands of thousands needed to tart-up their houses. They were familiarly like George. They did not see that old chamber pots catching drips, even those with crests and coronets, and dead jackdaws in fireplaces, do not add value to the experience. Brides' mothers and captains of industry might be put off from paying a deposit for a marquee on the old croquet lawn excavated by family terriers following moles' infrastructure, or the use of a dining room hung with as many Edwardian cobwebs as hunting scenes. We were too late for most.

From time to time, I took in students from the Royal Agricultural College and occasionally did B&B. I met people from all over the globe, whom I would never have met otherwise, gathered more friends, widened horizons, and had a lot of fun.

SEVENTEEN

BETTY

2004

Betty telephoned, asking whether I could be with her the following morning. Her psychiatrist was coming to assess her and she wanted support. I had become used to braving the fetid atmosphere of her house and I realised that she never opened windows because she was frightened of intruders. I had watched her measure water by the mugful into a chipped blue and black enamel saucepan so as not to waste gas in boiling more than was necessary. I knew that she only had one easy chair in her sitting room; nobody visited her so why would she need another? A foxed mirror in a dark wood frame was hung on a rusty chain from the picture rail, a timber tool chest supported a spider plant and the bookcase looked as though it had been made in a woodwork class. The books were crammed in horizontally as well as vertically. The dining room contained a flip-top desk, a blistered, gatelegged table and four rush-seated chairs. The window looked over a long garden of brambles and thistles. At the far end was a gnarled apple tree, probably planted in the early '30s, at the same time as the house. All perfect cover for an urban vixen to raise a litter. The avocado bathroom suite had crusty aquamarine stripes below the taps and the back bedroom, glimpsed through the half-closed door, was stacked with canvasses, her north facing studio. Betty's living conditions no longer concerned me; it was her home as she liked it.

Two women from the Warneford Hospital stood under the feature-brick arch of the porch. I introduced myself as I let them in. Betty as always, hung back, watching from the kitchen. Seeing that there were two of them she fetched a second chair from the dining room. I sat beside the pot plant on the chest. I was there to support not interfere. The lead was in her mid-twenties, probably recently qualified. I reckoned the older one was the mentor. It was unfortunate that the mentor had not told the mentee that she was inappropriately dressed for a consultation with someone from another era. She wore a micro, black, faux-leather skirt, black faux-leather boots that strained over her calves, and there was a great deal of black hosed flesh between them. The size of her thighs prevented her sitting with her knees together. Betty's face blanked the view.

"We are just here to review your medication, Betty. How are you feeling today?"

Betty had told me that she didn't like her medication as it had unfortunate side-effects. I hadn't wanted too much detail. Sometimes she remembered to take her pills, sometimes she did not. It didn't seem to make any difference to her 'mood' she said, but she needed me there to make sure they didn't force her into anything she didn't want.

After quarter of an hour of the lead trying, and failing, to elicit more than monosyllables from Betty, she changed tack.

"Oh Betteeeee, I see you have lots of books. Do you really read? Read books?"

Poor Betty. I couldn't keep zipped.

"Would it help if you knew that Betty's father was a barrister; that her younger brother was awarded a scholarship to Jesus College; that her sister was one of Fleet Street's leading journalists… as a family we all read books."

A smile glimmered on Betty's face. The psychologist pencilled notes and rather hastily assured Betty that her medication needed no adjustment. After I had closed the door behind them, Betty gave me the broadest smile I had seen her make.

"Thank goodness you were here. Thank you so much. They come here to bully me. I wish they'd leave me alone."

I don't think that they had any intention of bullying her. They simply had no idea how to handle Betty, who kept her verbal interaction to a minimum. Those with more experience than they, had deemed her schizophrenic. It was on file. In this day and age Care in the Community was thought preferable to incarceration and it was safer to keep up the dope than risk finding a banshee on their watch. Sometimes the silent ones were the worst. She might turn dangerously nuts without warning.

A few weeks later we were in a pub when Betty took a brown envelope from her shoulder bag and pushed it gingerly across the table.

"Would you come with me? Please."

It was from the oncology department of the John Radcliffe Hospital. Betty had been given an appointment with the consultant regarding the tumour in her breast. It was for the following day. As my mother had died of breast cancer, I'd often wondered whether I would follow suit. I had a pretty good idea of the fear; of what Betty must be going through.

As we sat in the waiting room it struck me how many people must have cancer if it needed to have so many chairs. We waited for her name to be called. She told me that she had been diagnosed some months before. She had known throughout the interview with those from the Warneford and she had not let on. While they had been thinking about what was happening in her head, she had been worrying about what was happening in her breast. Her name was called. I remained seated, I didn't know her well enough to get up so personal, so close, but she asked me to go with her. We traipsed to a side room.

The disarmingly young, and good-looking consultant drew the nylon curtain behind them, round the bed. I remained by the desk, watching shadows, hearing everything.

"Now, if you could take off your clothes, please. No, not your skirt that won't be necessary, just your top half. If you want help, Sister is here for you. While you're doing that, I'll put my hands under the tap to warm them up… perfect… is that alright? Not cold? Fine… sorry could you raise your arms please. Thank you… and there… slightly this way… and yes that's lovely. Thank you."

I wondered whether anyone had told Betty her breasts were lovely; had ever seen them or even looked at them; I doubted any man had ever touched them and I cringed with embarrassment for her. When, after she had dressed, the nurse had drawn back the curtains, the consultant said:

"I'm happy with you."

I wondered how long it had been since anyone had said that to her. I took her home and tried to be upbeat.

"I think it's good, Betty. He said he's pleased. It hasn't grown and at your age it's unlikely to grow fast anyway. Just keep taking the tablets and you should be OK. Great news. Marvellous!"

But the next month when I visited, she was distressed. She thought it must be the olanzapine the psychiatrists had given her that made her hands shake so much that she couldn't keep matches still enough to light her oven. The cooker, probably there since the house was built, looked ready to explode. I thought it a good thing she couldn't light the gas but she had not been eating hot food although the leaves were changing; the days were shortening and the evening air was distinctly chilled. I bought her a cheap microwave and a kettle from Tesco, enough ready meals to fill her fridge and asked Wiltshire Farm Foods to send a brochure.

A few weeks later I answered the telephone to somebody who identified herself as a friend from 'Betty's church'. I had been surprised that Betty had a church. None of our family, her family, had been church goers or even baptised, but she had told me with a smile that when she was in her sixties 'some missionaries' from the parish had persuaded her to join them. She said that she wasn't at all convinced but she enjoyed helping to decorate the church for the harvest festival.

"The browns and yellows glow when the sun shines through the South windows."

She added that sometimes the music was good, and they did an excellent line in moist sponge cakes and coffee, after services. She hinted that it was worth attending for the refreshments That said she didn't trust them, and she had given me years of bank statements, collected in SPAR carrier bags, to take away with me. One of the missionaries had suggested that he, rather than her high-street bank, could manage her finances and she suspected her church of being after her money. I had been astonished when I had seen how much money she had. The state pension, her teacher's pension and the income from a modest share portfolio bequeathed by a relative, was not being dented by the woman whose only recipe book was *Cooking for the Poor*. Capital had been accruing year on year.

"We are worried about Betty," said the friend from church. "She is not answering the telephone or our knocks on the door. Is she away do you know?"

I said I'd see whether she had gone to her brother in Devon and ring her back. Uncle had not heard from her. I returned her call.

"Perhaps she has fallen... is lying on the floor... may we have your permission to break in?"

I recalled the way Betty's mother had lain dead for no one knew how long. It would be awful for history to repeat itself. Maybe she had fallen and was only unconscious. Twenty minutes later they had broken in and found no sign of her. Her bed had not been slept in; her clothes had been neatly folded on the chair; her purse was on her dressing table.

By lunchtime there was still no sign and the missionaries had been round and boarded up the window they had broken. I reported her missing to the Oxford police. Yes, it was out of character; no, she had no other friends that I knew of; yes, she did have another relative, but he hadn't heard from her. Yes, her brother, but he was in his 90s and lived in Devon; and yes, I supposed after him I was her next of kin. I was allocated an Officer in Charge and the police carried out a door-to-door of neighbouring streets that afternoon. The Officer in Charge, 'call me Sandra', reported no sightings by dusk. She asked whether I could meet her at Betty's house the following morning. We promised to let each other know if we heard anything.

"I'm sure there's no need to worry and we have asked the bus companies and British Rail to keep an eye open just in case. Sometimes ladies of your aunt's age become confused and can't remember where they're going."

I pointed out that as her purse was still in the house it would have been difficult to buy a ticket.

"Mmm," said Sandra, "and I don't like the idea of anyone spending a night out in this weather." It had been a particularly wet November and the rain was turning to sleet.

We unscrewed the board on the broken window and Sandra climbed in. Everything was as the missionaries described: neat, tidy, and abandoned; there was not even a dirty mug waiting to be washed up. Her winter coat was hanging on the back of the kitchen door. Her key fob was missing but we found a spare Yale, that fitted the front door.

"Do you mind if I have a photograph?"

I foraged in the desk and found a photograph of Betty and Uncle, taken on top of some windswept hill.

"I'm afraid it's not very recent."

"Don't worry – it's better than nothing. We can cut out the man. Do you mind if we go public with this? Tell the press. Someone must have seen her. We need to find her."

That evening I had drifted asleep in front of the television when my son woke me.

"Mum… Mum… it's Betty she's on telly." And there she was, the cropped photograph larger than life, her oversized grey and white face filling the flatscreen, wisps of hair blown from her bun.

"Police are worried about a missing eighty-year-old Oxford woman…" said the reporter, "Elisabeth Grigs, who lives alone, hasn't been seen for three days."

Betty's face was replaced by footage of police in waders walking through flooded fields and prodding hedges and water-filled ditches with poles.

"Police have been searching the flooded recreation grounds near Miss Grigs' house and University Parks. If anyone has any information, please telephone Oxford ******."

The weather forecaster predicted a very cold night and the possibility of snow in the small hours as northeast winds brought down another front. If she was still alive, she was going to be hypothermic. I thought how embarrassed she would be to be the centre of attention. She had managed to pass unnoticed for most of her life.

"I thought I'd 'phone you before the weekend," said Sandra "No news I'm afraid. It's not looking good." There was no news the next Friday, nor the next but on the Saturday afternoon Sandra telephoned.

"I'm afraid it's bad news. I think she's been found."

"Where?"

"In the river at Abingdon, a dog-walker spotted her. We're not certain it's her but it fits her description. We're sending someone over now. I am so sorry."

"Thank you, Sandra, but I think we knew."

Sandra had told the desk sergeant to expect me and as he led me along an unlit passage a cheerful policewoman in her thirties walked towards me and outstretched her hand.

"Hello Mrs Bathurst, I'm Sandra."

"Sue, please."

"Er thank you… it's very good of you to drive over, especially on this horrible day. How were the roads?"

"A bit dodgy but I've got a four-by-four… I need one where we live."

"Good, well I'm sorry to say we're pretty sure it's your aunt. I am just having the keys that were found on her sent up to see whether you think they are hers – we've had them drying out on the boiler."

We talked about her daughters. One was keen to have her ears pierced.

"She is only nine, I think she's too young but she's always trying to keep up with her older sister… she's thirteen… so grown up. As soon as they go to secondary school you begin to lose them." She talked of her seven-year-old son who had played his first game of rugby at the weekend.

"He's a toughie, I think he's had to protect himself from his sisters!"

181

A colleague arrived with the rusty bunch of keys stuck to a fogged Bodleian Library fob. There was no doubt. We matched the Yale to the one we had found in her house.

"Looks like it then. The coroner needs her identified. Do you wish to do it?"

"Are you m-a-d? I'd rather remember her alive – not a fake Damien Hurst." Before my father died, they had removed his false teeth so that he didn't choke. It took months for me to be able to recall his lovely smiling face and not that of his gaping mouth with the one remaining top tooth.

"Of course you don't have to. I took some hair from her hairbrush. We can use DNA."

"Thank God for that!"

"The other thing I have to ask you is do you want her clothing?"

"You are joking?"

"I have to ask."

I was sorry to say goodbye to Sandra as she shook my hand on the station steps. In three weeks, she had become a friendly voice; tactful and helpful and fun. Her children were lucky to have her, so had I been.

By the middle of the next week, she telephoned again.

"Sue, the coroner has finished with Betty, he wants her taken away. The mortuary is rather full. It's the weather, car crashes and those living rough."

I hadn't thought about the next move.

"Oh, so I need an undertaker, can you recommend one? It's a bit far from here. I don't know any."

"I'm not meant to recommend, but try the Co-Op. They're always helpful."

My incorrigible, party-going Godmother, only five years younger than Betty, lived near Oxford and I had missed our regular pub-lunches during the Betty drama.

"Sally – would you like to come to the undertaker?"

"Oh Darling – have I died?"

"I don't know. Have you gone to heaven? Seriously, I must sort out Betty. I thought we could have lunch afterwards. I'll pick you up. Silly to have two cars: parking is hell in Headington."

The plastic flowers in the funeral parlour were identical to those in Cheltenham crematorium; the pink velour swabs on the Sheraton 'style' chairs were like the curtains that had closed round Daddy's coffin as it had squeaked off to the oven. The walls were Uncle Derick's green. It was as though some universities did arts degrees in 'Colour Schemes for the Dying and Dead'.

Olive, a woman in her mid-sixties with laughter lines fanning from her eyes, an unlikely funeral director, put her folder on the varnished, heavy boardroom table, probably made in Vietnam, and *sotto voce* signalled we should sit down. I could imagine an entire family sitting round it, resembling footage from The Godfather, arguing over the departure of a departed.

"Just to fill you in," I said, "Betty was my aunt but I didn't know her until near the end of her life, we weren't emotionally involved. I'm sad she died, committed suicide, well that's what it looks like, but I'm not about to burst into tears."

Olive looked relieved, although she must have been used to handling tsunamis of tears from the sincere and the less sincere; the withdrawn and theatrical.

"Ah… that'll make it easier, there's questions that have to be asked."

She asked me to confirm names; addresses; relationship. There was the option of burial or cremation. Cremation usually required two doctors' death certificates, but the coroner already had what he needed. There was no doubt she was dead. I had no idea what Betty wanted but I knew she wouldn't want to take up space.

"Cremation? That's fine but we are getting very near Christmas. There aren't a lot of slots left."

"That's OK, can we fit her in?"

"You don't mind when?"

"No, let's get her done."

"What about the vicar?"

"Do we need one?"

"They love being involved. They get expenses. They know the exact mileage from the rectory to the crematorium."

Olive was called to the telephone. When she returned she was laughing.

"That was the vicar! They seem to have a hot line to the coroner, let alone God! They know exactly where the business has gone."

We all laughed. Sally had been a Godmother of expedience when I needed to be baptised before I married. George had wanted it. Love knew no bounds. Sally and I never discussed God.

"He can go sing. I'll let them have a service for Betty after Christmas."

"OK. I'll see what we can arrange. Now do you want to see her, to say goodbye?" When she saw my expression she added

"You see, if relatives want to say goodbye to the deceased, we must wash them, embalm them. We can do that for you, for Betty."

"That's really thoughtful but no thanks! Anyway, as she's been in the river for three weeks, I don't imagine she needs much washing."

As we were leaving, Sally, always fascinated by people, asked Olive how on earth she, an obviously cosy grandmother, had become a funeral director. At her retirement party, after decades selling nails, staples, and turpentine in the hardware department of the Co-Op, they had asked her what she was going to do with herself in retirement. She had no idea. With nine grandchildren wanting Christmas presents she would have to find something. She was offered the job on trial and found she loved it. They loved her. She had people skills.

We had a delicious lunch at the Cherwell Boat House. Both of us wondered whether it was an appropriate place to be. From our table we could see the meadows across the Cherwell where a month earlier the police had been searching. If Betty had thrown herself in, it would have been downstream opposite Parson's Pleasure Bathing Place or Music Meadow. How fitting. The water swirled as it flowed past, fast; it looked very cold despite steaming into the freezing air. I hoped the shock had killed her and she had been spared the body's painful fight to reject the water as it forced its way into her lungs.

While I rummaged in Hades under Betty's sink in search of the mains, and ran the taps to drain the system, Sally fossicked through the chilled house. Neither of us had taken off our coats. She called from upstairs.

"Darling, have you seen these, her paintings. They're wonderful. Did you know? She was brilliant."

One by one, we took canvases from where they were stacked, leant them against the landing wall and stood back: a circus big top; a fair hurdy-gurdy; punting on the river; an outdoor market; children with balloons. A man strumming a guitar with a mangey dog curled at his feet and a woman with drooped head in the shade: a label peeling from its back had 'Recession – E Grigs. £50' typed on it. Canvasses too big to extract from the piles included women carrying wet sheets, bent over big tubs in a commercial laundry. I could feel the weight of sodden linen. Behind all the others an unframed square metre of canvas depicted men working in a tannery. Standing precariously balanced between the tanks of copper, salt, and urine, they prodded, stirred, and lifted hides. I could almost smell it. Sally was right. It was the way she'd seen people; got their stance; the angles of their shoulders; their weight properly distributed on their feet. She had been a brilliant draughtsman and she had studied people. The unobserved had been the observer.

Our noses and hands were cold; winter gloaming was coming down. I picked up the scattering of envelopes by the front door, not much post for a month, especially before Christmas, and drove Sally home.

"Of course, she committed suicide," I said, " if she thought the cancer might get her; that the macular degeneration would make her blind, that the drugs already made her hands shake so much she couldn't use a match to light the gas, so she couldn't have used a pencil. She had no reason to live."

I did not go to Betty's cremation the week before Christmas. Her soul had gone. She was no longer with us, and she wouldn't have wanted me to spend my birthday in the traffic jam between Cassington and the Oxford by-pass. When I collected her ashes, Olive told me the vicar and one member of his congregation had been at the crematorium. He didn't send a bill. She also told me she had had a lovely Christmas with her grandchildren.

The service to celebrate Betty's life was not very celebratory. There was a smouldering undercurrent of resentment that I hadn't made more of her death at the time so that the missionaries could have had a Christmas party at the crematorium. After the service we repaired to the village hall where there was a generous spread of sandwiches and sponge cakes. Betty would have enjoyed them. Sally and I spent most of the time talking to each other. The vicar had to attend another bereaved member of his flock and as people drifted off in his wake the wife of the person who had offered to look after Betty's finances came over and, having told me how sad they all were that her life ended as it did, she hesitantly enquired after Betty's will. I was able to tell her truthfully that we hadn't found a will. Perhaps Betty had been right.

EIGHTEEN

BAGENDON

2005

George had never accepted that we were divorced. He continued to invite me to accompany him to some family events. He had started to have what we decided later had been TIAs,[1] and he always gave my name as his next of kin when taken to hospital. Those who saw him thought it because he wasn't looking after himself properly. As his family showed no practical interest in his welfare our son and I invited him to live with us. Despite a stipulation of the divorce settlement being that I lived more than eight miles from him, he jumped at the idea. Before long he had given his ex-wife enduring power of attorney. Executorship of his living will and actual will, followed shortly.

Months later he had a full-blown stroke. After a few months in hospitals, he was discharged into a care home as he no longer warranted clinical care. He walked unsteadily with a Zimmer and had impaired speech, but it was clear that otherwise his brain worked as it ever had. He could tell us, stutteringly, the breeding and provenance of most of the first and second wives of Gloucestershire, as though they were hounds.

---

1   *Transient ischaemic attacks – temporary blood clots; mini strokes.*

He remained concerned about his older brother who had married an exceptionally acquisitive and unfortunate woman,[2] not a good appendage for one with thousands of acres, walls of de Lászlós and crates of ancestral porcelain. Despite being the physically compromised one, he still felt protective and strangely responsible for the misfortune that had befallen the family and estate. He felt he should have managed to talk Henry out of marrying Gloria and he had tried, but Henry was nothing if not stubborn.[3] Glum despair had diffused through the senior members of the family. Over a lunch at Eastnor, Aunt Finola (VA's sister) had persuaded George that the only hope of the marriage working was for us all to support it.

At the entrance to St Columba's in Pont Street there is a large stone tablet with the inscription: 'MY HOUSE SHALL BE CALLED THE HOUSE OF PRAYER'.

"It's going to need a great deal of that!" whispered George as we climbed the wooden stair to the first-floor church.

After the service Gloria had emerged into the sunshine, and as though in the spotlight for a role in Cabaret, had stopped on the shallow steps leading to the pavement and slowly raised her skirt, so that the waiting press could photograph the garter on her thigh. George winced. We had walked over the road for champagne in Denise, Lady Kilmarnock's house. Washing hands in the loo I stood next to a little old woman who introduced herself as Gloria's mother. I exclaimed what a happy day it was.

"No" she replied "Henry Bathurst is such a common little man."

---

2   Gloria Clarry was the daughter of an engineer and a Liverpudlian boarding house owner, who had emigrated to the USA during the war. A one-time Hartnell model, she had married the widowed David Rutherston, (of the famously artistic Rothenstein family), who had four very young children. On his death she discarded her stepchildren, by then in their teens, scooping up the wonderful collection of drawings and paintings as she departed. She married Henry, who gave her property in London and Gloucestershire and acres of the Bathurst Estate as well as paintings, jewellery, porcelain, and furniture collected over three centuries, some were personal gifts from Queen Anne and subsequent royals. She bequeathed it all to a friend. Rutherston paintings and the Bathurst artefacts, that VA had carefully managed to keep intact on the 7th Earl's death, were flicked across the world like chaff by the elegantly fingered female Christie's auctioneer. The day-long sale raised over £2,000,000.
3   One of Henry's nicer traits was to let his Etonian friends and fellow officers (10th Royal Hussars/Royal Gloucestershire Hussars) take estate tenancies. It made for a happy 'family' atmosphere and a fun estate shoot. Henry and Gloria's engagement caused wry regret – Judy had been universally popular. On the day the engagement was announced in the broadsheets, we were returning from exercise in the park when we met one such, the tenant of the Tunnel House pub. "Oh, dear George, what a pity, I see Henry is engaged to the regimental bicycle!"

The shoe had changed foot. About twenty of us sat down to a wedding breakfast of bland food and shallow merriment in the heavily draped private dining room of a Park Lane hotel. The deed had been done. A year later Gloria was with friends, without Henry, in a little restaurant in Sardinia, loudly proclaiming her delight in her new life.

"I've got Henry exactly where I want him!"

Unknown to her, the chic local resident dining with her husband at the next table was Nanny Bathurst's sister.[4] Gloria's conversation was relayed to Cirencester within hours. Even then we hadn't realised how the thumb screws were tightening.

*

George couldn't live in a house with stairs anymore, and there was no possibility of making a wet room on the ground floor. We managed to wing planning permission to replace a hideous garage block with a single storey place for him and a carer. Builders pulled out all the stops and we had him out of the care home and back with us in time for Christmas. In the summer, with the French windows open, the call and runner ducks came inside and sat on the stretcher of the big oak table. Occasionally at dusk, a fox trotted to the threshold and stood for a while, just to check him out.

In the meantime, we had remarried. One Sunday, he had pushed a little blue and gold box towards me across the kitchen chopping board. Inside was a wedding ring. His second proposal as romantic as his first thirty-two years earlier, but the ring contained three times as much gold. I had appreciated in value. We had an appointment with the registrar whose offices had been relocated to Cirencester's redundant hospital. With immigrants arranging

---

4   *Anne Hudson, one of three sisters, always wanted to look after children and to her parents' consternation trained as a Norland Nanny. One sister married a farmer and lived in Rhodesia. The other lived in grand style (the garden was featured in House & Garden) with her husband in Sardinia. Nanny rarely revealed her provenance but had some great quips. One was that her family's footmen had more elegant livery than the Bathursts' footmen. Nanny looked after all three of Henry and Judy's children from the Ninth Earl's birth in 1961 onward. She spent half of her life as their rock, and died a much-loved member of the family, in her nineties. All 'her' children some by then well into their sixties, attended her funeral.*

marriages to be able to remain in the country, questions had to be asked of the affianced separately, to make sure that they really did know each other. After a few minutes of the registrar failing to understand George's mumbled speech I was invited into the room to interpret.

"George, what was your father's occupation?"

"Farmer."

"George, he wasn't a farmer! He might have been a beneficiary of trusts involving land, but I doubt he ploughed a field after leaving Western Australia in 1925."

"Oh well what would you like me to put down as his occupation?"

"What do you want, George? Much decorated soldier? MP? PPS to various Ministers? Director of *The Morning Post*?"

George smiled.

"I'll put down Member of Parliament then."

The registrar addressed further questions to me, both about George's life and mine, and then said, "Well Mr and Mrs Bathurst, I am satisfied that you know each other, and you may get married."

While the interview had gone on, I had been studying her rather amused face, and I realised the reason I recognised her. She had been one of the Cirencester banks' cashiers. She had known all about us all the time. She probably knew George's bank statements better than he did. He never opened them. The list of upcoming marriages was pinned above the fireplace of the old hospital hall, and I asked whether our names could be put at the top, out of prying eyes. I didn't want the local press to send a photographer to snap George in his enfeebled state. I wanted him better remembered on a horse or opening the fête of the geriatric hospital's League of Friends, of which he'd been president.

Three weeks later we were married. We had persuaded Marie that she would rather be one of our witnesses than continue with the ironing. The three of us and our son piled into the car. While our son and Marie took the stairs to the first floor, George and I went in the lift. It had been purpose built, wide and thin to take stretcher cases up and the deceased down, including my father I thought as it ground up. After the 'short' ceremony, in what had been one of the two main wards of the hospital, now arranged with chairs across the middle instead of beds along the sides, the assistant registrar, embarrassed by the silence as the clerk completed the forms, asked our son whether he had been at his parents' first wedding. I hadn't dare look at his face. Back in Bagendon, the four of us cracked a bottle or two and Marie tried to concentrate on making straight creases.

*

Thirteen months after Betty died Sandra telephoned to say that she had reached the top of the coroner's list for an inquest and a date was set. We arranged to meet outside the Oxford Court House. It was good to see her cheery face again and we exchanged pleasantries about our respective families. Then she told me that owing to a big planning enquiry the Coroner's Court had been taken over and inquests had been transferred to the old assizes court.

"Don't worry it'll be fine," she said.

I was glad that she warned me. I was directed to a large empty courtroom. Frayed flags representing the seventeen Oxford Hundreds hung high from the walls. I wondered at the history. The wall-to-ceiling green flaking panelling; the ample seating for clerks, barristers, solicitors, witnesses, the press, and the public. The dais for the judges under the great coat of arms; the jury box, witness box and the box for the defendant from which some dozens had been led directly along a corridor to Oxford Gaol housed in the Norman castle, thence to drop from the gallows. There was a chill of evil despite the cobwebs gently stirred by warm air rising in the low winter sunshine.

With only nine of us present to help determine the reason a shy spinster's life had ended in her eightieth year, there were not enough human clothes to baffle sounds. Every foot that scuffled, the rustle of each sheet of paper that the clerk turned, could be heard. The unfortunate young policeman who had had to haul Betty from the water gave his evidence in private as he had a sickness bug. I imagined his chucking up when he found her. After three weeks drifting the eight miles through Christ Church Meadows, through the Iffley and Pound locks, snagging on roots and reeds, bouncing through the one hundred and seventy feet of Sanford Lock and then to be thrown down nearly nine feet like a rag doll, she would not have looked good. I had failed to ask Sandra where she had been found and was speculating whether she had reached Sanford Lasher or Swift Ditch. I was trying not to dwell on what must have confronted him, when the coroner called me to the witness box.

I said that I knew she was frightened of being taken back into psychiatric incarceration. The psychiatric experts, five sitting in a line, watched worried, as though I might point a finger of blame. That five had been sent from The Warneford indicated concern. I added that she had asked to have the tamoxifen reduced or replaced by another drug, but she hadn't been able to get a doctor's appointment.

"You see she was a painter and thought either it or the olanzapine made her hands shake. She could no longer do the one thing that gave her life meaning." The coroner decided that it was probable she committed suicide but there was no proof. He recorded an open verdict.

With the formalities over I was allowed to clear her house. I hired a skip, rented a white van and with two of my son's cricketing friends we went for it. Rule of thumb: all clothing, furnishings, carpets, and bed linen into the skip; everything from her studio into the van with the books and furniture. I would sort them once back home.

Jungle drums had alerted the missionaries who knocked on the open door. They asked whether they could have something to remember Betty by.

"Certainly, what would you like? A painting? I'm afraid we've already loaded some but do have a look."

Whatever their reasons they had kept an eye on her. While they rummaged through her studio Nigel beckoned me to follow him into the garden. In moving the Wellington Chest from her bedroom, a box had fallen out of the hidden cavity at the top.

"It seems to contain a great deal of money," he whispered. "What do you want me to do with it?"

"Keep it safe... we'll have a look when we are home, away from prying eyes. We'll share it."

The missionaries had chosen a canvas and had started going through her books in the sitting room.

"Ah, here you are. I see you found something. Good."

"Yes, thank you and can we take this book?"

"What is it?"

"Mary Day's Book."[5]

"Oh, I'm afraid not. It's my mother's." I had a few copies at home but ridiculously that copy mattered to me. It was a signed present to Betty from

---

5   In 1952 *Mary Day's Book* was published by Hulton Press. It is a selection of the pieces that my mother wrote for *Farmers Weekly 1934–1951*. When writing for *Farmers Weekly* she used the name 'Day' after her first stepmother.

her elder sister. The missionaries left, looking offended, without asking about her will. I felt guilty. I had answered them rather brusquely.

"What about all these shopping bags of papers, letters?" asked Nigel.

"There might be something fascinating there."

"Really? This is full of circulars about incontinence pads, funeral plans, equity release, Saga holidays. She's dated the receipt of every single one. They go back years."

"Ah, but a fifty pound note may be hiding among all that!"

Nick shouted from the kitchen, "There's no mains switch to turn off the gas. It's dangerous."

I telephoned the gas board to ask them to come and turn it off in the road. It reminded me to ask BT to disconnect. Nigel started clearing a path through the undergrowth so that potential house purchasers could see how far the garden extended.

"It's a good size."

No sooner had he got a bonfire going than someone turned up from the council. There had been complaints about smoke. Bonfires weren't allowed. Coming from villages in the country we had no idea. It was time to lock up and beat a retreat. We'd done enough.

"So," I said, as we sat round the garden table. "What about this money then?" Nigel produced the wooden box.

"Blimey that is a lot!" And in the evening sun I divided it into equal piles, and we cracked the couple of bottles of champagne that I'd bought in a petrol station on the way home.

From time to time, I'd go through another SPAR carrier bag of papers. I hoped to find out more about my mother and her family, my family, but there was very little. Endless letters from Uncle advising Betty how to do things 'better'. Everything from framing her paintings so that she could sell more to improving her life. He even suggested she should try and resume friendship with a long-lost male acquaintance so they could get married which, given his singular lack of success on that front, I thought a bit rich. She had gone through some of his letters underlining in pencil or covering in dayglo.

I found a letter from Uncle to Betty explaining why their father had disliked Daddy. He had thought my father, with the surname Messer,[6] was

---

6   *Messer is the German for knife. It was also the Scottish for a stockman, which Daddy's family had been in the 18thC*

a Jew therefore had 'hated him' (*quote*). I am not sure that this was true. I have found some very kind and affectionate letters from my mother's father written to mine after she died. Perhaps it was Uncle misconstruing the situation, as he sometimes did. I hope so.

NINETEEN

UNCLE

2007

Betty's mother's family had lived comfortably in Sussex and Betty had persuaded a maiden aunt to lend Uncle money. Uncle and Maud moved to a bungalow on the hill above Exmouth. It had a nice garden fore and aft with cordon fruit trees, currant and gooseberry bushes, flower beds and enough well-tilled earth for successful vegetables. The previous owner had loved gardening. There was no danger to the cats from traffic because there wasn't any traffic: not every bungalow in the *cul de sac* supported a car. Through a large picture window in the sitting room, they could glimpse the River Exe over the roofs of the bungalows opposite. It should have made for a warm, dry, content old age, but did not. When he wasn't train spotting; writing his war diaries, later sent to the Imperial War Museum; or involving himself in the local camera club, Uncle became a regular in-patient at the local hospital. He never revealed what was wrong with him.

"Tummy trouble, dear."

But as time crawled on it seemed that neither did the medics know. I began to wonder whether it was nerves caused by Maud, although in public he blamed Death Railway: perfectly plausible, except that the only time he telephoned either Betty or me had been on Tuesday afternoons when Maud

194

was out, having her hair crimped into tight curls. He had become frightened of her. It turned out with good reason.

One morning someone from Devon Social Services telephoned. Maud had gone for Uncle with the carving knife, and he had escaped the bungalow in his pyjamas. He had taken refuge with the sweet old couple who lived opposite. Please would I relieve them of him.

"Not to worry, Mrs Grigs has been taken into care. For her own *(sic)* safety." he added. I knew that she had been slipping into the murky pond of dementia for a while, but I also had fleeting sympathy: he must have been infuriating to live with. Nothing would have been right.

Three hours later I was with the neighbours. I felt no affection for the pathetic ninety-six-year-old man sitting hunched in the next room in his striped pyjamas and a borrowed dressing gown. He hadn't had to marry that woman or give the Japanese art away. He hadn't had endlessly to find fault with the young; doctors; bar staff; to criticise the standards of journalistic sub-editing; politicians. The list went on, but I had to face it: there was no dodging that Mummy's little brother had become my responsibility.

Driving back to Gloucestershire, I glanced at him. He was staring blankly at the Somerset levels as they rushed by. He looked crushed flat, like a stamped-on beverage can. Yet sitting beside me was someone who, somehow, had sidestepped being one of the over one hundred thousand who had died of torture and starvation while building the Death Railway. Once he must have been incredibly tough in every way. I wondered what he was thinking. Having seen how the Huns had decimated his father's generation in the First War he had signed-up in 1939 to help, as he saw it: "Stop the Bosch ripping through Europe".

But instead of facing Germans he had faced Japanese in Singapore. I thought how different our circumstances had been. Two closest living relatives forty years apart had grown so differently. He had been brought up by someone whom he thought was an anti-Semite; I had been brought up by someone who discriminated against no one. He, whose life had been surrendered to those who looked to him like aliens; I who saved up for adventure travel and entrusted my life to those with different features and skin colour.

Was he reflecting on forty-three years of marriage to Maud? Could he remember why he had married her? Had there even been good times or had he jumped in blind to cover his grief? He could never have imagined it would end like this. I wondered when he had started to feel threatened.

It must have seemed the culmination of a sad, frustrating, troubled life. He had been five when his mother died. He had just got used to, and presumably fond of, his stepmother and she died. Within twelve months he had another. I did quick maths. Ninety years earlier my mother had become his support, his proxy mother. She had been ten years old. At sixty I should be able to handle things for him. By the time we reached home I had talked myself into feeling protective.

A tryst to go on holiday with friends gave me the ideal deadline to locate space for him in a care home. Geriatric beds in Gloucestershire are always at a premium but I found a good-natured couple who had turned their house into a home for three adults. The residents had the run of all the rooms including the kitchen, which they were encouraged to use. There was a south-facing garden that overlooked fields. It contained a tree sagging under the weight of apples and a blackbird proudly proclaimed news of his latest family from the chimney. Garden chairs were arranged around a low table. It seemed ideal. Home from Home, and when Uncle asked whether he could help in the garden they were thrilled. I went away with a clear conscience.

Back in the departure lounge of the little airport, after a blissful fortnight of sun and Aegean Sea, my mobile picked up a signal and I realised we were in trouble. 'Ping' followed 'ping' followed 'ping' as successive messages from a Cirencester telephone number came across the airwaves. Uncle had indeed made himself at home in the kitchen, had found a kitchen knife and had taken himself to the apple tree where he had brandished it at anyone who tried to approach. Men in white coats had gently talked him into an ambulance and taken him off. He too was now in a mental hospital for his own safety, doubtless. What was it with that lot? MY lot.

I was apprehensive about visiting him. One of Granny's cousins had been the doctor in charge of the Middlesex County Asylum at Napsbury,[1] near St Alban's, built early in the 20th century to accommodate over one thousand patients. When I was nine years old, we had gone there for lunch. The cousin lived in an Arts and Crafts house in the grounds with its own garden and a goldfish pond, all very safe and suburban. However, after lunch, as I had behaved, (I always did behave with Granny) I was asked if, as a perceived treat for the farmer's daughter, I would like to see round the hospital farm. It

---

1   *It was converted into a 'leafy residential development' 2002 –2008 and is now called Napsbury Park.*

sounded more interesting than the pond with its pair of idly circulating fish. I'm not sure that even Granny realised that the farm workers were 'working patients' which presumably meant they were deemed safe. I thought that they were almost as terrifying as those we had passed on the way to the farm, screaming and shouting, caged in their exercise yards. Little exercise looked to be taken although some had been clawing the high chainlink fencing, trying to climb out. The working patients had followed us rather too closely in the dank, damp passage of the piggeries and when outside in daylight, just stood to one side, staring at us, unblinking. Those eyes followed me for years.

As a result, I was in no hurry to visit Uncle, but it had to be done. The hospital, on one of Stroud's steep hills, was small, light, and airy with southerly views across the valley to Minchinhampton Common. It felt more like a pensioners' social club. The patients sat around reading papers or playing dominoes. The staff were the sort of Christian people who make one feel guilty that one couldn't possibly do what they do. After a few months I found Uncle a room in another care home, and he was released. He lived there warm and well looked after for nearly a year. I visited him most weeks which gave him ample opportunity to complain about the things that were irritating him. I don't think he bothered to talk to anyone between my visits.

Three people attended his cremation in 2007 – me, his stepdaughter and someone from The Trainspotters Society. It was a sad, lonely end for an irritated life. Anyone who had survived Death Railway had deserved a reward. He had none.

TWENTY

CURTAIN

One day we realised that George was pushing his pills down the side of his chair to avoid swallowing them. He no longer wanted to be taken to watch polo or follow hounds. His doctor and I agreed that he was fed up with life.

"If he stops taking the medication, he will be dead within weeks."

"I think that's what he wants."

"So do I."

George didn't die within weeks. He suffered more strokes, each one more debilitating than the last. He could not speak at all, but his brain continued working and he could answer questions with thumbs up or down. He was Locked In. He became bed-ridden, not even able to turn over in it but, if propped up with pillows, he could feed himself and had a healthy appetite for home-cooked food. We moved his bed so that he could see the view down the valley, up to The Whiteway and on to the horizon and the treetops of Calmsden Gorse, a good mile away. The night after Storm Capella, thirty-three years earlier, we had had one of the best day's hunting from Tarlton. Many roads had been blocked by fallen trees and traffic was non-existent. It was the nearest my generation got to the hunting enjoyed in the early days of the motor car. Eventually hounds had lost their fox in Calmsden Gorse. It had been seven miles as the crow flies but more than double as hounds ran. I asked George whether he remembered it. With a huge smile he gave a thumbs up.

George's life had become intolerable, although he was in no position to do anything other than tolerate it. Eighteen months after he had swallowed the last pill he died. Following the service of thanksgiving for his life, and his release from it, I walked up Blackjack Street to The Mansion, his family home. It was a perfect sunny end-of-March day. The swallows had arrived that morning. The two-hundred-and-fifty-year-old church bells rang out across the town for him. I looked up at the cloudless sky. If there was a heaven up there, he would be able to hear them. I hoped he could.

George had not been the obvious candidate for strokes. Not an ounce overweight, he could still wear his Eton tails. The frayed, silk buttons required deft work with a felt tip pen before weddings and funerals. He took regular exercise; did not drink unless absentmindedly with food; did not smoke cigarettes and was not that fussed about after-dinner cigars. I took lots of exercise and hadn't smoked since leaving art school, but neither did I count units. It struck me I might be next. I was sixty-four. By the time I reached the opened wooden doors in the highest yew hedge in the world, to go into the wake and thank everybody for coming, I had decided to make the most of any time I had left. I would travel off-piste on horses, while I still could.

It was time to resume Laughing and Splashing.

POSTSCRIPT

MALCOLM MESSER

After my father died there were obituaries. Tristram Beresford, long-time farmer, journalist, and agricultural correspondent for the *Financial Times*, wrote to me in fury that the *Daily Telegraph* had given a deceased clown priority on the obituaries page. In his book *We Plough The Fields – Agriculture in Britain Today*,[1] Tristram had written that there had been:

> "...*men of genius who have supplied the needs of the creative minority in agriculture, and by diffusion affected the whole mass. A short list would include Harry Ferguson, the pioneer of hydraulics in agricultural machinery; Sir John Hammond, who broke new ground in livestock improvement; Sir George Stapledon, for his grassland work and for his life and thought; and Malcolm Messer, for twenty years the tutelary genius of the technical press.*"

The Times gave him four times the column inches more than the *Telegraph*. I think it was the person who wrote that obituary who sent me a personal letter in which he wrote:

---

1   *Published by Pelican Books ISBN 0 14 02 1872 6*

"Your father was unique, entering journalism by accident and managing to hold himself aloof from Fleet Street's turmoils. He even managed to avoid the troubles of literary composition. Perhaps because of this, as you know, he made an outstanding success of F.W. Up to the time he was thrown into the editorship, F.W. made little impression on the agricultural world, but by his vision and integrity of outlook, he made it secure. Malcolm regarded it as his first duty to serve the long-term interests of British agriculture as critical to the national economy; he thought that if he did so regardless of day-to-day expediency or popularity, F.W. would prosper. His confidence and sincerity were rewarded. So was British agriculture."

Frank Butcher wrote the obituary for *Farmers Weekly*. A few weeks after Daddy's death he sent me a sheaf of papers. In his covering letter he wrote:

"Obits and appreciations all too often say more about the writer than about the subject. I tried to avoid that trap but can assure you that MM marked me for life. After editing rural weeklies, I joined the paper as a reporter at 38 – and then learned what journalism was about."

I treasure what Frank, someone who worked with my father and knew him so well, wrote for *Farmers Weekly*:

"Malcolm Messer CBE died on Thursday May 31st, 1984, in the golden jubilee year of the paper, which is a living memorial to his wisdom, to his foresight, and to the loyalty he commanded from those of us who worked for him.

"As technical editor from 1934 to 1938 he helped to shape the newly launched Farmers Weekly. From 1938 to 1966, as editor, he helped the infant to grow into sturdy, independent manhood. Characteristically he shrugged off any credit for this. At a presentation marking his silver jubilee he responded with an apology 'When I came here I gave it a year. After four years I took over the editor's chair. There was nobody else to do it'.

"That was typical of the shy genius who, almost secretly, master-minded an adventure in farming journalism which challenged tradition while setting trends that became traditions in their own right.

"He was no platform performer. Far from it. When there was no escape from public speaking he was plainly, and sometimes inaudibly,

uncomfortable – so different from the stimulating conversationalist who, in private, was at his best talking off the record over what he called 'a dish of the great emollient'.

"Looking back one wonders whether he directed the weekly by telepathy. He was seldom seen or heard – no fuss, no fury, and yet his influence ever present. In some mysterious way he invested the paper with a character which made its own demands reflecting his guiding principles: journalistic integrity, sense of mission, ability to sniff 'climate' and to see what was 'at the other side of the wall'.

"Malcolm Messer was wary of political nostrums. He realised that a strong British agriculture could not be built on political measures alone and that these could do little more than bring about conditions in which farming could develop economically and technically. Under his editorship the Weekly advocated new techniques and new ideas in organisation and marketing.

"He was among the first to direct farmers' thoughts to the potential of Britain's grasslands and to ways of unlocking it. Under his direction Farmers Weekly staged pioneer demonstrations on the use of aircraft in agriculture, campaigned for the restoration of under-used or waste land, encouraged conservation – for farming – of fenland, and supported structural reform to raise productivity and improve incomes.

"It was Malcolm Messer who first involved Farmers Weekly in farming – as owner-occupier and as tenant on the hills and on lower land. The aim was not to teach but to learn and to enable readers to learn from FW farms' mistakes and to benefit from their successes. Beyond the trading accounts he saw the social needs. Back in the 1950s, before anyone had defined a 'less favoured area' he had sized up the deprivation and offered a prescription: 'give them a bathroom, hot and cold water and a chain to pull'.

"He achieved much, not by beating his drum, but by discussion with farmers and scientists who shared his intellectual approach and by asking questions.

"He described his own attitude as one of informed scepticism. As a shy man he disliked arrogance in others and chose to carry his readers along by persuasion and discussion rather than by use of what he called 'the bludgeon treatment'. The maxim he commended to his staff was 'Never be pompous – and no poodle-faking'.

"Members of that staff will never forget his insistence on complete editorial independence and freedom. He refused to debase his standards

either to comfort the critical or to satisfy commercial interests. He was unswerving in his commitment to these ideals even when sections of his readership fell out with him. It was by no means unusual to find pedigree breeders irately brandishing a copy of Farmers Weekly at a public meeting and roundly condemning the editorial opinion expressed in 'the yellow peril'. In time many of the ideas and policies advocated against the grain of some interest or another proved to be right and gained acceptance.

"Malcolm Messer unfailingly disguised his natural kindness, sometimes with his own brand of dry humour and occasionally with a not-too-convincing show of crustiness. Those who worked with him for the paper remember the man and his manner with an affection which he would have found acutely embarrassing. And they marvel that he succeeded in keeping so great a talent out of the public eye."

It had become a bit of a joke that my father would never retire. In 1963 there was a party in the office to celebrate his quarter century as editor. Among those present were staff from the Sun Printers at Watford, including Arthur Seeley the composing room 'clicker'. Among the papers Frank had kept, and sent me, was a page from the Sun Printer's house magazine, reporting the event. It ends:

"We at the Sun are proud to print the Farmers Weekly. When in May 1935 we did the trial run we were told by other printers that we could not turn out the paper week after week by rotary gravure, but as so often happens the critics have been proved very wrong. This in large measure, is due to the esteem, one might also say affection, that is felt by the whole works – the composing room in particular – for Malcolm Messer and his staff.

Sir, we salute you."

This was written when the print unions were flexing their muscles and starting to lock horns with Fleet Street. Within 15 years, Marmaduke Hussey,[2] then chief executive and managing director of Times Newspapers, had shut down *The Times* to bring the printers 'to heel'.

---

2   *Lord Hussey, later chairman of the BBC. Ennobled 1996.*

NOTE TO SOPHIE

It is 2022. You are not yet three years old, and I am in my seventy seventh year. In about forty years, when you have children, possibly grandchildren of your own, you may wonder about the generations that went before. I will be under the sod and your parents will be older than I am now. I hope, should you come across this on the shelves, you dip into it, and might even get this far. If I lived long enough, you may remember your father's mother, by then probably muttering to herself in the corner, holding her glass in both hands, trying not to spill it. I hope I recognised you when you came through the door, and that we laughed together, even if you had no idea what I was on about.

As this memoir shows, despite living at a time of enormous change, in conditions that may seem from another century (they were), I would have changed little of my life. I am not convinced that 'things happen for a reason' but they often give the experience to help handle the events that follow. Make the most of the company of those you are with while you have them. Grab the moment.

When, seven decades after your great grandmother's death, people learned that she died when I was barely five years old, they usually exclaimed, "Oh! You poor little mite, what a tragedy!"

It was not a tragedy for me. The tragedy was for your great grandfather, he adored her. Your great grandfather never visited his misery on me, and I had the happiest childhood of anyone I know. I hope such tragedies avoid you, but if not try to remember – the dynamics of relationships change, but it is not the end of the world, it simply is the beginning of a different one.

There is a sign at the entrance to Ravlar Khempur near Udaipur:
   'Everything will be alright in the end. If it's not alright it's not yet the end.'

APOLOGIES

Having reached the age when I cannot remember the reason I climbed the stairs, I am grateful to remember anything at all. I apologise if I have remembered things differently to those who were there and have survived to read this.

ACKNOWLEDGEMENTS

I would not have entertained the idea of writing anything longer than a bread-and-butter letter if I hadn't received such encouragement from Patricia Lord, Georgie Vassiltchikov and Philip Willmett. Stella Barnes booted me on whenever I waivered and without her input this would never have got off the ground, let alone into print.

I'm very grateful to Tim Boswell for welcoming me back to Lower Grounds Farm at Aynho; Hilary Northcote for filling me in on the variety of climber at Bishton; Dilys Hart for confirming Laureate's date and Brenda Ferry for helping with details about her parents.

Everyone at Jericho Writers has been forbearing and very helpful. Sam Jordison's course on non-fiction was great fun and essential. Dexter Petley kindly ploughed through the whole manuscript and made pertinent suggestions and gave me terrific encouragement and Jo Hall had a go at my punctuation. They all have helped make this readable and Beth Archer at Troubador Publishing was essential at getting the show on the road.

I owe immeasurable gratitude to all my friends, lifelong and more recent, who have given me so many hilarious moments and continuous laughing and splashing. Nobody deserved such generosity of spirit and table.

My parents engendered the attitude to life that has enabled me to brook the lows and revel in the highs, and unwittingly gave me the genes to enable what I have done and, astonishingly, continue to be able to do.

I unceasingly thank my beloved father, the biggest treat, my lodestar.

After she was widowed in 2010 Sue started travelling off-piste on horses.
She has ridden across the Thar Desert in India, in northern Mongolia
to visit the Tsaatan (reindeer people), in Cuba, Bhutan, across the Andes,
and in the Georgian Caucasus and Romanian Carpathians.

In 2013 she rode in Kyrgyzstan in the Tien Shan Mountains and fell in love
with the country returning year on year until Covid.

Her next book

KYRGYZSTAN & THE JAILOO
(Four Rides in The Mountains of Heaven)

will be published in 2023 and illustrated with many full colour
photographs.

In it she not only describes Kyrgyzstan but tells of four rides in the Tien Shan
and Talas Mountains. During those rides with English and Kyrgyz friends, she
crossed twenty passes, most between 9,000 feet
and 13,000 feet; rode through flower-filled alpine meadows
too inaccessible to be grazed by herds; negotiated precipitous gorges
and the boulder-strewn rivers of cascading snowmelt.

In 2017 armed with special permits from the Kyrgyz government, they rode for
over 150 miles down what was the USSR/Chinese border
and remains a no-go zone. They were stopped at five army checkpoints and
humoured two mounted border patrols.

Wherever they went they were welcomed by the shepherds
and their families.